In this fascinating and accessible book. David Wiles introduces ancient Greek theatre to students and enthusiasts interested in knowing how the plays were first performed. Theatre was a ceremony bound up with fundamental activities in classical Athenian life and Wiles explores those elements which created the theatre of the time. Actors rather than writers are the book's main concern and Wiles examines how the actor used the resources of storytelling, dance, mask, song and visual action to create a large-scale event that would shape the life of the citizen community. The book assumes no prior knowledge of the ancient world, and is written to answer the questions of those who want to know how the plays were performed, what they meant in their original social context, what they might mean in a modern performance and what can be learned from and achieved by performances of Greek plays today.

DAVID WILES is Professor of Theatre at Royal Holloway, University of London. In addition to numerous articles on classical drama, he has published *The Masks of Menander: sign and meaning in Greek and Roman performance* (Cambridge, 1991) and *Tragedy in Athens: performance space and theatrical meaning* (Cambridge, 1997). He also writes on festive aspects of Tudor drama and has published *The Early Plays of Robin Hood* (1981), *Shakespeare's clown: actor and text in the Elizabethan playhouse* (Cambridge, 1987) and *Shakespeare's almanac: 'A Midsummer Night's Dream', marriage and the Elizabethan calendar* (1993). He has contributed a chapter on Roman and medieval drama to the *Oxford Illustrated History of Theatre* (1995).

GREEK THEATRE PERFORMANCE

An Introduction

DAVID WILES

CAMBRIDGE
UNIVERSITY PRESS

CAMBRIDGE UNIVERSITY PRESS
Cambridge, New York, Melbourne, Madrid, Cape Town, Singapore, São Paulo, Delhi

Cambridge University Press
The Edinburgh Building, Cambridge CB2 8RU, UK

Published in the United States of America by Cambridge University Press, New York

www.cambridge.org
Information on this title: www.cambridge.org/9780521640275

First published 2000
Eighth printing 2008

Printed in the United Kingdom at the University Press, Cambridge

A catalogue record for this publication is available from the British Library

Library of Congress Cataloguing in Publication data
Wiles, David.
Greek theatre performance: an introduction / by David Wiles.
p.   cm.
Includes index.
ISBN 0 521 64027 X (hardback) – ISBN 0 521 64857 2 (paperback)
1. Theatre – Greece – Production and direction – History.
2. Greek drama – History and criticism.
3. Theatre – Greece – History.   I. Title.
PA3201.W53   2000
792'.0938 – dc21   99–043723

ISBN 978-0-521-64027-5 hardback
ISBN 978-0-521-64857-8 paperback

Contents

Illustrations

PLATES

FIGURES

Most of the drawings are taken from photographs. A few are adapted and modified from modern drawings: figure 6 after *Diction-naire des antiquités*; figure 11 after Richard Leacroft; figure 12 after Emil Orlik; figure 14 after George Izenour; and figure 20 after Yannis Kokkos.

Acknowledgements

I am grateful to those who have commented on parts of this book in draft form. Richard Seaford offered advice on five of the chapters. Colleagues at Royal Holloway have read shorter sections: Lene Rubinstein (who gave invaluable help on the subject of Athenian politics), Jacky Bratton, Richard Cave, Richard Hawley, Dan Rebellato, and Rosalind Thomas. I have learned much from my students, and it is their questions which I have tried to answer in this book. Eugenia Arsenis helped in obtaining photographs from Greece, and I am also grateful to Eric Handley, Costas Tsianos and Thanos Vovolis. I have profited from reading unpublished dissertations by Katerina Arvaniti, Marina Kotzamani, Karina Mitens, and Elizabeth Papacostantinou. Vicki Cooper at Cambridge University Press has been a continuing source of encouragement and support. Gayna Wiles provided the drawings and tutored me in visual awareness.

Note on the text

Translations in this book are my own, unless otherwise stated. There is an international system of standard page/line references for Greek texts based on the first manuscript or edition, which allows almost any academic translation to be consulted. I have given references to two useful collections of primary material in translation, though I have used my own translations in this book:

ALC   *Ancient Literary Criticism: the principal texts in new translations*, ed. D. A. Russell and M. Winterbottom (Oxford University Press, 1972)

COAD   *Contexts of Ancient Drama*, ed. Eric Csapo and William J. Slater (University of Michigan Press, 1995)

I also refer frequently to three collections of essays:

MTAG   Jean-Pierre Vernant and Pierre Vidal Naquet, *Myth and Tragedy in Ancient Greece*, tr. J. Lloyd (New York: Zone Books, 1990)

NTDWD   *Nothing To Do With Dionysos? Athenian drama in its social context*, ed. John J. Winkler and Froma Zeitlin (Princeton University Press, 1992)

CCGT   *The Cambridge Companion to Greek Tragedy*, ed. P. E. Easterling (Cambridge University Press, 1997)

Greek names are nowadays sometimes transliterated according to the traditional Latin system (e.g. Aeschylus) and sometimes directly from the Greek (e.g. Aiskhylos). Since we do not know quite what the Greek sounded like, I have used the form that felt most familiar. I have also used the translated titles that seem most recognizable, e.g.

Aristophanes, *Women at the Thesmophoria* rather than *Thesmophoria-zousae* (the Latinized Greek title) or *The Poet and the Women* (Penguin edition); Sophocles, *Oedipus the King* rather than *Oedipus Tyrannus* (Latinized Greek), *Oedipus Rex* (Latin), or *Oedipus the Tyrant*.

Introduction

Does the new century need a new introduction to Greek theatre? There are good books on the market. Several are written by directors of Greek plays, who are particularly well equipped to show you how to read plays in accordance with their sole original purpose: to make sense in performance. There has not been any avalanche of new discoveries, new hard information. The ancient world has not changed ... How could it? Yet *we* have changed. Our assumptions are different, and our questions are different. Here are some of my own assumptions that led me to embark on this book.

(1) A new readership has emerged from the new academic discipline of theatre studies. I have written supposing that the reader of this book knows nothing about ancient Greece, but has some sophistication in the analysis of performance. I hope that readers coming from classical studies will nevertheless find themselves interested by questions that emerge from a different academic agenda. I regard this book as an interdisciplinary study.

(2) As soon as theatre studies emerged as a discipline, it became clear that no one within the discipline actually knew what 'theatre' was. Performance reaches into all areas of life and it is an arbitrary convention which dubs one activity 'theatre', another circus, a wrestling match, a job interview. There is a danger of circularity. We know what 'theatre' and 'drama' are because we derive those words and concepts from the Greeks; armed with that knowledge, we return to the Greeks and analyse their 'theatre' accordingly. I have not, in this book, assumed that I know where theatre stops and mere 'performance' begins. I have tried to understand tragedy and comedy as two activities within a remarkable culture that fostered many types of performance.

(3) Practitioners of theatre must not claim too boldly the privilege of knowing how their artistic medium works, for Greek theatre was

not understood as 'art' in any recognizable modern terms. We can no longer study the history of Greek *theatre* in conceptual isolation. Theatre was an integral part of Athenian *culture*, whose values and practices differed profoundly from those of the modern west. This anthropological premise lies behind much important recent research within classical studies; it is shared, for example, by the contributors to the *Cambridge Companion to Greek Tragedy*.

(4) I do not believe that Greece was the cradle of *my* civilization because I inhabit an increasingly globalized culture. In many ways Greek civilization seems to me much closer to India or Japan, in its attitude to the harmony of mind and body for example, and its assumption that the universe is inhabited by gods and demigods. The idea that we should study Greek plays because that is how 'our' theatre began seems less and less compelling. The main reason now for studying Greek plays is the opportunity which they provide to create performances in the present. Of course, their ability to communicate today is tied to their history, and the fact that they are familiar. Geographically Greece is a place where east meets west, and it is not today a hegemonic power like the land of Shakespeare, so the drama of Greece is well placed to become a shared cultural possession, a vehicle for communication.

(5) To study Greek theatre anthropologically, i.e. as a social practice, is to throw out the old separation of form and content. It is no longer good enough to think we can first study the *context* – i.e. the Greek world-view, the conventions of performance, the historical facts – and then move on to *the plays themselves*, to see what the plays are *saying*. The form of Greek plays is inseparable from what they meant and mean.

(6) History can never be objective. As a way of establishing meaningful links between bits of data, we tell stories about the past, and those stories reflect how *we* see our own world. To describe the past is partly but not exclusively to describe ourselves. Theatre poses acute problems for the historian at the best of times because it is always finished and lost before anyone can put into words what it was. In order to create my personal picture of how Greek theatre *was*, I return unavoidably to the way Greek theatre has been performed in the twentieth century. Each modern performance embodies a new understanding of the past, and offers a new perspective. My sense of how things were in the past is informed by my sense of what theatre can do in the present, and my dreams of

what it might do. The theatrical culture which I inhabit is, if not a thriving one, at least a pluralist one, with no single dominant notion of how theatre ought to be, so it is easier for me than for a scholar a hundred years ago to weigh and evaluate different possibilities, and to probe the boundaries which separate modern practices from the radically different practices of the past.

(7) I share widespread contemporary embarrassment at the notion of 'great art' because I know that the aesthetic taste of one generation, class or culture is rarely shared by the next. I prefer to say that I admire Greek plays because they have so many possibilities. They can be handled as movement pieces, performance poetry or intellectual arguments. They confront themes like war, gender, democracy and the limits of materialism which seem to matter in the present. The unique qualities of Greek dramatic writing are bound up with the uniqueness of the Greek political experiment, which engaged the public as participants in rather than spectators of all public events.

(8) The true authors were the Athenian public. The conflicts and perplexities of some 30,000 men were articulated through a small number of writers and a rather larger number of performers. My shortest chapter is the one devoted to the handful of Athenians who served their city as dramatic poets, for I see theatre as a collaborative process. Without the skills of the performers and the emotional commitment of the spectators, the scripts that we now read could not have been written.

(9) It is an accident of history that our knowledge of Greek drama has been transmitted by words on papyrus, and not by the tomb paintings of the Egyptians, the picture writing of the Aztecs or the celluloid and magnetic tape of the twentieth century.

The first half of this book is devoted to modes of performance in classical Athens: (1) the recounting of stories or 'myths'; (2) ceremonies devoted to the gods; (3) speeches designed to sway an assembly towards the speaker's point of view; and (4) everyday life, with the particular example of how gender is performed. These modes of performance shape both the form and the content of Greek drama. Since theatre is a relationship between actors and spectators at one moment in time, I consider in chapter 5 the physical basis of that relationship. Chapter 6 is perhaps the core of the book, for the live and spectacular presence of the performer distinguishes theatre and dance from other artistic media. The fact

that theatre does not *need* writing is precisely what makes the writer an interesting figure to study in chapter 7. I finish by trying to unravel some of the issues that arise when performers *now* try to understand *their* theatre *then*.

CHAPTER I

Myth

SUBJECT MATTER

Mythos

According to Aristotle – and we agree there – narrative is the soul of drama. (Brecht)[1]

For the philosopher Aristotle the life-spirit of a play was its *mythos* – a word we can variously translate as story, plot, narrative, myth or simply an act of speaking. I shall start this analysis of Greek theatre with its storytelling – the core skill that kept an audience on the front of its wooden seats through a long day. It is sometimes stated that Greek audiences knew the stories, and knew what was fated to happen. This is misleading. The myths of classical Greece were highly malleable, and the job of the dramatist was not to reproduce myths but to recreate them. Compared with today, there was more possibility of surprise for there were no reviews, no published texts, and plays were written for a one-off performance. There is also the simple fact that good theatre relies on suspense. The expert story-teller can hold a listener who has heard the tale many times before. Take this account of a scene by Euripides:

Remember how Merope in the tragedy raised her axe against her son because she mistook him for his own murderer. When she cries: 'This blow will cost you dearer than the one you gave!' what uproar she causes in the auditorium, lifting them to their feet in terror, in case she does the boy an injury before the old man can stop her.[2]

This may be a folk memory of the first performance. More likely it describes an effect regularly reproduced after the play had become a classic known to all, thanks to the skill of the dramatist and actors, and the quality of audience involvement.

5

Gods

The Greek term *mythos* covered a spectrum of meanings from a palpable falsehood to a story of deep symbolic and religious significance. The tragedians had at their disposal a stock of 'myths' or traditional story lines about gods and heroes, and a short introduction to these more-than-human beings is essential. The presence of the divine can be accepted, rationalized or simply eliminated in modern performance. In 1968 Richard Schechner's adaptation of *The Bacchae* challenged the audience to question their humanist assumptions and accept the divine. The actor playing the god Dionysos introduced himself by giving his own name:

Good evening, I see you found your seats. My name is William Finley. I was born twenty-seven years ago and two months after my birth the hospital in which I was born burned to the ground. I've come here tonight for three important reasons. The first and most important of these is to announce my divinity. The second is to establish my rites and rituals. And the third is to be born, if you'll excuse me.

During the birth ritual, Finley continued his commentary:

Now I noticed some untoward snickering when I announced the fact that I was a god. I realize that in 1968 it is hard to fathom the idea that gods walk the earth again. However, to say that I am not a god would be the same as saying that this is not a theatre ... Now for those of you who believe what I just told you, that I am a god, you are going to have a terrific evening. The rest of you are in trouble.[3]

With this warning in mind, let us consider how the modern mind can relate to the Greek gods. At one extreme were the Olympians, whom we may consider the highest form of divine life, victors in a long process of natural selection, looking and behaving like humans, and residing – at least notionally – on top of Greece's highest mountain, Olympus. Then there were demons, like the Furies or Erinyes whom Aeschylus describes as black, tangled with snakes, eyes oozing blood.[4] These demons were of greater antiquity than the Olympians, and lived within the earth. It was a major innovation when Aeschylus asked human actors to impersonate creatures that could scarcely be imagined in any human form. At a further level of abstraction, forces such as Atê (blind destruction), Dikê (justice) and Anankê (compulsion) could be imagined as semi-personal deities. The system was fluid enough to allow Euripides, for example, to stage creatures called Death and Madness – part divinities, part allegorical symbols.

There are different ways of understanding the Olympians. The simplest approach is biographical. Zeus, king of the gods, came to power at a certain point when he ousted the previous regime of Titans. He rules as lord of the manor alongside his wife Hera, and goes around fathering children upon the female tenants of his earthly estate. His underemployed children by different liaisons – Apollo, Artemis, Ares, Athene, Aphrodite, Dionysos, Hephaistos, Hermes – quarrel amongst themselves and create chaos by dabbling in human affairs. His siblings rule lesser estates: Hades the underworld, Poseidon the sea, Demeter the cornfields, Hestia the indoor world. It follows that we can also associate the Olympians with different aspects of space. Zeus rules the sky, his weapon is a bolt of lightning, and he fertilizes the female earth with rain. Artemis the huntress roams in the uncultivated wilderness. Hermes is concerned with movement across boundaries from place to place, whilst Dionysos dissolves boundaries, moving freely from drinking parties to wild mountain tops. This spatial analysis is more satisfactory than the biographical mode because it recognizes that the Greek gods were a means of describing the world and explaining it. The gods can also be understood as social and psychological projections. Female experience is associated with a series of goddesses – Hera: the frustrations of the married state; Athene: the asexual world of domestic production; Hestia: seclusion in the home; Aphrodite: the exercise of erotic attraction; Demeter: reproduction; Artemis: the wildness of adolescence, the pain, fertility and taboos associated with menstruation. Male experience incorporates Zeus as power, Hermes as travel, Ares as fighting, Dionysos as drinking, Hephaistos as manual labour, Apollo as artistic and intellectual endeavour. Of course, male aspects impinge upon women, and vice versa. Each god has a complex series of attributes which resonate in many directions.

A comparison between Apollo and Dionysos will illustrate some of these complexities. Dionysos shared Apollo's holiest shrine at Delphi, and reigned in the four winter months whilst Apollo retreated to a sunnier clime. Apollo is associated with light, thus intellectual enlightenment, and far-sighted prophecy. Dionysos the wine-god is associated with darkness, with nocturnal drinking bouts, and the loss of mental clarity in moments of collective emotion, with the loss of boundaries around the self experienced in a crowd, and the hiding of self behind a theatrical mask. Apollo makes music with the measured chords of his lyre, whilst the instrument of Dionysos is

the haunting double oboe which can whip up wild dances. The worshippers of Apollo tend to be male, those of Dionysos more often female. In the field of performance, Apollo is responsible for epic poetry, which is to say the disciplined recitation of a classic text by a single performer. Dionysos is responsible for theatre, with its collective performance, its freedom of bodily expression, its unpredictable content, its anarchic assemblage of different verse forms, and its projection of a moral void.

It is often said that there can be no such thing as a Christian tragedy. Christianity posits that God is good and does not contradict himself; hence in every moral dilemma there is ultimately a right and wrong. In Greek religion, the gods have no morality, and represent irreconcilable opposites. In Greek tragedy conflict amongst humans is often mirrored by conflict amongst the gods: for example, Artemis (chastity) opposes Aphrodite (sexual fulfilment) in the *Hippolytus*. These gods are powerful and have to be honoured, but they have no concern with the criteria of right and wrong. They usually like their worshippers to be pure, not physically polluted by a crime like murder, but that is not the same thing as morality, a sense developed by human beings alone. Tragedy allowed Greeks to extrapolate from the anarchy of their religion a viable moral code.

Modern readers are often shocked by the cruelty or (in comedy) the ridiculousness of Greek gods, and wonder if the author responsible was an atheist or a blasphemer. This is to miss the point, for the only true crime against the Greek gods was to dishonour them by denying their power. Although modern criticism has yielded techniques for rationalizing the Greek gods, we must remember that gods are, ultimately, gods and it is their nature to resist explanation.

Translators of Greek plays have a serious problem with the gods, since they are forced in some measure to standardize a host of variant names. The translator's dilemma is whether to strip much of the religious content from the text so it becomes comprehensible, or to lace the text with beautiful and exotic names that create an aura of numinous mystery. Directors also have to take a stance. David Rudkin and Ron Daniels opted for rationalism in their version of the *Hippolytus* presented by the Royal Shakespeare Company in 1978, a period much less sympathetic to mysticism than 1968. Rudkin argued: 'It is quite natural for man to make human form of the abstracts and intangibles he feels in his experience.' Thus 'Greek tragedy does not deal with mythology at all. It deals with the world.'

Figure 1 Dionysos in *The Frogs* wearing the lion skin of Herakles. The slave Xanthias carries his baggage. From a vase of about 375–350 BC.

Rudkin arrives at a troubling paradox: 'we can only approach the original "Greek" experience of the play by expunging all that is culture-specifically Greek in it.'[5] The assumption that Artemis and Aphrodite are merely aspects of psychological experience resulted in a certain quality of performance. Juliet Stevenson played both roles, a still, human presence in the middle of an intimate theatre, voicing thoughts. By contrast, Silviu Purcarete's Romanian production which visited England in 1995 offered an Artemis who paced restlessly about the stage swathed in bandages from head to toe with no eyes visible. Here was a figure that could not be explained in any rational terms, barely human, with a menace that suggested the power of a totalitarian regime.[6]

Heroes

Whilst gods hover on the margins of Greek tragedy, the plots focus upon heroes, men and women of a distant time that can neither be

called myth nor history. The Greeks knew that the heroes existed not only from innumerable tales, but also because they could see the vestiges of their palaces built of gigantic boulders, and the grave mounds beneath which they were buried. It was felt that such ancestors could exert some power upon their descendants, so heroes were often worshipped at these graves. The difference between heroes and gods was that gods live for ever. Euripides in his play *Orestes* shows Apollo transforming Helen of Troy at death into a star – but this is not the same thing as living forever, for as a star Helen can no longer intervene in human affairs. The unique instance of a hero who successfully became a god is Herakles. As a hero, this man of incomparable strength is at the centre of two surviving plays; as a god, he makes a brief appearance in the resolution of *Philoctetes*, and in *Alcestis* he straddles both categories, fighting a god in order to save the heroine.

The plays that survive are dominated by three story cycles. (1) The war against Troy: two brothers, Agamemnon, king of Argos and Menelaus, king of Sparta, lead a Greek expedition to Troy on the Turkish coast, where they fight to recapture Helen, wife of Menelaus. After a siege of ten years, the Greeks destroy the city amidst scenes of much brutality. (2) The Orestes story: the same Agamemnon returns to the city of Argos, where his wife Clytaemnestra has taken up with another man. Clytaemnestra murders her husband in his bath, and in punishment is murdered by her vengeful son Orestes, who is aided and abetted by her daughter Electra. (3) The Oedipus story: in the city of Thebes Oedipus, having unknowingly killed his father, unknowingly fathers four children upon his mother. The curse of Oedipus destroys the next generation. His two sons fall out, and one leads an army from Argos to lay siege to Thebes, where the pair kill each other in single combat. These three story cycles, containing two wars and every permutation of intrafamilial conflict, provided the material for hundreds of plays. There were always new points of view to be found, new shifts of sympathy, new interpretations of motive, and new moral dilemmas. Although other story cycles were used – cycles associated with figures like Herakles, Theseus founder of Athens, Cadmus founder of Thebes and Jason the Argonaut, the number of stories was finite. Dramatists kept returning to the same core narratives.

The dramatists found infinite variety in these stories through superimposing the present upon the template of the past. In theory

the plays are set in a distant bronze age milieu, but the characters inhabit the mental universe of the audience, and their values are substantially those of the democratic period. We might compare the way Shakespeare set his history plays in the feudal era, but used them to discuss an Elizabethan regime. An extreme example of this double-time-scale is provided by Euripides' *Orestes*. In earlier tellings of the story, Orestes killed his mother in pursuance of the unwritten laws of vendetta, but in Euripides' play Orestes is castigated for not referring the matter to a democratic law court. A modern society based upon the rule of law is superimposed upon an ancient society based upon codes of honour. In more subtle ways, all Greek tragedies observed the same principle, refracting the past through the present to make old stories generate an infinite number of new meanings.

The first tragedies about which we know anything useful dealt with recent history: the great wars in which the united Greeks fought off the Persians. Aeschylus' *Persians* survives, depicting how news of final defeat was brought to the Persian court. Another early tragedian wrote a play about genocide in the Greek city of Miletus. The audience wept, and the author was fined for 'reminding them of a disaster which touched them so closely'.[7] Empathy was all too easy when the Athenians lay under the same Persian threat, and tears did not fortify the spirit of resistance. Mythic subject matter was not a residue of old tradition, but was introduced into tragedy as a means of generating critical distance, so issues of the moment could be turned into issues of principle. By transferring immediate political hopes and fears to the world of myth, tragedians encouraged their audience to judge as well as to feel. Or rather, to feel from more than one point of view, with tears born of sympathy, not empathy.

MYTH AS PERFORMANCE

The Greek tragedies that we possess were, so far as we know, written for the city of Athens, and date from the years 472 BC (the performance of Aeschylus' *Persians*) to 406 BC when Sophocles and Euripides died.[8] These dates fall close to two major political turning points, the defeat of the Persians by the Greeks in 479 and the fall of Athens to Sparta in 404. For convenience of reference, I shall refer to this as the 'classical' period.

Oral tradition

The audience of the classical period had no basis for conceiving the text as something separable from performance. When Aristophanes stages in *The Frogs* a contest between Aeschylus and Euripides, the writers have the words inside their heads and render them complete with rhythms, music, choreography and a description of costume. Writing was needed for words intended to remain forever in the public gaze – laws and memorials to the dead – but was only incidental to the business of creating plays. Myth was the product of an oral society. The very word *mythos* implies 'something spoken'. For the classical Greek audience, myths were, only and always, *performances*. There was no sacred text declaring the truth about the gods, equivalent to the Bible, the Torah or the Koran. No definitive version of any Greek myth fixed the story forever in writing. Myths in multiple variants were transmitted and circulated through songs, dances, recitations of poetry and pictures. In an oral culture, the performers of myths were free to reshape their material in response to new audiences and situations.

Women's tales

The first stories which a child encountered were told by women. Plato writes, when laying out his programme for a utopian society: 'We shall persuade mothers and nurses to tell our selected myths to their children, to mould minds by means of stories rather than bodies by physical handling. Of the stories they tell now, most will have to be censored.'[9] Plato was convinced that stories heard in early childhood had a major impact upon adult behaviour. Women had the job of rearing children, and no television or books to help them develop a child's language and imagination. They had more time for stories than men did, and they were a repository of mythological lore. This is one reason why Greek choruses were so often female. At any point women could dip into their fund of stories to find analogies for present events.

The opening chorus of Euripides' *Hypsipyle* illustrates this story culture. An enslaved princess sings simple words to a baby and laments that she is not at home on the island of her birth, where she would now be working on the loom and exchanging indigenous songs with her companions. As she sweeps the courtyard, women

arrive and expect to hear her singing of Jason, her lover who fetched the golden fleece. When soldiers are seen nearby, the slave princess retreats into the past and her fund of romantic stories about Jason and the Argonauts. The women try to comfort her by pulling from their stock two stories of exiled women that have happy endings, the myths of Europa and Io, but the slave caps them with a third that has a gloomy ending. Sharing repetitive work, Greek women devoted much mental energy to stories, and memories shaded easily into myths.

Choruses

A 'chorus' was a group that both danced and sang in unison. At a festival belonging to a god or hero, choruses of men or women would recount stories of that god or hero. On the island of Delos maidens in early times used to sing hymns to Apollo at his mythical birthplace, and groups would come to the island to compete in a choral competition. An ancient hymn to Apollo describes how the dancers would sing of Apollo, and about heroes of yesteryear, imitating male and female voices in a wholly plausible way.[10] Athens revived and regulated the competition in the classical period. The custom was that choruses had to start singing the moment they set foot on the sacred island, so the Athenian Nikias, famous both for his wealth and his piety in the classical period, decided to build a pontoon bridge to the next island, allowing his chorus at the moment of sunrise to make a grand theatrical entry, fully costumed and in good order. Nikias knew about theatre, and prided himself on the fact that his choruses were always victorious.[11] Whilst tradition had to be respected, the framework of competition acted as a powerful stimulus to creativity. On Delos, as so often in traditional choral dances, women had a key role as performers.

Before the performance of tragedies and comedies at the festival of Dionysos, ten choruses of fifty boys apiece and ten similar choruses of men competed with songs in honour of Dionysos, called 'dithyrambs'. Costume and rehearsal entailed enormous expense. The opening chorus of Euripides' *Bacchae* seems to imitate the traditional form of a dithyramb. The chorus clear a passage, bring on an image of the god and call blessings on his followers. They tell the story of Dionysos' birth from the thigh of Zeus, and a second narrative sequence tells the history of the drum upon which they

beat their rhythms. A dance of the kind which we see in *Bacchae* would have become monotonous if performed twenty times, and it seems that many different myths were recounted under the pressure of pleasing a panel of amateur judges. The proverbial phrase 'Nothing to do with Dionysos!' emerged in response to the fact that stories sung and danced in honour of this god strayed outside his own cycle of myths.

Epic

The recitation of epic poems was an old performance art that continued to flourish during the classical period. Homer's *Iliad* dealt with the siege of Troy, and events that stemmed from the anger of Achilles, the most charismatic warrior in the Greek army. Homer's *Odyssey* dealt with the return of the Greek warrior Odysseus to his island home after Troy had fallen. The subject matter of the *Iliad* gave it special cultural importance, for numerous Greek states sent contingents to the Asian city of Troy, and the *Iliad* thus opened up questions about collective Greek identity. Odysseus served as a Greek everyman thanks partly to the fact that he came from an island of no political significance.

Set down in writing two or three centuries before the classical period, Homer's poems were not a bible, but helped to fix a collective understanding of the gods. The Greek gods were worshipped under many titles in many different sanctuaries, and different statues embodied different visual images, but Homer implied that behind these local practices lay in each case a single figure of human appearance. A goddess called Aphrodite, for example, emerged from the poems with distinctive physical features (golden hair) and a distinctive psychological character. Even here, though, the Greeks had to balance Homer against another epic poet, Hesiod, who provided Aphrodite with a quite different ancestry. For Homer, she is the daughter of Zeus; for Hesiod she is born from the semen of Zeus' grandfather, the sky-god.

Homer appears to construct a self-portrait when he depicts the blind bard Demodokos singing to the lyre in a royal court where Odysseus is being entertained. Outdoors, the bard sings another tale of the gods whilst athletic young men interpret his story in dance.[12] However, these pictures belong to an earlier society, and have little bearing on the urbanized classical world, where a 'rhapsode'

performed competitively before a huge public audience. The rhapsode stood on a platform, with a rod in his hand to give him presence
and prevent the use of gesture. Everything turned upon the unaccompanied voice. Plato has left us a vivid portrait of a professional
rhapsode returning victorious from a competition in honour of the
god Asclepius, ambitious to win in the Panathenaia, Athens' greatest
festival held in honour of the city's patron Athene (see p. 153
below).[13] Homeric recitation was a centrepiece of the festival,
perhaps because Homer belonged to all the Greeks and Athens
wanted to make a statement about cultural supremacy. In the later
classical period, performance probably took place in the Odeon, a
hall next to the theatre where some 6,000 people could sit and listen,
shaded from the summer sun, though some could not see for the
pillars. The competitors had to have the complete text of both
poems committed to memory, and had to take up at whatever point
the previous competitor in random sequence left off. It is likely that
the present form of the poems, each divided into twenty-four books,
derives from the Panathenaic contest. In addition to vocal skills and
the ability to create suspense in an audience that knew the text
intimately, the rhapsode also needed skills of character building, for
much of Homer's text takes the form of direct speech. The rhapsode
had somehow to assume the character of the person speaking.

Homer was seen as a founding father of tragedy.[14] The tragedians
drew from his work a distinctive milieu: a heroic world in which
gods from time to time reveal themselves to mortals, an aristocratic
society unlike the present and thus ripe for challenge. The horror
and glory of war collide in Homer, but enough glory remains for
dramatists to question his vision. Although Greeks triumph over
Asiatics in Homer, they do so through greater cunning and a higher
level of divine support, but not superior moral virtues. Homer thus
prepared the way for tragedy where rights and wrongs are evenly
divided. The tragedians also learned from Homer the technique of
compressing action into a narrow timeframe, for much of the *Iliad* is
packed into four days. They learned the art of constructing dramatic
situations, but for the most part avoided using Homer's actual
stories. Though Homer's text was not sacred, his interpretation of
events was too powerful to meddle with, and the playwrights drew
most of their material from a corpus of lesser poems, all now
vanished, dealing with the Trojan war, Herakles, Oedipus and the
city of Thebes. Here dramatists could tinker freely with contexts,

Figure 2 A rhapsode reciting Homer at the Panathenaia, watched by a rival in the competition. From an oil jar of about 510 BC.

motives and the order of events, creating a new interpretation of the past that would carry as much authority as the older account.

The convention of the 'messenger speech' owes much to the art of the rhapsode. At the climax of almost every Greek tragedy, a single speaker's voice describes a violent death: how Oedipus blinds himself, Hippolytus is killed by a bull that charges from the sea, or Pentheus torn apart on the mountain by his female relatives. These speeches are not a sign that tragedy lacked enough visual resources; rather, they were an opportunity for the actor to display an ancient skill. Messenger speeches have great emotional power. Having accepted a certain storyline, having visualized certain characters, the spectator was forced by words alone to imagine the unimaginable.

Life amidst myth

The phrase 'a forest of myths' has been coined to evoke the world of the classical Greeks.[15] Images from myth met the eye on personal jewellery, on drinking cups, on statues in the street, and on wall paintings in the market place. Myths were associated with every form of ceremony. Roland Barthes has used the term 'mythologies' to evoke the complex of messages emanating from television, film, magazines, posters and cookery books in French bourgeois culture.[16] The Greeks were subject to the same kind of saturation, and life outside the parameters of myth was inconceivable. In what sense, then, did the Greeks 'believe' in their myths? We could dismiss the question as irrelevant. People whose perceptions of life today are *shaped* by Hollywood do not in any meaningful sense *believe* in Hollywood. Yet there are differences between then and now. Greek myths told of heroes whose graves were physically present. The historical notion that there was once a war against Troy and a king of Thebes called Oedipus lay beyond dispute. It was in relation to the gods that the question of belief became sensitive.

Plato is a helpful guide to Athenian opinion. Here is part of a lecture that he imagined himself giving to a hot-headed young atheist:

Neither you nor your friends are the first to have held this view of the gods. The disease is a constant, though not the number of sufferers. I've met a great many. Let me assure you that no one convinced early in life that gods don't exist has ever retained that belief into old age. Two feelings about religion can hold their grip, however, not frequently but often enough: first, the gods do exist but are indifferent to human affairs; and second, the gods do indeed care and in a moment can be won over by our sacrifices and prayers.[17]

Plato sketches out a range of contemporary positions, from atheism to superstition or an agnostic belief in gods who never intervene, and he has to look back to Minoan Crete in the heroic age to find a period of religious consensus.[18] Plato's own view was a revisionist one. He was a man of deep religious sensibility, but believed the gods were fundamentally good, and thus that much of Homer and traditional mythology ought to be abandoned. Tragedy would also have to be censored. He quotes, for example, one of Aeschylus' plays in which a sea-goddess laments the death of her son Achilles at Troy, declaring that Apollo sang a song of blessing on her child, and then

broke his word by causing her son's death. 'If a poet says this sort of thing about the gods,' declares Plato, 'we shall be angry and refuse to let him produce his play; nor shall we allow it to be used to educate our children.'[19] The logic of Plato's argument became notorious, namely that tragedy and comedy have no place in an ideal society.

In the classical period when Plato grew up, every Greek intellectual was an expert in deconstructing myth. Back in 530 BC Xenophanes was already declaiming in Homeric style poems which stated that Homer's gods were pure fiction. If horses could paint, Xenophanes argued, they would paint the gods as horses, and cattle would paint the gods as cattle. A gulf became increasingly pronounced between the intelligentsia and ordinary citizens. For the benefit of a mass audience, Aristophanes' play *The Clouds* mocked the activities of free-thinking intellectuals. The philosopher Socrates was seen in the play suspended in a basket trying to view the sky more closely, having determined to worship the clouds – which are of course a nice symbol of mental vacuity. Many years later, because he had associated himself with elitist politicians, the real Socrates was brought to trial for his unorthodox religious teachings and put to death.

We must avoid the trap of supposing that 'the Greeks' all shared the same core of beliefs. They did not – and that is why the plays are so interesting. Take the example of Sophocles' *Antigone*: when the chorus sang of all that humans had achieved in navigation, agriculture, hunting, fishing and housing, many would have sensed a humanist message, a message which the play goes on to question. In the play, Antigone buries her brother in defiance of a decree that a traitor must remain unburied. Because Antigone seems to be the individual pitted against the state, following her heart rather than her head, it is rather easy for modern readers and directors to spring to the assumption that Antigone is right and her uncle Creon wrong. The play seems to demonstrate, to a consciousness informed by Christianity, that the gods, i.e. right, are on Antigone's side. In the classical period things were much more complicated. There were several decrees at the time refusing burial to traitors. Plato, who was a religious man but also an enthusiast for state control, had no qualms in urging that a religious fraudster should be cast over the border unburied.[20] Sophocles glosses over the crucial question of borders, so the play did not turn on a technicality but was open to

multiple interpretations. His plays drew their creative energy from the fact that there was no consensus within his audience about the most fundamental religious issues.

Variant versions

Greek myths were endlessly malleable. The Athenians, for example, gradually transformed Theseus into their national hero:[21] the Theseus who saved Athenian girls from the minotaur was reshaped to become the founder of a centralized democratic regime. The purpose of such myth-making was to validate political changes, and make them harder for a later generation to reverse. A famous painting in Athens represented Theseus rising from the earth to participate in the battle of Marathon. A line was slipped into the still malleable text of the *Odyssey* in order that Theseus should appear on a roll-call of the great that all Greece respected. At the start of the classical period a politician called Kimon, who liked to associate himself with Theseus, wanted to colonize the island of Skyros and remove its native population. Having advertised the myth that Theseus was killed on Skyros, he duly excavated the bones of a long-dead warrior of huge build, and ceremoniously brought them back to Athens.

The tragedians were part of this on-going process of myth-making. An orator remarks: 'Who does not know, who has not heard from the tragic teachers at the Dionysia about the misfortunes of Adrastus at Thebes?'[22] The story in question told of how Adrastus, king of Argos, needed the help of Athens in order to recover his war dead. Increasingly the main way in which Athenians absorbed myths in the classical period was through the performance of tragedy. When written words carried no authority, the poet was seen to be a guru, the personal embodiment of knowledge. Aeschylus wrote a tragedy in which Theseus persuaded the Thebans to hand over the bodies to Adrastus, and allowed the Argive commanders to be buried on Athenian soil. Aeschylus' Theseus embodied the ideal of peace and reconciliation. In the surviving version by Euripides, Theseus goes to war for the bodies, which are finally sent home amidst fierce oaths about what will happen to Argos if it reneges on its debt to Athens. Athens at the time of Euripides' play was at war

with Thebes, and Argos had reneged or was about to renege on its treaty with Athens.[23] In a new political context, the myth had to be rewritten, validating Athens' policies in a new situation. Euripides' version was not more or less authentic than that of Aeschylus. Both were part of a continuing process.

In one instance we can read three versions of a myth alongside each other: Aeschylus' *Libation Bearers*, Euripides' *Electra* and Sophocles' *Electra*. In these plays we can trace different attitudes to monarchical rule, moral responsibility and the state of mind that allows a child to kill its parent. When we read a play like *Oedipus the King*, which only survives in Sophocles' version, we have to remember that the first audience viewed the play in relation to the way Aeschylus had told the story. Whilst for us Sophocles recounts *the* myth, to the Athenians he offered his own particular, nuanced interpretation. In Homer and the lost epic *Oedipodeia*, Oedipus marries his mother called Epicasta not Jocasta, he remains king of Thebes after discovering the incest, and has his four children by a second marriage.[24] Aeschylus and Sophocles developed the tragic situation of Oedipus, and made his downfall political. In Aeschylus it is likely that the fate of Oedipus resulted from the crime of Oedipus' father Laius, who raped a prince. Sophocles' emphasis on the rationality of Oedipus and the arbitrariness of fate would be seen as a new interpretation. The plague which starts Sophocles' play was in all likelihood inspired by a great plague which decimated the Athenian population at the time of writing, caused by refugees crowding into the city in insanitary conditions.[25] We cannot understand the play as the Athenians did because we have lost the earlier versions of the myth, and can only glimpse the political context.

Intertextuality

In a comedy called *Poetics*, Comedy declares that tragedians have an easy life:

Tragedy is a blessed art in every way, since its plots are well known to the audience before anyone begins to speak. A poet need only remind. I have just to say, 'Oedipus', and they know all the rest: father, Laius; mother, Jocasta; their sons and daughters; what he will suffer; what he has done.[26]

The statement is comical because it exceeds the truth. Whether Oedipus will be driven into exile, imprisoned in Thebes or left on

the throne remains open for the dramatist to determine. But there is still a sense in which tragedy was a 'blessed art', for the use of a limited core of stories allowed every viewing to be 'intertextual', and thus dense. Behind the lines and images of one play the audience could always discern another. In the postmodern age, Jacques Derrida suggests that we should reject originality as a creative ideal, and value instead what he punningly calls *différance* – the idea that meaning is (a) constituted by distinctions, and (b) always deferred, thrown back upon previous meanings *ad infinitum.*[27]

Let me put one tiny example beneath the microscope: an exchange from Euripides' *Phoenician Women.* Antigone stands on the walls of Thebes with her tutor, surveying the army that has come to destroy the city. When she asks the position of her brother, the tutor replies: 'By the tomb of the seven maiden daughters of Niobe.' From their knowledge of the theatrical repertory, the Athenian audience would have brought to bear on this exchange layers of knowledge about: (1) the forthcoming assault on the seven gates of Thebes; (2) the likelihood that a less naïve Antigone would die in consequence of burying this brother; (3) how Niobe's daughters were shot by Artemis. The death of these innocent Theban princesses long ago – familiar to the audience from the *Niobe* of Aeschylus and the *Niobe* of Sophocles – foreshadows the fate that awaits an innocent girl like Antigone if the city falls. The use of myth allows this tiny but typical fragment of dialogue to possess a richness of texture and play of meaning that would be impossible in an 'original' story.

Not that any story is ever truly original. The pleasure of an audience always depends upon its ability to predict. The cinema-goer will always place a Hollywood film in a genre, and genre provides assurances about how the story will end. The chase sequence marks the fact that the story has entered its final phase. The viewer's pleasure is the greater the more he or she knows the rules of the form. And so it is with tragedy.

MODERN VIEWS OF MYTH

Psychoanalysis

As in the time of Plato, so today the analysis of myth is a major academic industry. Scholars have tried at different times to interpret myths as a corrupted form of history or a pre-scientific way of

explaining the universe. It was the fashion at the start of the twentieth century to relate all myths to a universal myth about a 'year-god' who dies and returns in spring. When Peter Brook in 1967 chose to end his production of *Oedipus* (in Seneca's Roman version) with an image of a huge golden phallus, he was influenced by the now outmoded idea that all myths deal with fertility and the cycle of death and rebirth. Two currents in twentieth-century thought remain today particularly influential: psychoanalysis and structuralism.

Psychoanalysis proposes that we have an unconscious mind, a conception which the Greeks would have found incomprehensible. Freud, as is well known, thought that the power of Sophocles' *Oedipus the King* relates to the drive of every child to kill its father and marry its mother, so people enjoy the play because it releases a repressed wish.[28] One of the many flaws in Freud's theory is the fact that Sophocles' play obsessed European theatre directors around 1900 more than it did Greeks in the classical period. Greek vase painters were far more interested in representing Oedipus' encounter with the Sphinx than his parricide or incest. Since the Sphinx is female, one might have thought that killing a Sphinx is rather like killing a mother figure – if Freud's theory did not dictate otherwise. Psychoanalytic criticism has become much more sophisticated since the time of Freud, and the broad notion that myth relates to conflicts within the psyche cannot be so easily dismissed.

Freud's theory was conditioned by the theatrical realities of his day. He was inspired by Sophocles' play in the emotive production of Mounet-Sully, where the star actor was everything, the chorus was nothing.[29] The proscenium theatre can be regarded as a model for Freud's conception of mind: the isolated ego fully visible in the foreground, with gloom, murk and shadowy shapes in the background. In his one essay devoted to theatre, Freud tries to explain why people enjoy tragedy. The spectator will 'identify himself with a hero', whilst at the same time knowing that it is 'someone other than himself who is acting and suffering on the stage'. Pleasure in identifying with a man of greatness is mixed with masochistic satisfaction in seeing the hero suffer. Heroes like Prometheus, Ajax and Philoctetes, Freud believed, engaged in a primal rebellion 'against God or something divine'.[30] Such statements accord with conventions of performance at the end of the nineteenth century: the star actor is picked out by footlights which amplify his features;

the spectator forgets in the now darkened auditorium that she or he is part of a community, and identifies with the solitary hero.

Structuralism

Structuralism starts from the proposition that meaning is created only when distinctions are set up within a *structure*. If we study the mythological *system* of any pre-literate society, and find the structural logic underpinning that system, then we see how myth fulfils the para-scientific function of describing society and nature. Structuralism has no interest in the problem of consciousness, in what people think about myth, and maintains rather that myths think themselves through people.

The structural anthropologist Claude Lévi-Strauss undertook a famous analysis of the Oedipus myth as a way of explaining his method. Although his analysis has been discredited in its detail, his method of working has exerted a huge influence. Lévi-Strauss has no interest in the narrative order of the story, but arranges the separate components of the story into bundles. He assembles enough bundles to show that the myth generates two sets of 'binary oppositions'. Bundle one, which concerns people who love their relatives too much (incest, breaking the law to bury a brother), is set in opposition to bundle two, which concerns those who love relatives too little (killing a father, a brother). The nature of the family is at issue here as Freud recognized. Bundle three is concerned with the killing of monsters such as the Sphinx, while bundle four is concerned with images of lameness, exemplified by the nailed feet of Oedipus when left as a baby on the mountainside. Lévi-Strauss argued that these images of lameness relate to the idea that human beings began as vegetables growing from the earth. The Sphinx, Lévi-Strauss goes on, is an earth monster, and in killing her Oedipus demonstrates that humans are different in kind from all that belongs to the earth. The myth is thus a way of questioning what it is to be human: is bisexual reproduction an inherent part of being human, or a kind of anomaly?[31]

It all sounds very strange – but that was precisely Lévi-Strauss' point. If we are to understand myth, we have to discard twentieth-century common sense and find a thread through a chaotic mass of detail. Observe the difficulty which modern readers usually have with Euripides' play *Ion*. Ion's Athenian mother is associated, thanks

to her parentage and the poison of a monstrous Gorgon in her amulet, with a dangerous earth-monster. Ion almost kills his mother, but recognizes her in the nick of time. It is easy for us to read the play as an ironic situation comedy. It is much harder to see how Euripides in his day was juggling two myths about the Athenians: the myth that they descended from the eastern *Ion*ian Greeks, and another newer myth that they descended from the earth-serpent Cecrops. The idea that Athenians sprang from their own soil had huge emotional appeal in an age of migrant peoples, and served to validate Athens' place as the supreme power in the Greek world. The structuralist method helps us to adjust to an unfamiliar, pre-scientific mind-set.[32]

In *Antigone*, a conflict of personality between Antigone and Creon correlates on the political level with a conflict of family and state, and on the level of myth with a conflict between dark, feminine earth goddesses and luminous, patriarchal Olympian gods. Antigone is buried alive in a cave, which helps associate her with subterranean divinities. The main binary oppositions of the play can be tabulated:

Creon	Antigone
city	household
human law	divine law
Zeus (sky-god)	earth-goddesses
male	female
daylight	darkness
exposure	burial[33]

The advantage of a simple structuralist analysis of this kind is that it prevents us from seeing the play reductively as just a psychological battle of wills, or just a conflict between individual and state. Mythic thought bound together psychological, political and religious thinking into an organic whole. The easy modern choice is to compartmentalize these categories.

COMEDY

Comic plots

Tragedians have life easy, lamented the voice of Comedy in *Poetics*, because their plots are given. A god can be flown in at the end to tie everything up . . . 'None of that for us. We have to invent everything: new names, then the previous circumstances, present situation,

resolution, prologue.' The elderly writer and novice alike are hissed if their invention fails in comedy.[34] In fact, the tragedian's skill lay precisely in inventing new situations. The greater originality of comic plots is an illusion, for the comedian will be hissed if he fails to deliver novelty according to the expected formula.

The heroic milieu of tragedy was transmuted into laughter in a short piece called a satyr play, which followed the performance of three tragedies – but more of this in the next chapter. Comedy in the classical period was set in the world of the Athenian audience, and could venture if it chose into the realm of the gods, but avoided the heroic world of tragedy and the satyr play. Comedy defined its identity not through being funny (for the satyr play was also funny) but through being the opposite of tragedy. Comedy in an immediate and direct way commented on the circumstances of the audience. Often, as in *Poetics*, comedies called attention to their own status as live performances.

Whilst tragedies are closed structures, in terms of both space and plot, comedies are open and linear. Characters journey from place to place, and the end is not sealed off by death or divine judgement, but opens into a future shared by the audience. Aristophanes is the only comic writer of the period to have left us more than fragments, and his play *Peace* demonstrates how minimal comic plotting could be. As in most of his comedies, an Athenian everyman figure goes in quest of something which citizens need. The comic hero, tired of war, rides to Olympus on a dung beetle and brings back the goddess Peace in the form of a statue. This storyline was inspired by Euripides' play about Bellerophon, who tried to fly to Olympus on a winged horse, and the fetching of the statue probably recalls a play by Sophocles, in which Odysseus smuggles a statue of war-like Athene out of Troy via the sewers. Aristophanes' 'original' plot was thus generated by the tragedies which it parodies. The second half of *Peace* has effectively no narrative at all, but enacts rituals around the installation of the statue, interrupted by frustrated warmongers.

In the last decades of the century which followed the classical period, comedy underwent a revolution. Menander and his contemporaries wrote tightly structured five-act plays on the boy-meets-girl theme. Their plots owe much to the tragedy of Euripides, and almost nothing to classical comedy.

CHAPTER 2

Ritual

THE NATURE OF RITUAL

Modern preconceptions

We have lost all sense of ritual and ceremony – whether it be connected with Christmas, birthdays or funerals – but the words remain with us and old impulses stir in the marrow ... So the artist sometimes attempts to find new rituals with only his imagination as his source ... The result is rarely convincing. (Peter Brook)[1]

Artaud expressed more passionately and forcefully than anyone else in the twentieth century the idea that psychological theatre is physically inert and spiritually sterile. He witnessed his ideal of 'pure' theatre when Balinese dancers visited a colonial exhibition in Paris in 1931, and he declared that their performance had 'the solemnity of a holy ritual'. In a sense this decontextualized dance-drama moved Artaud precisely because he could not understand it. He discerned 'a horde of ritualized gestures in it to which we have no key', and because he had no key, he was free to see these gestures as 'strange signs matching some dark prodigious reality we have repressed once and for all here in the West'.[2] Perhaps Artaud would have reacted in the same way if, somehow, ancient Greek actors transported from the past had invaded the colonial exhibition. Perhaps he would have loaded on to the past the same romantic longing that he attached to the Orient, for a life that was spiritual rather than alienated. Many classicists in the early twentieth century had interpreted Greek tragedy as a ritual form, preparing the way for Artaud's vision of the Balinese. There is a question that refuses to go away: were the Greeks fundamentally *like us*, being our ancestors who created the same theatre that *we* have inherited, or were they embodiments of *the other*, exotic, spiritually richer, and capable of

26

creating a theatre that was more total and more pure than anything we possess today?

Classical Greek society was more overtly ritualized than modern European and American society. Christianity, particularly the Protestant tradition, emphasizes the interior quality of faith, and the importance of the Bible as a revelation of God's will. Greek religion had no holy books and no interest in what individuals privately believed. Piety was a matter of performing ritual acts in honour of the gods, and these acts were the glue that held society together. Aristophanes in *The Frogs* has no scruple in showing the god Dionysos shitting himself in terror before a door-keeper. It mattered little what stories people told about the gods in a comedy and what people believed in their hearts. What did matter was reverencing Dionysos' ancient wooden statue, processing on the right day, and appointing a woman of true Athenian lineage as his official spouse. The oracle of Apollo at Delphi decreed that the Athenians were to honour Dionysos by dancing in a melée in the streets, putting garlands on their heads beside the altar, placing bowls of wine by the roadside, and raising their arms to the sky.[3] To abide by such customs was an absolute obligation within Athenian society.

Analyzing ritual

The modern world has found many different ways of understanding 'ritual', and I shall summarize three of the most important. Emile Durkheim, the father of modern sociology, was clear that ritual rather than belief was the basis of religion. He saw religion as a collective activity with a social purpose. The function of religion, he argued, 'is to make us act, and to help us to live. The believer ... is a man who is *stronger*'. Durkheim seeks to understand religious belief and practice in terms of its observed effect on society. 'If religion gave birth to all that is essential in society, that is so because the idea of society is the soul of religion.'[4] Religion, in other words, both creates and reflects society.

The structuralist method is to search in ritual for a system of symbolic meanings. The gestures of a Balinese dancer have a coded meaning which the indigenous Balinese or a trained anthropologist know how to decipher, but Artaud does not. 'The culture of a people is an ensemble of texts,' writes an American anthropologist at the end of a famous essay on the Balinese ritual of cockfighting.[5]

Reduced to a set of texts, every ritual becomes an explanatory story told by members of a group to their fellows.

The phenomenologist starts by trying to understand the individual's subjective experience of *the sacred*. Durkheim resisted this tendency, arguing that a psychic state involving feelings of the sacred stems from an intense collective activity. Much discussion of how Greeks subjectively experienced the ritual of theatre turns upon the word *catharsis*, which means purging or purification. Aristotle uses the word to describe what happens when people in a trance, feeling they are possessed by the gods, are brought back to normality through the playing of frenzied music, and he explains the pleasures of theatre in similar therapeutic terms.[6]

RITUAL AND PERFORMANCE

An example of ritual: the day of pitchers

The wine-drinking competition dramatized at the end of Aristophanes' play *The Acharnians* will serve as a representative Greek ritual. In Athens this ceremony marked the opening in spring of the previous autumn's vintage. It formed part of a festival of Dionysos the wine-god that had nothing directly to do with performing tragedies and comedies.

Aristophanes' play depicts the efforts of a peasant farmer to effect peace between Athens and Sparta. The farmer attempts to involve his household in the annual 'rural Dionysia', processing behind a giant phallus, but the community embodied by the chorus disrupts his celebration. In his solitary quest for peace against the wishes of his community, the farmer turns to the wine-drinking contest which allows him to function as an individual. Instead of sharing in the meat cut from a sacrificial animal and drinking from the communal wine bowl passed around the circle, each participant in the 'Day of Pitchers' brought his own picnic and drank from his own jug. The custom was explained by a myth – dramatized, by Aeschylus in his *Eumenides*. According to the myth, Orestes, after killing his mother, sought refuge in Athens, placing the Athenians in a dilemma: should they welcome him as the man of justice, or turn him away as a man polluted by matricide? According to the story honoured by the festival (which here differed from Aeschylus), the Athenians compromised by devising a new ceremony to display their hospitality.

Instead of the wine bowl being passed around the circle in a convivial manner, each man drank alone in silence at his private table from his own jug. Doors were shut and temples closed on this day because spirits of the dead were thought to circulate. The annual drinking contest was a kind of drama commemorating the way Orestes was simultaneously admitted to the community, and isolated as an individual. We can choose whether we want to analyze this paratheatrical event in terms of its social function, its symbolic meanings or the feelings which it engendered in the participants.

Ritual and theatre

The Athenians engaged in a multitude of such rituals, which helped to breed a theatrical imagination. These were a resource for the playwright, allowing chains of association that a modern audience cannot easily share. When Aristophanes' farmer announces that he has drained his jug (which incidentally held over two litres) he adds that the wine was neat. The skin of wine symbolizes an offer of peace. If we know about Greek rituals which governed wine drinking, we can interpret this information. The wine which Dionysos gave to mortals was thought to be a dangerous gift, so neat wine was always mixed with water. The farmer is not simply a hero who knows how to hold his drink, but a breaker of ritual rules, a man acting like an uncivilized northerner. Perhaps Aristophanes meant that the Spartan peace should not be accepted in an undiluted form, that true peace is for gods and not mortals. Ritual provided dramatists with a means of exploring complex ideas through scenes of symbolic action.

Although Aristophanes frames his comedy around a set of rituals, there is no clear dividing line between theatre and ritual. A comic performance was itself a competitive ritual performed in honour of the god Dionysos. At the end of *The Acharnians*, the farmer approaches the priest of Dionysos responsible for the theatre festival, and asks him for the prize as fastest drinker. The character at this point became the actor, seeking victory in the theatrical competition of 425 BC.

To distinguish 'ritual' from 'theatre' on the grounds that one is always repeated and the other is always different would be naïve. To take a modern example: in a church service, the sermon is always newly scripted, whilst in a performance of *Hamlet* the text is always the same – so which is ritual? Dionysos demanded new plays just as

he demanded a new bull and not one that had been sacrificed before. One of the striking things about Greek ritual is its capacity for innovation. When the Spartans wanted to demoralize a neighbouring state, they smuggled out of that state the bones of a bronze-age warrior whom they claimed to be Orestes, and set up appropriate rituals, just as the Athenians did when they commandeered the bones of 'Theseus'. Any form of political innovation in Athens required a religious correlative. The practice of establishing new rituals for political purposes is often glimpsed in Aristophanes: the founder of a law court designs a new rite around the emblem of Apollo on his doorstep; antiwar protestors dig up a statue of a goddess called Peace, bring it to Athens, and sacrifice before it; the founders of an Athenian colony decide to worship birds.

There remains one important sense in which the Dionysiac ritual of performing tragedies and comedies was exceptional: the god was or became separated from the stories enacted in his honour. Dionysos was associated with shifting mental states, a feature of wine drinking as much as theatre, and with the emotions that derive from being in a crowd. It was not the content of the stories that constituted the Dionysiac ritual, but the act of masked impersonation before a crowd.

Whether drama originated in the telling of stories, i.e. myth, or in Dionysiac dances, i.e. ritual, has been hotly debated. According to the first theory, the attachment of drama to Dionysos was a historical accident. The only hard evidence favours the second hypothesis. Aristotle states that drama began in improvization, when the leaders of choruses began an interchange with the group. Tragedy, says Aristotle, derived from dithyrambs, danced narratives about Dionysos, whilst comedy derived from songs sung around phallic emblems.[7] The on-going debate about myth and ritual focusses an issue that is crucial for practitioners. Who has primacy: the author/ storyteller, or the dancer/performer? language or body?

THE CITY DIONYSIA

Timetable

The major dramatic festival, the City Dionysia, took place in spring – though there was also a minor festival in winter called the Lenaia. The sun was a source of warmth but not sun-stroke, visitors could

safely sail to Athens, countrymen could travel to the city and sleep in the open, and feasting out of doors at night had become possible. The festival was not an ancient one, but sprang up on the eve of democratization.

The normal timetable for the City Dionysia was probably as follows:

Day −1	pre-contest
Day 0 (eve)	leading-in
Day 1	procession
	and 10 boys' dithyrambs + 10 men's dithyrambs
Day 2	5 comedies
Day 3	3 tragedies + satyr play
Day 4	3 tragedies + satyr play
Day 5	3 tragedies + satyr play

During the war with Sparta, it seems likely that day two was cancelled, and one comedy was performed after each satyr play.[8]

Preparations

In the pre-contest or *proagon* the tragedians appeared with their casts, who were out of costume, and described their plays. The modern printed theatre programme fulfils something of the same function. Next day, normal life began to close down at dusk, and regular political and legal activity came to a halt. We hear of one crisis in 271 BC when the plays were not ready. Rather than dishonour the god by changing his day, the Athenians simply stopped their calendar for five days.

The festival proper began with the leading-in of the wooden statue of the god from a shrine outside the city walls (the *eisagoge*). The statue entered the city by torchlight escorted by young men, in a ritual that symbolized the arrival of the god in Athens. The story told of how Dionysos was rejected when he first visited Athens with his dangerous gift of wine, so he punished the men by condemning them to a permanent state of erection.[9] An erect phallus thus became a central emblem of the festival.

In the procession proper next morning (the *pompe*), the city put its political structure on display. The citizens were divided into their ten tribes, and each tribe brought its sacrificial bulls. Groups such as young men on military training and the executive Council would also have been demarcated. Foreign residents were marked out by

scarlet costumes, showing that they were both part and not part of the city. The citizens carried skins of wine, whilst the foreign residents carried mixing bowls to mix the wine with water – a symbol of their place in society. Besides wine, the other major emblem of the festival was the erect phallus. We have a chance record of one northern colony required to send a phallus as a sign of its membership of the wider Athenian community. For further details we can only guess on the basis of vase paintings and a later description of a Dionysiac procession in Alexandria. The latter included floats depicting scenes from the life of Dionysos, utensils for cooking and drinking, a display of masks, groups of actors, poets and priests, women dressed as followers of Dionysos ('maenads') and many groups of men dressed as satyrs.[10]

The Athenian procession passed through the marketplace (the *Agora*), where there were dances in honour of the twelve Olympians, symbolizing the concern of the festival with all the gods and the whole community. It ended at the altar below the theatre, where bulls were sacrificed. Before, during or after the sacrifices dithyrambs were danced. These dances were performed by groups of fifty males and narrated an event from the life of Dionysos or (as the repertoire ran dry) some other appropriate mythical figure. The piper stood in the centre whilst the chorus circled around him. The dithyramb was a competition between the tribes, so the street procession flowed naturally into its climax: a processional performance in the theatre. Since the prize was a bull, it is reasonable to guess that the victorious dancers had the honour of making the first sacrifice on behalf of their tribe. We know all too little about dithyrambs since the texts were not salvaged in later antiquity, but the numbers are striking. Since 1,000 citizens participated in this festival alone, and choruses performed in many other contexts, most of the men who watched tragedy did so not as passive consumers but as sometime performers with experience in singing and dancing before a huge audience.

Members of the audience were participants as much as spectators at the start of the festival. They ate meat from Dionysos' bull in the evening, they wore garlands of ivy, another emblem of the god, and of course they drank the wine that was Dionysos' gift. The link between wine and theatre was fixed by the myth that Dionysos first brought wine to the mountain village of Ikarion. Ikarion was the home of Thespis, reputedly the first actor/author of tragedies, and we have documentary evidence of tragedies being performed in this

village in the classical period.[11] A later Athenian historian writes of
the Athenians drinking before leaving for the festival in the morning.
'Throughout the competition wine was poured and snacks were
passed around.' He goes on to describe the choruses of the
dithyramb: 'As the choruses went in, wine was poured for them, and
when they had finished competing, and were coming out, wine was
poured again.'[12] This drinking sealed the bond of the dancers with
the god and with the spectators.

Comedy

The day of comedies must also have been a day of hangovers. Its
central Dionysiac emblem was the long limp phallus sewn to the
tights of male characters. The phallus was a constant opportunity for
comic business, and made heroism a physical impossibility. The
central character in comedy is usually an Athenian everyman figure
with an eccentric solution to the city's problems. At the core of the
comedy was a set-piece address to the audience, when the chorus on
behalf of the poet would relate the meaning of the play to the
immediate problems of Athens. The writer of comedy had a special
freedom to slander individuals in the audience, and to ridicule the
behaviour of the gods. Insult was the celebratory core of classical
comedy, and symbolized the freedom of speech allowed by democracy. Aristotle's formulation is succinct: 'Comedy simulates people
worse than they are today, tragedy better.'[13]

Comedy was set in contemporary Athens with all its follies,
tragedy in the world of heroic myth. The processions on day one of
the festival invested the city with glory. Comedy on day two acknowl-
edged divisions, but found wild fantasies to resolve those divisions.
Day three moved into the world of myth. The immediate reality of
Athens was pushed further away, but fantastic solutions were no
longer available. Whilst the characters of tragedy are for the most
part sealed within the world of the play, the characters of comedy
acknowledge the world of the audience. Laughter stemmed from the
collision of utopian dreams with the harsh political reality of the
here and now. While tragedy dealt with the experience of being
trapped, comedy allowed all forms of transformation and escape.
The choral dancers might escape from human identity by becoming
gnats, birds, frogs, riders of horses, ostriches, dolphins, clouds or
boats. The notion of a participatory festival underpins all comedies,

and they customarily end with a party that involves wine, food and usually sex, echoing the way actors and audience celebrated together a festival of Dionysos.

Tragedy

Officially, tragedies and comedies were contests between choruses, groups singing and dancing in unison. The word *tragedy* meaning literally 'goat song' derives, it is thought, from the prize of a goat for which the first tragic choruses competed. When tragedy began, the author was simply the chorus leader who set up an interchange with his followers. Only one man was considered to be the 'actor' in a given play in memory of the original conditions (see p. 159 below). A wealthy citizen called the *choregos* financed the production costs, selected the chorus-men and trained them in his house. He would doubtless have chosen the chorus from his own community, and he had the power to compel them to serve.[14] 'Actors' were allocated to plays by lot and paid from state funds, for a covert auction would have undermined the spirit of equal competition. The choregos had to spend his money visibly, on rigorous training and lavish costumes. He could if he chose dance himself in the chorus, and he must always have led his chorus in the street procession. The author remained the director ('teacher' was the ancient term), for only he possessed the script, and he held the music and unwritten stage directions in his head. In the course of time a new specialist role emerged for the chorus trainer.

It was the job of a state official, selected by lot, to choose the three tragic poets for the festival. Each poet had to write three tragedies followed by a satyr play. Aeschylus wrote tetralogies, four plays that effectively form a single epic play, and his *Oresteia* survives as a unique example of three tragedies in sequence. How far the lost satyr play *Proteus* comprised a fourth act as distinct from an epilogue is unclear. The plays of Sophocles and Euripides a generation later were for the most part free-standing. The tetralogy was ideal for depicting a society in historical evolution, but a generation later the Athenians felt they had arrived; how their culture came into being was of less consequence than immediate problems of survival. The self-contained play was a more powerful vehicle for dealing with the individual, and his or her relationship to the established city-state. A new competition for best actor was introduced in 449 BC, once

authors had generally withdrawn from performing in their own plays. Three independent plays gave the actor more scope to demonstrate his versatility.

The same state official allocated each poet to a choregos. The play had been vetted on behalf of the state, and the choregos had no control over content. The tragic choregos was chosen, rather exceptionally, by the state and not by his tribe, because it would have been quite inappropriate if different parts of the audience had cheered on their own representatives. In tragedy the poet spoke to the whole community, as well as outsiders who had come to view the community, so it was imperative that the plays should not be seen as partisan. The poet was a kind of appointed guru, and the space of the festival allowed him a special freedom of speech. This was a freedom to look into the void: to confront personal death; on occasion to confront also the possibility that an entire community might be extinguished; and to confront the moral void, where right meets right and there are no answers.

The ritual environment of a tragedy was part of its meaning. The spectators were able to look at situations from multiple points of view because they had ceremonially taken leave of immediate personal concerns. A collective affirmation of unity prepared the city to contemplate unhealed rifts within itself. An affirmation of divine power prepared the city for the recognition of human limits. The sight of slaughtered bulls on the altar prepared for the contemplation of human death.

Satyr play

Having danced in three successive tragedies, a feat of considerable athletic prowess not to mention memory, the chorus-men transformed themselves for a wild finale into servants of Dionysos called satyrs. Satyrs were part divine, part human, and part bestial, having the ears and tail of a horse and the same permanently erect phallus that Dionysos once inflicted upon the Athenians. Only one text survives intact – Euripides' *Cyclops* – but many paintings of satyrs survive on wine bowls because satyrs are a point of connexion between wine drinking, Dionysos and theatre. In the satyr play a chorus of beings obsessed with drinking and copulation was inserted into the world of heroic myth, with farcical consequences. (The word *comic* has to be avoided here because the genre of 'comedy' was

entirely separate.) The satyr play did not puncture the world of tragedy, but anchored it to the figure of Dionysos. It released the spectators from the emotional trauma of tragedy, and reinserted them in a world of celebration. Whilst comedy deflated pretension, the mood of the satyr play, like its dance steps and its phallic appendages, was uplifting. For the dancers who had reached the end of a long and draining process, the satyr uniform must have helped them experience possession by the god, with all feeling of ego gone. It was doubtless in the costume of the satyr that they wound down and celebrated in the sanctuary of Dionysos after the play. They took leave of the roles they had played in the tragedy by placing their masks in the temple as offerings.

Tony Harrison built his play *Trackers of Oxyrhynchus* around the remains of a satyr play by Sophocles, and found an equivalent to satyr dancing in Yorkshire clog dancing.[15] His satyrs were working class rather than animalistic, they wore the long hanging phallus of comedy, and their dancing was rooted to the earth. Harrison construed his satyrs as victims of colonialism, and representatives of northern popular culture. His experiment illustrates just how difficult it is to find any modern equivalent to these products of a Greek religious environment.

TRAGEDY AND RITUAL

Narrated ritual

For Richard Schechner, conventional western theatre tends merely to entertain, whereas rituals change people. 'The basic polarity is between efficacy and entertainment, not between ritual and theater'.[16] Schechner reformulates the old ritual/theatre divide because his ideal is a theatre capable of changing people. Greek plays portray *efficacious* ritual practices, which become in a sense rituals within a ritual. Greek plays may also be described as *efficacious myths*, shaping the way the Athenian audience understood rituals which it performed outside the Dionysia.

Some rituals in Greek drama are merely described as unseen action. In Euripides' *Electra*, Orestes returns in disguise to kill Aegisthus, the murderer of his father, and finds him engaged in a sacrifice. The messenger reports that Aegisthus welcomes Orestes in accordance with the ritual obligation to show hospitality. The usual

elaborate practices sanctify the killing of an animal and remove guilt from the killer: the knife is hidden in a basket, grain is thrown about the altar, and hairs of the animal are cut. Aegisthus inspects the organs of the dead animal, and finds that part of the liver is missing, an evil omen. The climax comes when Orestes finishes chopping up the meat and kills Aegisthus. The play is concerned with Orestes' loss of innocence, and the messenger pictures a symbolically appropriate sacrifice – beside unpolluted water in honour of river nymphs. Nymphs are unlikely protectors against attack, so the setting hints at the vulnerability of Aegisthus, an unarmed man killed by his guest. Aegisthus sacrifices a young male animal so the nymphs will protect him from the young Orestes, and the corrupt innards of the bullock hint at the way Orestes is inwardly corrupted. The audience hear how Orestes attempts to separate his killing from the holy sacrifice by refusing to wash his hands, failing to join the prayer, and substituting the sacred knife for another. Instead of cutting Aegisthus' throat over the altar like the bullock, Orestes stabs him in the back. Characteristically, tragedy here describes a perversion of normal ritual practice. Ritual opened up a vein of symbolism for the dramatist to exploit, drawing on a language of symbols that was part of Greek culture.

Tragedy as explanation of ritual

Greek tragedies often end with the establishment of a ritual familiar to the audience, so the play functions as an explanatory myth. At the end of Aeschylus' *Oresteia*, the goddess Athene institutes her major Athenian festival, the Panathenaia. The Furies, female avenging spirits, are given purple robes to wear in the closing procession, equating them with the real foreign residents of Athens who wore such robes in the Panathenaia. The play thus clarified and validated Athens' cautious but positive attitude to rich foreigners. Sophocles' *Oedipus at Colonus* is also concerned with the Furies, and the action is set in their shrine a mile outside Athens. The play describes the death of Oedipus close by the shrine, and Sophocles plainly intended that his tragedy should help to sanctify a known cave by portraying it as a route to the underworld. The play claimed that Oedipus' body lay beneath Athenian soil, and would serve as a magical prophylactic, protecting the Athenians in the darkest days of the Peloponnesian war. This is one of our clearest instances of efficacious theatre (see p. 176 below).

Many plays not set in Athens are given a slant which relates them to Athenian ritual. Euripides' *Herakles* is a blatant hijack of the Herakles myth. After the famous strongman has killed his children in a fit of madness, Euripides has the Athenian folk hero Theseus come to Thebes to rescue him. Theseus promises that a monument will be built and sacrifices made to Herakles, and Athens will win honour from all of Greece. The 'monument' alludes to the temple at Marathon, where Athens fought in her finest hour against the Persians. Athens made her headquarters in the sanctuary, and the god supposedly helped the Athenians in the battle. The play implies that the cult of Herakles belongs to Athens more than to rival states. Behind the propaganda lay a level of popular religious belief that Herakles would again help Athens in her hour of need.

Ritual as paradigm for tragedy

Ritual may provide the underlying model for the narrative of a tragedy. The sacrifice of animals is an obvious instance, since tragedy usually focusses on a killing. In *The Oresteia* one reason why Clytaemnestra kills Agamemnon is Agamemnon's agreement ten years ago to sacrifice their daughter on an altar of Artemis. The murders in the play are all described in the language of sacrifice, and the plot can be seen as a sequence of perverted rituals. Behind Euripides' *Bacchae*, where Pentheus, king of Thebes is torn apart by women, many have seen rites of Dionysos that involved women in trance tearing live animals apart. A more problematic example is *Oedipus the King*, where critics have looked for signs of the scapegoat ritual, which required that one ugly man, after a brief period of royal treatment, should be beaten from the city to remove its evil. The problem is that Oedipus at the end of Sophocles' play does not actually leave the city. It is generally more constructive to search for the detailed and specific meanings of ritual than simplify Greek plays by searching for monolithic explanations.

RITUAL IN TRAGEDY

The inherent theatricality of rituals made them attractive to practi-tioners of the particular ritual we call 'theatre'. I shall examine a few of the most important.

Supplication

In a world of small city-states with no shared legal code but a shared religion, rites of supplication were a means of ensuring personal protection. To supplicate an individual, you abased yourself and clung to their knees. If the individual was an older male, your left arm clasped his knees, and your right hand reached for his beard. To hurt suppliants or force them away was considered shameful. At the end of the *Iliad*, the aged King of Troy manages to supplicate the young Greek warrior Achilles, a humiliating act and hard to effect in conditions of warfare. Achilles' acceptance of the suppliant brings the Homeric story to a close. Euripides' Medea performs the rite twice to secure the concessions she needs, and tragedy offers countless other examples. Another ritual act available to a woman was the baring of a single breast, to signal her function as mother and life-giver. In *The Oresteia*, Clytaemnestra appeals by this means to the son who is about to kill her. The physical scale of the theatre and distance of the audience made it possible for a male actor to play the gesture.

The other form of supplication – rare in Homer but much more common in daily life in the classical period – was to take refuge on ground that belonged to a god. The tragedians liked to represent people clinging to altars or idols because this created an intense visual focus on the centre of the acting area. To drag a suppliant away from holy ground was a crime against Zeus, god of suppliants. After murdering his mother, Orestes in *The Oresteia* embraces first the navel stone of Apollo in Delphi and then the statue of Athene in Athens whilst the Furies pace menacingly about him. Athene takes on the role of the priest, who often in the Greek world had to establish peace between a suppliant and those who regarded him or her as a criminal. Suppliants could advertise their ritual status by carrying branches of olive wreathed in wool, and boys in plague-stricken Thebes perform the rite in this way at the start of *Oedipus the King*. On the face of it they are pleading with the gods for mercy, but the context turns their gesture into a political demonstration designed to stir the king into action.

A historical example underlines the theatricality of ritual. When Athens fell to Sparta at the end of the classical period, a junta took control and started assassinating the opposition and robbing the foreign community. There was a showdown between two members

of the junta in front of the 500 rich men who nominally formed the ruling council. Critias the extremist brought his band of young thugs to stand with weapons at the back of the audience, and stationed foreign troops outside. Theramenes the moderate, having lost the argument, took refuge on the altar of Zeus Councillor, the ceremonial hearth close to the rostrum. It was the boldest of the thugs who dragged him from the altar as he cried out to the gods. Theramenes was killed but the nature of his protest helped undermine the regime.[17]

Funeral practice

In the *Odyssey* Odysseus sails to the edge of the world and digs a pit.[18] Into the pit he pours liquid offerings of wine, honey, milk and water to feed the dead, followed by the blood of a sheep. These 'libations' prompt the shades of the dead to come flocking, and those who drink the blood receive a sufficient injection of life to talk, though they cannot touch one who is alive. All the shades inhabit a gloomy limbo, anxious about their sons, and often embittered by their experiences on earth. Agamemnon, for example, tells Odysseus never to trust women; Achilles states that he would rather be a living serf than king of the dead. First to appear is a restless spirit whose body has not been buried.

This was the dominant picture of death in the classical period. Burial rites were crucial if the dead were to find peace. In Euripides' *Hecuba* an unburied man flies in to haunt his mother; Sophocles' *Antigone* buries her brother in defiance of an edict, knowing that even a few handfuls of earth will accomplish the ritual. Plays like Sophocles' *Ajax* are rarely performed today because the modern audience cannot easily accept that the place where a body is buried matters so much. In the Greek world the dead never forget the living. The second play of *The Oresteia* is called *Libation Bearers* because Clytaemnestra has sent women to pour liquids onto the grave of her husband, to placate him with drops of life. At burial Clytaemnestra cut off Agamemnon's hands to rob him of residual power, but he is still able to haunt her. Orestes kills his mother because he has been warned that otherwise spirits from below the earth will pursue him. The dead were both far away and ever present. They could not intervene in any personal sense, but their bodies exerted a certain physical power. The physical sense of the

Figure 3 A chorus of women lamenting a death. Tomb painting from Ruvo.

earth as home of the dead is constantly exploited in Greek theatre. The actors performed on a floor of beaten earth, and their feet created dust and a characteristic thud.

In the traditional funeral, women had a dominant role as keeners. Aristotle explains their practices as a form of homeopathy:[19] by beating their breasts, shaving their heads, tearing their clothes and lacerating their faces with their fingernails, women took death upon themselves, and thus were able to put the experience behind them. Greek tragedy contains many formal demonstrations of grief, often accompanied by ritual vocalizations like 'i-o', 'ai-ai'. The basis of keening was a chanted interchange between the leading mourner and a choral group which echoes but controls the leader's emotion. The most famous theatrical example is the lament (*kommos*) in *Libation Bearers* (306–478), where the two children of Agamemnon have their emotions wound up to the point where they can kill. Greek mourning rituals are strictly efficacious. Some two generations before tragedy emerged in Athens, we hear in another city that a ritual lament at the tomb of a hero was for political reasons transformed into 'tragic' dancing for Dionysos, and this scrap of evidence suggests something important about the origins of tragedy.[20]

Before the classical age, funerals asserted the power and solidarity of the extended family, but with the development of the city-state legislation curbed private demonstrations of grief in favour of public

funerals. Extravagant keening posed society with a problem because it undermined the collective ethos. The Greek dramatists did not represent the raw power of keening for its own sake, but addressed the context in which keening takes place. The killings triggered by the kommos in *Libation Bearers* are not praiseworthy, and it is significant that the mourners are Asiatic war captives, not democratic Athenians.

Purification

Death was experienced as a source of pollution, a kind of filth which contaminated those who came close to it. Mourners attacked their own bodies and might even, like the King of Troy in the *Iliad*, rub dung into their hair; they took on literal or symbolic filth so they could then wash themselves clean and put the death of a loved one behind them. We have seen how the Day of Pitchers commemorated one solution to contamination: the Athenians received Orestes the murderer, but avoided speaking to him or sharing wine with him. Killing was the worst source of pollution, and we have seen how Aegisthus took the traditional steps to protect himself when sacrificing a bullock. A man accused of homicide in classical Athens was barred from holy ground, and was tried in the open air so that no juror could be contaminated by contact. The deliberate killing of a slave was legally equivalent to the accidental killing of a citizen, for both acts incurred the same pollution.

In *The Oresteia* Aeschylus depicted for the first time in human form the earth spirits known as the Erinyes or Furies. These ugly creatures were a personification of the clinging filth that stems from murder. In the play, ritual purification at Delphi proves inadequate, and formal acquittal in a court of law is needed. By bringing the forces of pollution to life, Aeschylus laid the foundations for a new concept of democratic justice. While all Greeks responded emotionally to the idea of pollution, its nature was highly debatable. Apart from Orestes, the most important polluted figure in Greek tragedy is Oedipus. The plague which descends on Thebes in *Oedipus the King* externalizes the contamination which Oedipus incurs through incest and killing his father. Around the time of the play, when Athens was infected with plague, the Spartans claimed that Pericles, the main political leader of Athens, was still polluted by murders committed generations earlier by his mother's family. The Athenians rejected

the claim, but the Spartan ploy is evidence of how powerful the notion was.

Purification was a preliminary to most ritual acts. Before a political assembly a young pig was killed, its blood was sprinkled on the seats around the podium and it was then castrated. A similar ritual took place in the theatre in order to sacralize the space of performance. The word *catharsis* means purification. Aristotle's famous proposition that the audience undergoes catharsis of the emotions can be related to the idea that suffering in the play does not contaminate the onlookers. The refusal of Greek plays to portray acts of killing in front of the audience must be related to the fear of pollution.

Prayer

Christian prayer differs from Greek prayer in two main ways. Firstly, humility was not considered a virtue in the Greek world, and kneeling belongs to supplication rather than prayer. The Greeks preferred to make noisy demands upon their gods, reminding them of their moral obligations. Secondly, the modern Christian God is considered to be everywhere, whereas in Greek religion any particular god is *somewhere*. To pray is to reach out physically to where the god is, to create silence and then call the god by his or her proper title in order to be heard. Aegisthus went out to the water meadows to sacrifice to the nymphs, because that is where river nymphs live. There was a basic distinction between gods above the earth, whose symbolic home was on Mount Olympus, and forces beneath the earth – 'chthonic' gods like the Furies, and heroes in their tombs. To reach the former you held out your arms to the sky, to reach the latter you touched or pounded the earth. Prayer was usually tied to other rituals, like sacrifice or pouring wine into the earth, for a gift to the gods imposed an obligation on them to reciprocate.

Greek temples were houses for statues. The most ancient statues were small and made of wood, like that of Dionysos brought from his temple to watch plays in the theatre. Prayers are often addressed to statues. At the start of *Hippolytus*, hunters offer a hymn to the statue of Artemis, goddess of hunting, and sing of Artemis dwelling in the sky. Hippolytus declares, gazing at the statue before crowning it with flowers, that the goddess speaks to him but he has never seen her face. The statue was a symbol embodying a variable degree of

Figure 4 A half-chorus of six men dancing in front of a tomb, probably to raise
a ghost. Athenian wine mixing bowl of about 490 BC.

divine presence. Hindus regard statues in a very similar manner.
Like Artaud, modern practitioners in search of an appropriate ritual
language often turn to the east for inspiration.

The opening chorus of *Oedipus the King* is a sustained prayer, asking
the gods to deliver Thebes from plague, and send an answer through
Apollo's oracle. There is no grovelling here or sense of sin, but a set
of fierce demands. Untranslatable cries like 'paian', 'i-o', 'popoi',
'euion' create the flavour of familiar ritual practices. Anyone performing the sequence has to begin by analyzing its structure.

(1A) A prayer to the voice of Zeus which passes through Apollo's
      oracle. This section is a *paean*, a choral form traditionally used
      when asking Apollo to bring healing.

(1B) A formal demand to three gods whose statues face the Theban
      market place, asking them to appear.

(2A) A lament, building up to a picture of spirits of the dead flying
      towards the sunset.

(2B) A description of women lamenting, building up to a prayer, in
      language which links Athene to the sunrise.

(3A) A curse upon Ares the war god, much worshipped in Thebes. The chorus sense his presence and want him removed by Zeus, god of thunder and lightning.

(3B) A prayer to Apollo as warrior, to Artemis, who is now imagined on the mountains, and to Theban Dionysos, asking them to drive out Ares.

The structure is precise and symmetrical. Section 1: gods located somewhere beyond the exits to left and right of the playing area are urged to appear. Section 2: a formal lament builds into gestures reaching for the sky. Section 3: gods up above, in the sky or mountains, are called upon to curse Ares. In the final section, the Thebes of the play shades into the Athens of the audience, for Athens was suffering from war and plague.[21] Gestures towards the sky pointed to the Parthenon, Athene's temple high above the audience. The final prayer to Dionysos must have been directed out front, towards the wooden Dionysos in the auditorium. The boundary between 'theatre' and 'ritual' was far from clear in the Greek world.

Ritual theatre: the case of Peter Hall

Twentieth-century productions often aspire to being ritualistic. Some follow Artaud and seek through ritual a route to raw emotion, while others are inspired by the formality of Greek tragedy. Peter Hall's *Oresteia* (1981) and *Oedipus Plays* (1996) fall into the second category, and are often regarded as 'ritualistic' because of their emphasis on masked acting and rhythmic verse. Hall conceives tragedy in a generalized way as 'a profoundly spiritual experience' designed to 'teach us about the tragedy of life',[22] and he avoids developing any kind of ritual vocabulary drawn from a specific culture. The gods in his dramatic world are a non-personal force that blindly subjects humans to fate, and cannot really be reached through prayer. The implications are illustrated by Hall's treatment of the prayer sequence in *Oedipus the King*. Sections of prayer to multiple gods (1B and 3B) were cut, to emphasize the human emotion of suffering. Zeus was imagined above by the choreographer, Apollo vaguely in all directions, and Athene precisely stage left, with no clear rationale, and the designer provided no altar of Apollo to create a sense of sacred space on the stage. Old-fashioned assumptions about the universality of Greek tragedy made it im-

Plate 1 Orestes and Electra in *The Oresteia*, directed by Karolos Koun. 1982.

possible for Hall to satisfy the actor's need for a specific physical
language appropriate to the text.

Hall provoked political controversy with one gesture in the
direction of ritual theatre, when he decided to burn drums of
kerosene in the theatre of Epidaurus in Greece, where the production opened. Hall states in his memoirs that 'Epidaurus still feels
what it was originally – a holy place, a place of healing.'[23] The
visitor to the adjacent museum can see the texts of many paeans
performed in the theatre to give thanks for healing. Yet Hall offered
his Greek audience, escaping from the sulphurous air of Athens,
pollution rather than *catharsis*. Hall's fire-light was an intellectual
metaphor for Oedipus' blindness, and a feast for the eyes. It was a
theatrical sign of ritual which failed to turn the actual performance
event into a ritual. Part of the problem is that Hall does not belong
to a culture with a strong ritual tradition. When the Greek director
Karolos Koun used Christian candles to signify the tomb of Aga-

memnon (Epidaurus, 1982), he set up links between past and present that offered more chance of creative interplay. All too often the desire to ritualize Greek tragedy results in emptiness, and the imposition of a homogeneous style.

CHAPTER 3

Politics

ATHENIAN DEMOCRACY

History

'Democracy' means 'rule by the people'. In modern democracy millions elect a few representatives who will govern them for a fixed number of years. In ancient democracy, men ruled themselves, and the modern system would not have been considered 'democratic'. The Athenians went to extraordinary lengths to distribute power amongst a group of some 40,000 or more men so that no individuals could tyrannize the rest. The exclusion of women and non-Athenian males from the category of 'the people' should not blind us to the nature of the achievement. The poor wielded the power of their votes, and the rich to a significant extent acquiesced, finding ways of retaining their influence. It is no coincidence that democracy and tragedy were born at the same historical moment. Each member of the Athenian democracy in the classical period was aware of his own responsibility as a maker of decisions, and knew there was no god-given model of the good society. Tragedy was a device which allowed the Athenians to come together and collectively think through their problems. The Greek word *polis* means a 'city-state' or community of citizens. Greek tragedy was necessarily 'political': its subject matter was the well being of the polis, and its performance was part of what turned a collection of men into a polis.

Democracy was an evolving rather than a static system in the classical period, and I shall trace some of the landmarks.

Solon. Early 500s BC   Solon established a full assembly and trial by jury. He legislated against enslaving citizens for debt, so once a citizen, always a citizen. The city was no longer ruled by a hereditary

aristocracy, but was organized on the basis of four types of men who work the land. These correspond roughly to four military capacities: (1) leadership in battle; (2) fighting on horseback; (3) fighting in armour; (4) rowing a ship. Through the classical period the polis remained a military clan, fighting for prosperity or survival.

Cleisthenes. Late 500s BC   After a period of dictatorship came a new constitution. Each citizen had to belong to a local community or *deme*. The demes were grouped to form ten tribes, with an equal weighting of representation from the city, coastal settlements and the hinterland. These tribes were the basis for all forms of organization: political, military and festive. The dithyrambs, for example, were competitions that engendered fierce tribal loyalties. Tribal loyalty transformed a natural bonding with family and local community into a wider sense of belonging, and prevented class interests and old systems of patronage from dividing the polis.

Major issues were debated in an open assembly, with a quorum of 6,000 required for the most important decisions. As the system evolved, delegates from each deme were chosen by lottery to serve for a year on an executive council of 500, and 50 men at any one time (5 per tribe) sat in full-time session, so most citizens eventually took their turn here at the centre of government. Lottery was in general considered more democratic than election, since it prevented wealth from buying influence. The crucial post which remained elective was that of 'general': ten military leaders were elected, one from each tribe, and this offered scope for men of wealth and family to assert their personal qualities of leadership. It was recognized that fighting wars required authoritarian control, but unlike today, generals were held to account by their men at the end of a year's term of office. Large democratic juries were also introduced, though we do not know quite how the system worked in the classical period.

The Persian wars. 500–479 BC   Athens defeated the invading Persian army at Marathon (490 BC) and Persian navy at Salamis (480 BC). Whilst the first victory was essentially won by the elite who could afford armour, the second was won by the poor who manned the ships, and is vividly described by Aeschylus in his *Persians*. These victories established the moral and military hegemony of Athens within the Greek world.

Empire The process of liberating Aegean islands from Persian control turned steadily into something more sinister, an Athenian empire. Men and ships contributed to the collective defence programme were replaced by money, and this money helped to fund buildings like the Parthenon. From around 460 BC until 429 BC, Pericles was a driving force in Athens, because his expansionist policies succeeded in reconciling rich and poor. The empire provided the salaries for countless office holders and for oarsmen in the expanding fleet. Empire was not simply maintained by force, for Athens supported democratic regimes in her 'allied' states. A sharp ideological divide emerged within the Greek world between democracy and 'oligarchy' – 'rule by the few'.

The Peloponnesian war. 431–404 BC Athens' great rival was Sparta, where the 'few' were firmly in control. Intermittent warfare gave way to sustained hostilities in 431 BC. The policy of Pericles was to control the seas and abandon indefensible borders on land. This was popular with the poor, who found work in the city and in the fleet, but unpopular with the landowning classes. In his plays *Acharnians* and *Peace*, Aristophanes paints a vivid picture of once prosperous landed peasants desperate for an armistice. Athens fell victim to plague, exacerbated by urban overcrowding, to a failed attempt to annex Sicily, and above all to internal divisions. With the surrender of the city, a viciously repressive oligarchy was imposed, but democracy proved too deeply embedded for such a regime to survive.

THEATRE AS PART OF THE DEMOCRATIC STRUCTURE

The choregia

In aristocratic societies wealth is not valued just for itself, but mainly as a means of obtaining honour. Sophocles pictures a typical piece of aristocratic display in *Electra* (68off.): Orestes goes to the athletics contest at Delphi, and emerges full of honour from the foot race, winning every succeeding contest also. The announcer credits him as a man of Argos, Orestes, son of the great Agamemnon, and so divides the pool of honour evenly between the individual, the individual's country, and the individual's aristocratic family. Orestes finally comes a cropper in the most exclusive because most expensive

contest, the chariot race. Naturally, because Sophocles is writing for Athens, it is a canny Athenian who wins. This aristocratic hunger for honour had to be diverted in the democratic period, so that individual ambitions could serve the polis as a whole, and not just family groupings. Chariot racing was overshadowed by new forms of competition, such as tragedy and comedy. Greek drama was democratic because the competing choruses comprised ordinary, anonymous men who received a fee for their services; but it was also funded by a rich choregos, and thus satisfied the aristocratic desire for honour.

A negative view of this system of funding is provided by an anonymous opponent of the democratic system. Athletics, warfare and theatre are placed in a single conceptual frame.

Training in athletics and pursuit of the arts have been abolished by the democrats, who see nothing fine in them because they are incapable of such activities. As for funding choruses, and torch races, and warships, they know that the rich will serve as choregos, and the people will be beneficiaries, the rich will muster races, and the people will have their ships, enjoy their races. The people are happy to accept cash for singing and running and dancing and sailing so they can be the gainers while the rich grow poorer.[1]

In this reactionary view, an aesthetic disdain for the new art forms is mixed up with an economic protest that such forms involve the redistribution of wealth. The writer laments that democratic Athens has more festivals than any other Greek city, and public business keeps grinding to a halt. The views of this man exemplify the divided nature of Athenian society. Tragedy was engendered not by solidarity but by the need to reconcile such divisions.

In the democratic backlash which followed the removal of the oligarchs in 403 BC, a rich defendant on a corruption charge desperately sets out the attitude to funding which the democratic jury wanted to hear.[2] He prefers to spend his money on the state rather than on himself, he claims, for there is no honour in inherited wealth, and if he impoverishes his children, so be it. His list of contributions begins with tragedy. He was *choregos* at the Dionysia in 410 BC upon coming of age, and as an athletic youth probably led the chorus in the actual performance. His contributions in the next six years were:

- four dithyrambs: victory at the Dionysia involved the extra expense of setting up a monument on behalf of his tribe

- comedy: victory meant the extra expense of a ceremony to dedicate the masks to Dionysos
- a torch race in honour of Prometheus
- a procession bearing the robe of Athene
- racing a warship in honour of Poseidon
- two war dances
- seven years equipping and captaining a warship: the most costly commitment.

There is a deep sense of aristocratic pride as this wealthy man asserts that he had the best warship in the fleet, the best helmsman and crew, and generals quarrelled for the chance of sailing on his vessel. He must have felt similar pride when he launched himself into public life with three tragedies and a satyr play, though plainly he did not win the prize. His catalogue covers the desperate final years of the war, when huge sums of money went on being devoted to festivals, countless man-hours were invested in preparation and more invested in watching, while the city risked annihilation. These priorities will seem astonishing if we place politics, warfare and entertainment in separate boxes. For the Athenians dancing in a tragic chorus involved the same discipline as dancing a war dance, a form of military parade. The pipes which controlled the rhythm of the tragic chorus would control the same men as they rowed their warship fast enough to ram a Spartan. The survival of the city relied upon the collective solidarity engendered by tragedy.

Political display at the Dionysia

The assembly was notionally a gathering of the whole adult male population, but more people, perhaps three times as many, came to the Dionysia. Some of the extra numbers came from far-flung demes, some were resident foreigners, others were visitors to Athens. The occasion was used for ceremonies which Athens wanted the rest of Greece to witness. When an armistice with Sparta was arranged and renewed, it was at the Dionysia that the solemn ceremony of pouring wine into the earth took place. In the period of empire the 'allies' all had to bring their tribute to the Dionysia, where it was laid out on the ground in units so its amount was visible to all. The occasion was also used to present suits of armour to young men upon coming of age, if their fathers had died fighting for the city. It is likely enough that the young choregos in 410 BC was one of these.

The generals appeared before the audience to pour libations. At the Dionysia, Athens put her power on display to the world, which was another reason for sustaining performances through the worst days of the war.

Classical tragedies presented Athens to the world. Aristophanes was charged with 'slandering the polis in front of foreigners'[3] when he put on his first comedy at the Dionysia, and it seems no coincidence that his most hard-hitting attacks on political policy – in *Acharnians*, *Knights*, *Lysistrata* and *Frogs* – were written for the Lenaia, the smaller festival of Dionysos held in January when the world was not gathered to watch. The Lenaia was regarded as a second-class event in respect of tragedy because the festival was purely for an Athenian audience. The Dionysia was not just a show-case any more than Shakespeare's *Macbeth* was *just* a tribute to the Jacobean monarchy – but inescapably the political context of Greek perform-ance shaped the meaning the plays had for their audience.

Democratic procedures at the Dionysia

The rich choregos was allowed no control over the content of the plays he produced, and procedures for judging were equally demo-cratic. A list of jurors was submitted by each tribe, and one individual was chosen from each shortly before the performance to limit the possibility of bribery. Ten judges voted, but only five ballots were counted, leaving the gods with an element of responsibility for the final decision. Although the jurors swore an oath of impartiality, there was obvious pressure placed upon them by the response of the crowd. A review of the festival was conducted in the theatre immediately after celebrations had ended, and any acts of violence or corruption were dealt with, while those who had organized well were commended.[4]

Plato's anti-democratic analysis of the Dionysia is an interesting one. We saw how the choral prayer at the start of *Oedipus the King* mixes traditional forms: the paean, the lament, the dithyramb to Dionysos and perhaps also what Plato calls a 'hymn' (see above, pp. 44–5). Such mixing of forms means, according to Plato, that experts can no longer pronounce. No one can define on the basis of tradition what makes a good play, so the only criterion of merit is what the common man enjoys. 'Artistic anarchy was instilled into the masses, and the bold belief that they were fit to pass judgement. And so the

silent auditorium became a place of shouting, claiming to tell good art from bad. An aristocracy of taste gave way to low-class theatrocracy.'[5] This behaviour in the theatre, Plato claims, with everyone heckling to influence the judges, was the starting point for anti-authoritarian behaviour and ethical free-thinking in society at large. Plato's hostility to theatre stems from a recognition that theatre mattered. It shaped the mentality of the audience, and was inseparable from the democratic way of life.

RHETORIC

The importance of rhetoric

It was the essence of democracy that every citizen had to be a decision maker. Citizens devoted a massive amount of their time to making and assessing speeches. The historian Thucydides offers us two contrasting views. He makes Pericles' voice an idealized democratic position.

> Our policies are considered and evaluated. We do not believe that talking endangers action. The real danger comes when we do not talk the plan through before doing what has to be done. We are unique in the way we combine bravado with reasoned debate about every project.[6]

The view that Athens is a talking-shop is given to Cleon, who addresses the assembly in an attempt to guillotine discussion. This democratic radical, like Plato, identifies democracy as a kind of theatrocracy.

> It is your fault. You set up politics as a competition, so you can be spectators of speeches, listeners about actions ... You would each like to speak for yourself, but if you cannot, you compete by trying to think one step ahead of the speaker ... You are chasing after something that is not, shall I say, real life, and you ignore the here and now. In brief, you have surrendered to the pleasure of being a listener and you sit there like spectators of the sophists, not political decision makers.[7]

The sophists were men who taught the art of public speaking, and offered improvized speeches about imaginary situations as a form of public entertainment. Political rhetoric became a kind of art form, and the tragedians, particularly Euripides, exploited this public taste for speech-making. Plato declared tragedy to be a form of public speaking that had the sole objective of gratifying the audience,[8] but

we may take a more positive view. The audience which evaluated speeches in the fictional context of tragedy became more adept at discerning ideological platitudes in Thucydides' first speaker, hypocrisy in the second. The more theatrical the assembly became, the more necessary was tragedy.

Orations

Rhetoric was the art of persuasion. There were three major forms: set-piece orations, debating speeches in assemblies, and speeches in court. The oration performed in honour of the war orphans at the Dionysia is an example of the first. Plato describes, satirically, the response which eloquent speeches over the dead evoked in a typical Athenian:

I take on a noble character in response to the praise. Each time I hear them I am bewitched and believe instantly that I am taller and nobler and more handsome. And there are normally foreigners with me and listening alongside, which gives me instant dignity. They feel the same emotions as me, about myself and about Athens, which they think more wonderful than ever, seduced by the speech maker.[9]

One function of plays at the Dionysia was surely to provoke this kind of response.

The assembly

In theory any Athenian could speak in the assembly. In reality only a minority can have had the courage to step up on to the podium, put on a wreath, and speak more or less off the cuff to a noisy and critical audience of some 6,000, not to mention other onlookers on the hillside outside the demarcated area where votes were counted. A powerful voice was essential, and voices improve with the benefit of expensive training. Humbler citizens would be more likely to speak when serving on the Council, or in local assemblies in their demes. Speaking in political debates was thus not limited to an elite.

Athens' assembly-place was on a hill called the Pnyx (see figure 9). The scale and disposition of the assembly resemble the theatre. The audience sat on crude seats on the hillside and looked down upon the city whose future they were debating. The fact that the speaker was physically below his audience made it hard for him to dominate the crowd, and enormous skill was needed. We hear (from a Sicilian)

how the most famous of the sophists came as an ambassador from Sicily, requesting military aid. 'With his exotic style he astounded the Athenians, who are so fashionable and devoted to language.' He secured the vote of the mass assembly with a set of verbal tricks such as carefully balanced antitheses, which would in a few years come to seem ludicrously artificial.[10]

Mass emotion was the great danger. Cleon's speech, cited above, followed a hasty decision to slaughter the entire adult male population of a rebellious island. He attempts to dismiss as irrational sentimentality a move to reconsider. Mass emotion is again best analyzed by Plato, democracy's most perceptive critic.

When the public sit crowded together in assemblies, or law courts, theatres, military encampments or any other gathering of the masses, there is a huge volume of noise. Some speeches or decisions are condemned, others applauded. Shouting and clapping are unrestrained. Echoes from the rocks and surroundings double the hubbub of complaint or approval. In such a situation, how can a young fellow do what his heart dictates? What education can hold him? ... He will be swept along by the force of the current.[11]

Mass emotion was a danger, but also a source of the collective will that made Athens so powerful. The god Dionysos personifies the loss of ego that is a feature of being in such a crowd. Greek theatre in performance gained much of its power playing to a close-packed audience of some 15,000 to 20,000. Peter Hall writes vividly about the energy given to actors by the audience at Epidaurus. 'I stood behind the scene with the actors just before the performance began and listened to the expectant roar of all those thousands of people. The sound was voracious, but it was reassuring in its need. It wanted us to begin.'[12]

The law court

Aristotle tells us that speeches in the law court offered most scope for trickery since, he claims, the jurors were likely to attend for the pure pleasure of hearing a good speech.[13] Aristophanes' *Wasps* portrays a man who is hooked on jury service, always arriving early for a front seat. Aristophanes' jurors are like wasps, noisy and eager to inflict pain. The law courts underpinned the democratic system – but they also offered Athenians the pleasures of soap opera, glimpses into domestic dramas that are normally secret.

Speeches in the law court were more theatrical than speeches in the assembly because they could be fully rehearsed in advance. The speaker would often memorize a speech written for him by a specialist, but he would pretend to improvize, calling himself an amateur in the matter of public speaking. No paid advocates were allowed. A woman could not speak, so a relative would have to speak for her. There were also no professional judges to interpret the law, so the amateur jury had to reach its own instant decision. Naturally body language was crucial. A speaker was better advised to project the integrity of his own character and smear his opponent than bore the audience with intricate points of law.

Plaintiff and defendant stood on two platforms facing the audience. Each was given an equal amount of time, controlled by a water clock that could be halted for citations of the law and statements by witnesses. The men on the platforms were engaged in a process of self-dramatization. The defendant would sometimes bring his children on to his small stage, creating a tableau designed to provoke the sympathy of the jury. In *Wasps* one dog prosecutes another for failing to share a stolen cheese. The democratic juror favours the plaintiff, which is well behaved because it has food to eat, and condemns the defendant because of the way it bares its teeth. However, he acquits the defendant when a brood of puppies melts his heart. Aristophanes' parody should not blind us to the real pleasure which jurors must have taken in the cut and thrust of rational argument.

Tragedies derive part of their formal structure from the law court. Regularly we find two individuals pitted against each other, and each makes a long speech of approximately equal length. Speakers in the law court could use part of their precious time to interrogate their opponent, and a short intense interchange at the end of a pair of speeches is a common feature in drama. Often a long speech in tragedy is followed by a seemingly banal comment from the chorus – like: 'Sir, you should, if he is talking sense, pay some heed, and so should you of him. Both have spoken well.'[14] Such tags are a sign that a kind of jury has been weighing the arguments and trying to reach a collective decision. Almost everything said in Greek drama is said with a view to impressing the chorus.

Long speeches are often a problem for modern western actors. Stanislavskian theatre is concerned with how the actor relates to the role, and with secret motivations that drive the character forward. While Stanislavski is actor-centred, rhetorical theory was audience-

centred. Greek theorists of public speaking tried to analyze the emotions and rational processes of an audience in order to persuade the audience to vote for them and not the opposition. They were interested not in the drive behind words but in the effect of words. Stanislavskian actors are trained to clarify emotion, not reason, and the modern corrective, inevitably, is Brecht. Asking himself why middle-class people blamed him for having so little feeling, Brecht responded: 'His use of reason stirred no emotion in their souls. Indeed, their feelings rebelled against him and his reason.'[15] The rational arguments which characters develop in tragedy are designed to stimulate emotions, particularly feelings of outrage about ideas expressed.

THEATRE AS POLITICAL INTERVENTION

'The Eumenides' and 'Orestes'

Aeschylus' *Oresteia*, our one surviving trilogy, traces society through three phases: (1) Agamemnon rules as a hereditary monarch; (2) Aegisthus imposes a dictatorship, symbolized in performance by the arrival of his bodyguard; (3) a law-court is established, the core component of democracy. Orestes kills his mother because he is required to do so by the old-fashioned laws of vendetta, a social code based upon honour and obligations to relatives. The cycle of violence is broken when the duty of imposing justice is transferred from relatives to the polis. Whilst the first two plays of *The Oresteia* are set in the distant past in Argos, *The Eumenides* is set in Athens, the world of the audience.

In 462 BC democracy took an important step forwards when an aristocratic body called the Council of the Areopagus was stripped of its constitutional powers. The democrats allowed the Areopagus to remain as a religious court with the power to try cases of sacrilege and intentional homicide. Aeschylus' play celebrates that new role which the Areopagus performed on behalf of the people, and on the face of it approves the new status quo which prevailed in 458 BC.

Performed exactly fifty years later, Euripides' *Orestes* is a response to the optimistic vision of *The Oresteia*. Orestes is portrayed not as a man of integrity saved by the democratic system but as an isolated aristocrat who culpably ignores the democratic process. He is hauled

before the assembly, where men of different political complexions debate how he should be punished, and his own speech being a feeble one, he is condemned to death. After taking hostages, he brings his house down about him in flames. In Aeschylus' play the marginalized outsiders, the Furies or 'Eumenides', are absorbed into the procession that symbolizes the Athenian community, but in Euripides the community is divided irreconcilably. On the one hand embittered aristocrats seem willing to allow their whole world to crash down with them; on the other, a democratic assembly is controlled by those who have the greatest facility with words. The Athens of Aeschylus is the city that defeated the Persians; the Argos of Euripides' *Orestes* evokes an Athens that was losing its empire, an Athens in which the elite had recently staged a coup and would soon try again.

Whilst Aeschylus' play enacts the democratic processes of speaking and casting ballots, Euripides has a messenger describe the assembly, which seems part of an alien world over which individuals have little control – though Orestes does secure one small concession. Euripides' chorus become sympathetic onlookers with no active involvement in the plot. The audience's mode of viewing thus changes. In Euripides' play only private life is visible to the spectator. There is no sense of interaction between the individual and the collective. A gulf has appeared between a man's personal identity and his public identity as a citizen.

'Knights' and 'Trojan Women'

When Aristophanes and Euripides attack the horrors of war, their plays reflect the trauma of the Peloponnesian war. Many critics have wondered how far these plays align the author with a particular political stance. The context, as we have seen, is that the commercial classes and the poor who lived on state payments supported an aggressive policy of expanding the empire, whilst farmers had good reason to oppose this policy. Cleon succeeded Pericles as the driving force in Athenian politics, continuing the policy of war and empire, and Aristophanes' *Knights* appears to be a direct personal attack upon him. Cleon is satirized as a slave manipulating his master 'Demos', who personifies the democratic assembly. The slave is ousted from power by a grotesque sausage-maker who carries Cleon's methods to a logical extreme. This sausage-maker reconsti-

tutes old and scatty Demos as a dashing youth from the good old days when Athens beat the Persians.

There are two ways of reading *Knights*: as a contribution to the class war, or as a carnival celebration based around motifs of anti-authoritarianism, food and rebirth. In defence of the carnivalesque reading, it is often pointed out that the Athenians awarded Aristophanes first prize but promptly elected Cleon to the post of general.[16] *Knights* may end with a peace treaty because Aristophanes spoke for landowners, or it may end with peace because comedy as a genre was bound to celebrate eating, drinking and sexual pleasure. Human beings in comedy are corpulent, illogical, subject to biological drives and plainly incapable of fighting a heroic war. Much the same issue arises in respect of tragedy, which in the nature of the genre must portray war as the source of suffering.

In 415 BC Euripides' *Trojan Women* portrayed the plight of women enslaved at the end of the Trojan war; the men of Troy have all been executed, and a boy-child is killed in the climax of the play. Euripides shows that the Greeks responsible for the massacre will be punished by the gods. The audience and actors of the play knew that Athens had in the course of that winter massacred the adult males and enslaved the women of Melos, after the island's ruling elite had resisted Athens too long. Euripides could not have known of the genocide at the time of writing, but he knew of earlier massacres and he knew that Athens was poised to send an invasion force to Sicily. At the same time, memories were strong of how the Persians, around the time when Euripides was born, had driven the Athenians from their city and destroyed it. The women of Troy could thus stand as a metaphor not only for the victims of Athenian genocide, but also for the Athenians themselves. The Athenians listened to Euripides, and perhaps the play impressed them, but they still went to war, and it was fortunate for them that the Spartans proved merciful when Athens eventually surrendered.

In modern times the theme of war has given the play particular appeal. Jean-Paul Sartre, for example, was impressed by a production which attacked French military policy in Algeria and adapted the play to point up the dangers of nuclear war in 1965.[17] In turn, an Israeli adaptation of Sartre's text in 1983 attacked Israel's invasion of Lebanon.[18] The production was directed by a German, and the image of a glass cage identified Helen with Eichmann the German war criminal. Greek myth thus became a vehicle for

pointing up that which could not otherwise be contemplated: similarities between the crimes of the Nazis and present Israeli policy. Women of ancient Troy became an acceptable mirror in which both Jews and Palestinians could be glimpsed. The masks of Trojan women probably served a similar function in Euripides' Athens, allowing Athenians to glimpse themselves in the person of the other.

'*Oedipus the King*'

It seems self-evident today that *Trojan Women* makes a political statement, but the same cannot be said of Sophocles' *Oedipus*. The play was censored in Britain until 1910 because of its treatment of incest, and Freud's theory of the Oedipus complex emerged out of this great moral panic of the Victorian age (see above, p. 22). Freud's reading of Sophocles suggests that the play has a universal power because it acts out psychological drives buried within every individual. Freud indicates (1) that the meanings of the play are not culture-specific, (2) that the focus is the isolated central character, and (3) that Sophocles depicts what is fated and not Oedipus' free moral choices. Modern theatre practitioners have tended to read the play as post-Freudians, and to obliterate its politics.

In Peter Hall's 'ritual' version of *Oedipus the King* the elimination of any political aspect was furthered by some key directorial decisions. In Sophocles the chorus represent an assembly of senior Theban citizens, but in Hall's production the chorus were a mixture of males and females, indistinguishable from the helpless suppliant children of the opening tableau; there was no sense, therefore, that Oedipus has to justify himself at every point to the voters who put him in power. Because the play was followed in a double-bill by *Oedipus at Colonus*, it became the saga of one human individual. In staging the play, Hall placed Oedipus on top of a projecting platform, so the actor stood high above the chorus, making little eye contact with them. Attention was thus focussed on the solitary figure of the larger than life hero, whose fate alone concerned the audience. When rehearsing the text, Hall concentrated on the musicality of Ranjit Bolt's rhyming couplets, which with their insistent and predictable rhymes created a sense of inevitability. The translator assured the cast that 'Sophocles was a very pessimistic, melancholy man who represents a dark view of life',[19] and this old-fashioned doom-and-

gloom view of Greek tragedy left no space for recognition that the chorus make democratic decisions, that they emerge wiser from their experience, and that Thebes is saved from the plague.

Oedipus becomes a political play when we focus on the interaction of actor and chorus, and see how the chorus form a democratic mass jury. Each sequence of dialogue takes the form of a contest for the chorus' sympathy, with Oedipus sliding from the role of prosecutor to that of defendant, and each choral dance offers a provisional verdict. After Oedipus' set-to with Teiresias the sooth-sayer, the chorus decide to trust Oedipus on the basis of his past record; after his argument with his brother-in-law Creon, the chorus show their distress and urge compromise. Once Oedipus has confessed to a killing and Jocasta has declared that oracles have no force, the chorus are forced to think about political tyranny, torn between respect for divine law and trust in their rulers. In the next dance they assume that the contradiction is resolved and Oedipus has turned out to be the son of a god. Finally a slave's evidence reveals that the man most honoured by society is in fact the least to be envied. The political implications are clear: there is no space in democratic society for such as Oedipus. Athenians, like the chorus of the play, must reject the temptation to believe one man can calculate the future.

There are echoes in the play of two significant events in the Peloponnesian war. Pericles' imperialist policies were undermined by the plague which decimated the city; and the Spartans challenged Pericles on the grounds that his family was polluted by murder (see above, p. 42). The play was not an allegory, but a myth dealing with the pressing issue of charismatic leadership in the days of Pericles' decline. It was a myth about the polis. If the politics of *Oedipus* has been underplayed in the twentieth century, the reason is not simply a lack of historical information. Brecht ironically remarks that within the bourgeois theatre 'in a performance of *Oedipus* one has for all practical purposes an auditorium full of little Oedipuses'.[20] The urge to identify with the individual hero rather than the collective has been endemic.

'Antigone'

Sophocles' *Antigone* begins in the aftermath of war. Thebes has beaten off an attack by Polyneices, son of Oedipus. Creon, who now

rules Thebes, decrees that Polyneices' body will be left unburied, but Antigone, his niece and Polyneices' sister, buries the body and is punished by death. In the nineteenth century *Antigone* was usually seen as play about balance. In a famous analysis, the German philosopher Hegel argued that the ideal society could only be created through a synthesis of the two principles which Sophocles' play opposes. Thus the play was chosen in 1841 by a progressive Prussian monarch to be the first authentic rendition of a Greek tragedy.[21] Many twentieth-century theatre practitioners have turned to Sophocles' play in order to articulate new visions of how the individual relates to the state. Antigone normally becomes the heroine resisting state oppression. A celebrated example is the performance undertaken in the prison where Nelson Mandela was held captive by the white South African regime. Athol Fugard reconstructed this event in his play *The Island* (1972).

In occupied Paris during the Second World War, Jean Anouilh created, beneath a radical veneer, a 'boulevard' version of the play which demonstrates the futility of political engagement.[22] Creon, whose aim is to keep the system running, wins the intellectual argument, but Antigone still elects to die as an expression of personal rebellion against the values of bourgeois society. Anouilh created in Antigone a figure whose existential angst seemed deeply familiar to a middle-class European audience. The New York production of 1946 found it necessary to modify the text to make Antigone a more thoroughgoing heroine. The Nazi censors felt comfortable with this play, which pointed the finger not at political repression but at bourgeois malaise. When turning *Antigone* into a work for the commercial theatre, Anouilh's decisive move was to eliminate the collective voice of the chorus. A single prologue figure (played by Laurence Olivier in the London version of 1949) intervenes to speak of tragedy as a well-oiled machine. Personal decisions in Anouilh's world are inconsequential.

When Brecht adapted *Antigone* immediately after the war, he politicized the play by restoring the chorus of elders to a central position. His chorus represented the German majority who complained but never rebelled against fascism. Brecht's chorus distance themselves from Creon when the war goes badly, but prove unable to break with him. Antigone lambasts the chorus when they offer her sentimental pity and say that her death is fated. The four actors of the chorus dressed like Creon, shared the same acting space, and

Figure 5 Brecht's *Antigone* (1948). Antigone after her arrest confronts Creon
and the chorus.

spoke in a similar way. Their *Gestus* or social body language defined
at every point their attitude to the events which they witnessed.
Brecht was concerned to resist any tendency of the audience to
identify in a sentimental way with the heroine.

It is a considerable temptation for the actress of Antigone, in her exchange
with Creon, to play directly for the sympathy of the audience. If she yielded
to this temptation, she might obscure the audience's vision of the root
conflict within the ruling class – which the play exemplifies – and might
jeopardize speculations and emotions prompted by this vision.[23]

Brecht used the choral form of Greek tragedy as a device for creating
critical distance, and thus emotions of a more complex kind.

Brecht's text was first performed in English by the Living Theatre
in 1967.[24] This production expressed the values of a counter-culture
focussed around opposition to the Vietnam war. Julian Beck (director
and Creon) and Judith Malina (translator and Antigone) imposed on
Brecht's radicalism the new sixties notion that political liberation
meant liberation of the self. A correct analysis of the class struggle
was no longer enough, and Artaud's ideal of a total theatre had
somehow to be married to Marx. While Brecht placed his audience

outside the play as judges, Beck and Malina gave the audience a role inside the play as the invading army, denying them a position of intellectual detachment. Understanding mind and body as part of a single organism, they translated words into mimetic action at every point, creating a succession of fluid group images. While Brecht set his play in a remote half-oriental antiquity, Beck and Malina opted for jeans and T-shirt to emphasize that the performance event belonged to the here-and-now of 1967. In Brecht's stark production, both audience and actors listened to arguments and weighed them up, but in 1967 to be cerebral was to deny one's self. Brecht's vision was a materialist one, but Beck and Malina dissolved material reality to create visual metaphors: the corpse of Polyneices was present and thrown onto bodies representing the sea; Creon's feelings on realizing his error were represented by the chorus transforming themselves into the Hindu juggernaut of Vishnu and crushing him. What the Living Theatre surrendered was a faith in reason and the power of language to persuade, and Malina's Antigone inevitably became the heroine because she followed her feelings. Sophocles might have appreciated in Beck and Malina their sense that reason is insufficient. Sophocles' chorus were dancers as well as thinkers, and used their bodies to communicate a level of awareness beyond that of debate. In Athens the gods required due acknowledgement.

CHAPTER 4

Gender

WOMEN, POLITICS AND MYTH

The problem

> Amongst our qualities,
> god's gift of singing to the lyre
> was not granted us by Apollo, commander of music.
> Otherwise I'd have sung out my reply
> to the race of men.
> The past has as much to tell of woman's lot
> as it does of males. (chorus: *Medea*, 424–30)

The theatre of Athens was created by and for men, yet it is generally thought to contain some of the best female roles in the repertory. The contrast with Shakespearean theatre is a striking one. Why? The question has caused much concern in the late twentieth century.

The first surviving words of dramatic dialogue from the Greek world are actually written by a woman:

> – Virginity, virginity, you have left me: where have you gone?
> – I shall never return to you, never return.[1]

The singer of the first line represents a bride, and the reply is by an individual or more probably a chorus playing the bride's lost virginity. Sappho wrote this text for a wedding on the island of Lesbos, more than a century before Greek theatre as we know it came into being, and there is no reason to doubt that the performers were women. Another text by Sappho laments the annual death of the young god Adonis, and a singer representing the goddess Aphrodite (probably Sappho herself) is in dialogue with a chorus of girls:

> – Aphrodite! the delicate Adonis is dying: what should we do?
> – Strike yourselves, maidens, tear your tunics.[2]

66

In the classical period, the emergence of democracy meant that female voices like Sappho's were removed from the public domain. When the Athenian historian Thucydides places a democratic manifesto in the mouth of Pericles on the occasion of a state funeral, the only mention of women is a brief afterthought addressed to widows of the dead: 'Great is your glory if you prove not inferior to that nature that you have, and enjoy no kind of reputation among males either for good or for bad.'[3] In the pre-democratic age these silent widows without 'reputation' would have been the focus of attention, keening loudly and beating their bodies to purge their grief, to signal respect for their dead husbands, and if necessary to whip up the spirit of revenge; but in democratic Athens a sober speech by a male politician has supplanted those female voices and actions. Funerals in the old style identified the dead first and foremost as members of a family, but the new democratic funeral rendered the family invisible, and located the dead men as children of their city. The sons of these fallen warriors would now be reared by the state and not by their mothers. The logic that silenced these mourning widows of Athens also silenced women like Sappho, whose role included the creation of public performances at weddings. Like funerals, traditional weddings glorified the family and not the state. The enactment of female behaviour by men in Athenian drama has to be seen in its complex relationship to this great act of suppression by the male democratic state. Tears and lamentations that were no longer tolerated in real funerals seem to have been relocated in the theatre. Men who restrained themselves over the real bodies of their fallen comrades were content to weep in the theatre as they watched men dressed as women wailing and lamenting over simulated corpses.

There is no dispute that the roles in Athenian theatre were all taken by men. The audience has proved a more contentious issue, and jokes in Aristophanes have been dissected time and again in vain efforts to determine whether they seem funnier if there is indeed a female presence in the auditorium.[4] Certainly men did not go to the theatre escorting their wives as they did in ancient Rome, or in the modern bourgeois theatre. Athenian theatre was sponsored by the state, and thus men attended as members of the male community that embodied the state. If women were present, then it is generally assumed that those who came sat at the back, or maybe the sides, and the female presence was marginal. The plays were directed at male spectators.

Figure 6 The male Athenian audience. Some mature men and a youth admire
a young acrobat at the Panathenaian festival. Late 500s BC.

The best evidence for a female spectator is a seat which can be
inspected today in the theatre in Athens: a throne in the front row
for a priestess of Athene. There is no reason why this surviving
monument should not reflect time-honoured tradition. Male priests
represented the other goddesses, and this solitary woman seems to
be the exception who proves the rule – representing the goddess who
has no mother and no sexual relationships, and fights like a man. We
may consider her rather like the token white (a dummy if necessary)
whom Genet required to be present in the front row if ever his play
The Blacks was performed to a black audience.[5] Without the symbolic
presence of the other in the audience, the play's debate about
otherness would not have the same force. This token female seems to
lie behind the figure of Lysistrata, who in Aristophanes' comedy
inspired the women of Athens to declare a sex strike and barricade
themselves in the Acropolis in a bid to end the war. 'Lysistrata'
means 'dissolver of armies' and the real priestess who viewed the
performance was called Lysimache, 'dissolver of war'.[6]

Women in Athenian democracy

Penelope, the wife of Homer's Odysseus, spends her life weaving,
like most Athenian women, but the palace where she lives is a place
where important people assemble, and the price she pays is sexual

harassment when her husband is away at sea. In the democratic era, men removed themselves from the household to a new set of public spaces where the important business of life was now conducted. Women at the same time were removed from the public domain in which citizen males paraded their equality. Solon, in the early days of the city-state, imposed a series of controls upon Athenian women which included: regulation of women's festivals; restraints upon extravagant dress; a curfew for women after dark; smaller trousseaux to prevent bridegrooms from appearing to sell their bodies for money; no displays at funerals with hired mourners and self-flagellation. The funeral procession was to take place before daybreak, with women walking at the back, and traditional female mourning was dismissed as 'barbaric'.[7] Behind Solon's measures lay a democratic logic. In the new era of the city-state, rich men were not to flaunt their wealth by showing how women of their family could dress. The elite should not be tempted to use marriage to pool their wealth. The chastity of citizen women should be protected, so there could be no ambiguity about who was or was not a son of Athens.

The strength of the city-state was a matter of life and death. If the men of the city fought side by side as equals with complete commitment to the collective good, then the city became rich. If it was torn apart by in-fighting between rich and poor, the city could be annihilated. The suppression of women was therefore a means to an end. The place of Athenian women became the home – and even within the home they were excluded from rooms where men entertained male guests. The place of males became the market, the assembly, the law court, the gymnasium where they conversed and trained for war, and the theatre where they questioned in the most fundamental ways who they were and how they should live. The suppression of women is perhaps most obvious in the rules of the law court. Though citizen women could engage in the religious practice of swearing an oath, they could not otherwise speak, and had to be represented by the male relative who was their legal master. Their identities were effaced to the point that not even their names could be mentioned in public. We cannot tell how far women resented a political system which reduced them to non-persons, because their voices are lost.

Pericles' injunction that Athenian women should live in accordance with 'that nature that you have' begged a few questions. It would take a generation or two longer before democratic ideology

(by which term I refer to the work of philosophers, biologists and theatre-makers, amongst others) would bring the new socially constructed role of women into alignment with public perceptions of the natural and god-given. In the classical period there seemed nothing natural about the way Athenian women were required to behave, for too many alternative models were available. Myths of great antiquity showed goddesses resisting their husbands and driving chariots into battle. A woman like Aspasia, the mistress and intellectual companion of Pericles, was free to mingle with men because she was not Athenian but an Ionian Greek from Asia Minor. Customs were seen to be different in non-democratic societies. In Sparta, for example, women were educated, they could own property, they could dance in public and criticize the dancing displays of men.[8] Most famously, Spartan girls could run naked like men in athletic contests. A subject population took responsibility for most of the weaving, and the Spartan priority was that women should be physically fit to breed fit sons. In Athens, the debate about an ideal society could at no point sidestep the issue of woman's role and nature.

There was thus a conspicuous gap in classical Athens between sex and gender. Dramatists could construct new myths in order to efface this gap, or they could play upon the gap in order to explore deep tensions and contradictions within the democratic system. Aeschylus is often associated with the first strategy, Euripides and Aristophanes with the second.

Women in Aeschylus

Aeschylus' *Oresteia* portrayed a process of political change, starting in a Homeric, monarchical Argos, and finishing in a law court of democratic Athens (see above, p. 58). In Argos a woman, Clytaemnestra, rules for ten years while her husband Agamemnon is away at war, and she kills him when he returns, for reasons that seem to touch her as a woman: he made a human sacrifice of their daughter; he brings a concubine into her home; and he abandoned her without a male protector, so she has taken a man to replace her husband. In the second play of the trilogy their son Orestes returns and avenges his father by killing his mother. In baring her breast, Clytaemnestra emphasizes the biological bond of mother and child. In *Eumenides*, the third play, the affair is brought to trial before the sexually ambivalent figure of Athene. The issue is thus, whose crime

was the greater? That of the woman who broke the social bond by killing her husband, or that of the man who broke the biological bond by killing his mother? Athene determines, through her casting vote, that the social bond is more important. The overt moral is clear: in Greek democratic society, ties of family have to be subordinated to those socially constructed ties which constitute the political system.

In the trial scene, Orestes has as his advocate the male god Apollo, who commanded him to kill. Clytaemnestra's case is represented by twelve demonic Furies, who are associated with the earth and represent the forces of nature and reproduction. The core of Apollo's case is the argument that the womb is merely a container for the male seed: 'The so-called mother is not the parent of her child, but nurse to a freshly seeded foetus. The parent is he who mounts. The woman is a stranger who preserves the shoots of a stranger, if a god helps him.'[9]

Apollo's patriarchal biology drew upon new fashions of thought that were later consolidated by Aristotle, but flew in the face of normal thinking at the time, thinking embedded in medicine and in law. Seven years later, Pericles implemented a new marriage code which required that citizenship be restricted to those born of citizen mothers as well as citizen fathers, and such laws assumed that the mother had a significant role in the reproductive process. The harshness of Apollo's phrasing has led many interpreters to conclude that Aeschylus intended to generate a critical response and not simple assent.

In the final scene, Athene makes her peace with the Furies, and gives them a home in a cave beneath the Areopagus, the crag on which the court sat. The Furies become '*eumenides*', 'well-disposed'. The metaphor of the cave can be read in several ways. (1) Women are below and men above. (2) Women are now sequestered in the privacy of the home. (3) Women according to the formula used in the wedding ceremony are given to be ploughed for the propagation of legitimate children: the female Furies are thus associated with the fertility of the earth. (4) Women are equated with forces of political instability: if the lower orders of society are not accommodated, the power structure will collapse. Aeschylus' trilogy can be read as patriarchal propaganda, but it can also be read as an ironic and symbolic representation of sociopolitical changes currently taking place. Peter Stein was at pains to capture the complexity of the final

Plate 2   Silhouettes of the Furies on the roof of the house at the start of *Agamemnon*:
from *The Oresteia*, directed by Silviu Purcarete. Limoges, 1996.

image in his staging of the final scene. His Furies were bound up in
tight cloths to suggest both patriarchal rearing practices (foot-
binding, swaddling clothes) and the form of a chrysalis that would
one day hatch. His use of a Russian cast emphasized the vulnerability of the new Athenian order.[10] Silviu Purcarete with a Romanian cast had pregnant and faceless Furies lying on the ground to
emphasize their link with the earth. The ironic contrast between
their lyrical blessing song and their loss of freedom again tied post-
communist politics to the question of gender.[11]

Only the first play survives of Aeschylus' *Danaid* trilogy, but there
too Aeschylus uses a broad historical sweep to represent the
changing status of Greek women. In *Suppliants*, the surviving first
play of the trilogy, fifty wild but genetically Greek women (represented by twelve actors) arrive from North Africa as refugees from
an arranged marriage which they oppose. They dress with oriental
extravagance and engage in ritual displays of grief that include
tearing their veils, beating their breasts and lacerating their faces.

They engage, therefore, in practices which Athens and other Greek states tried to curb. The king of Argos decides to protect them, after minimal democratic consultations. In the lost second play, when Argos has been defeated in battle, the women murder their Egyptian husbands on their wedding night. One woman opts out of the conspiracy, perhaps because her husband declines to engage in marital rape. It appears that a new sexual regime is now implemented in Argos: whilst males give up Egyptian-style rapacity, women give up their autonomy. *Suppliants* dramatizes female qualities which alarmed Athenian males: the power to seduce and deceive, the power of emotion expressed through the body, the power and exclusiveness of women in a collective group.

Gender in *Suppliants* is bound up with ethnicity. It emerges as a Greek principle that the woman submits to her husband, and the husband controls his rapacious instincts. The barbaric east is associated time and again in Greek thinking with femininity and lack of self-control; oriental men were said to fawn before monarchs, dress luxuriously and indulge in emotional displays. The sexual regime of classical Athens relates not only to democracy but also to the ideology of race. The classical historian Herodotus sketched an Egypt where gender roles are reversed. Women urinate standing up, and sell goods in the market, leaving men at home to do the weaving. Most interestingly, Herodotus describes a dramatic festival dedicated to a god he recognized as Dionysos. Women, he says, processed from village to village operating marionettes equipped with a giant mobile phallus. The remarkable thing was not the obscenity, but the fact that women performed these obscenities before men.[12] Similar role inversion is a feature of Aeschylus' *Persians*, where the widowed queen performs her ritual functions with dignity and authority, but Xerxes her son, defeated by the Greeks in battle, leads the male chorus in a frenzied display of feminine emotion. The Persian males ululate, beat their breasts, tear at their hair, rip their clothing and weep in a manner antithetical to Greek notions of masculinity.

Women on the Parthenon

On the temple of Athene the 'Maiden' (Parthenos), sculptors fixed forever in stone myths about the foundation of civilization in general

and Athens in particular, myths which represent the viewpoint of those who controlled Athens in around 440 BC. On the four sides of the temple above the outside columns appear four archetypal conflicts: the Greeks sack Troy and retrieve Helen; men fight off centaurs trying to rape their women; Athenian men fight Amazons, with the fight evenly balanced; and the gods beat off primeval giants, with goddesses fighting alongside gods. The Parthenon thus declared women to be equals in the world of the gods, but not in the world of humans, where they may be a cause of trouble like Helen, or vulnerable beings who need protection from the animal lusts of centaurs. Yet women also have the potential to be Amazons strong as men, and there is nothing butch or overtly unfeminine about the way these Amazons are represented. Athene in *The Oresteia* reminds the audience that she establishes male rule on the very hill where the Amazons once camped when laying siege to the Acropolis.[13] These Amazons were an important folk memory, and the Amazon myth makes it clear that male dominance never existed in nature, but was at some point imposed. Phaedra, the heroine of Euripides' *Hippolytus*, is the daughter of an Amazon, and longs to ride a chariot and hunt in the mountains like a man. There is no sense in the play that these longings are unnatural.

The Parthenon is concerned with gender because it was a temple to Athene the Maiden, the female patron of a society ruled by men, and its sculptures explore the ambivalence of a goddess who transcends sexuality. The frieze above the main door depicted the most prestigious ceremony in which Athenian women participated, bringing newly woven robes every four years to dress the goddess's wooden statue. Yet Athene was not only the goddess of weaving but also a warrior. The east pediment depicted the birth of Athene from her single, male parent, and the west her fight with Poseidon. Inside the building, a magnificent statue of Athene the warrior stood on a base depicting Pandora, the first wife and a creature of foolish curiosity, consigned to low status. On Athene's shield, ringed by battling Amazons, was the face of the Gorgon, which turned all men to stone. The power and danger of women was a recurrent theme, and the figure of Athene is a reminder of how complex the male–female relationship actually was. Like the cult of Elizabeth in Shakespeare's England, the cult of Athene was a constant stimulus to the exploration of gender.

WOMEN AND RITUAL

The worship of goddesses

Under democracy women became legal and political non-entities. A woman in Euripides makes a case for equality on the grounds of her role in the religious life of the city:

Women are superior to men. I shall prove it ... In the matter of religion – the crux in my view – the major role is ours. In Apollo's oracles, women are prophetesses who speak the mind of the god. At the holy seat of Dodona, by the sacred oak-tree, womankind transmits the will of Zeus to all Greeks who want to attend. Rites dedicated to the Fates, or the Nameless Goddesses, would be impure if males took part, but invariably thrive when the participants are women. In religion the female receives her due. So why slander the race of women?[14]

As so often in tragedy, the speaker uses bad arguments to support a good case. It is a woman's psychic powers that allow her to act as mouthpiece for male gods, not her reason; and the Fates and Furies (the so-called 'nameless goddesses') are marginal figures, worshipped by women because of their association with death. Yet women did indeed play a major part in Athenian religion. The religious life of the democratic state was not centred on oracles in remote places or on primeval Fates and Furies, but on the worship of Olympian deities, particularly the canonical twelve. The twelve traditionally numbered six males and six females, reflecting an ancient quest for equilibrium, but in the democratic era, the sixth female, Hestia goddess of the domestic hearth, yielded up her place to Dionysos. So, for example, it was Dionysos who occupied the twelfth position above the entrance to the Parthenon. Male deities now outnumber females, so the symmetry of the sexes is broken. The goddess of the home is effaced, like her human counterparts, in favour of a god whose worship falls to the community as a whole.

Despite men's monopoly of the political sphere in the democratic period, numerous cults allowed women the chance to emerge from the home and engage in collective activities, often of a para-theatrical nature. Selected Athenian girls went to the outlying shrine of Brauron and donned bear masks in the worship of Artemis, a goddess associated with hunting in the wilderness. In the classical period, however, we cease to hear of Athenian girls at festivals of

Artemis giving public displays of dancing, for this type of performance, common in earlier times and in communities like Sparta, was
found incompatible with the democratic way of life.

All married Athenian women celebrated a festival of Demeter and
Persephone called the Thesmophoria, which linked the sowing of
seed in the autumn to female fertility. For three days the women of
Athens took over the Pnyx, the male assembly-place, and reverted to
a pre-civilized way of living, with no houses or fire for cooking. Males
were excluded. The events again symbolically recreated the disappearance of Persephone and her reappearance after the winter.
Much obscenity was involved in order to draw a smile from the
goddess, who wept for her lost daughter: in the rites of Demeter,
excessive feminine modesty was recognized as a bar to human
fertility. We can see the Thesmophoria either as a liberating event for
women or as a symbolic statement that woman equates with
barbarism. Aristophanes made this double-edged festival the setting
for a comedy in which Euripides is put on trial for insulting womankind.[15] Yet another festival of Demeter provides the occasion in
Aristophanes' *Assembly Women* when women conspire to take over the
city and share the available men on an egalitarian basis. Aristophanes' visions of sexual inversion are inspired by ritual practice.

Both men and women could be initiated into the 'Mysteries' at
Eleusis, where they received some kind of vision related to reproduction and the after-life. Aristophanes portrays separate male and
female processions singing and dancing in the procession.[16] At
Eleusis, two priestesses performed a kind of sacred drama: Demeter's
daughter Persephone disappeared into a cavern, supposedly ab-
ducted by the god of the underworld, and returned to her grieving
mother after the symbolic elapse of winter.[17] Women were not
prevented entirely from being performers in classical Athens.

Women and ritual in tragedy

There is a recurrent tension in Greek tragedy between women's
claim upon the ritual sphere and men's claim upon the political
sphere. A common focus is the role of women as public mourners. A
familiar example is *Antigone*, where Antigone insists upon the right to
bury her brother despite Creon's calculated decision to leave the
body unburied as an example to others. The moral of the play is
clearly that the Creons of this world need to take more account of

the female–ritual dimension. Since theatre was both an act of worship of a god and a kind of surrogate political assembly, it was in its nature to explore this middle ground between politics and ritual.

The woman's role as mourner, which the democratic city kept trying to check, was not simply a passive function. The chorus of Euripides' *Suppliants*, for example, are highly proactive. Argive women appear at the shrine of Demeter in Eleusis, demanding that Athens help them reclaim their dead from the siege of Thebes, so that burial may take place. The king of Athens succumbs to collective female pressure and rescues the corpses, but does nothing to stop the cycle of violence repeating in the next generation. In *The Libation Bearers*, the chorus of Trojan slave-women prove equally efficacious when they dance their lament around the tomb of Agamemnon, whipping up Orestes to a point of frenzy that allows him to kill. The democratic city suppressed ritual mourning not only because it lent status to aristocratic families, but also because the practice caused actions to be taken on the basis of emotion and codes of honour rather than calculation of the collective interest.

In Aeschylus' *Seven Against Thebes* the male warrior and politician Eteocles protests at a different kind of ritual. The women of the besieged city insist upon dressing the statues of the Theban gods in robes and garlands, in a rite that recalls for example the dressing of Athene at the Panathenaia. Eteocles condemns the women's howling as bad for morale, and declares that he will never share a house with anyone of the 'female race'; the woman's place is indoors, he insists, and she should express no opinions about the outdoor world of men. He proceeds to give the women a lecture on ritual practice: they should ululate in an upbeat manner to demoralize the enemy, and then make a cool-headed bargain with the gods, promising a fixed number of sacrifices in return for divine aid. The irony of course is that the women prove right. Eteocles' fate has been determined by the gods because his forebears have transgressed the sexual code. No voice of male authority is left at the end of the play to check the female lament over Eteocles' corpse. As always in Greek tragedy, the rational, male world view proves itself insufficient.

Women and Dionysos

The devotions of Athenian women were, broadly speaking, focussed upon goddesses. Dionysos as twelfth Olympian is something of an

anomaly, and according to tradition was worshipped by women who wandered the mountains in a state approaching trance. Athenian vases depict such 'maenads' encircling the robe and mask of Dionysos set on top of a pole. Whether these maenads are figures from myth or figures from some contemporary ritual remains unclear. In plate 3 the maenads have their hair loose and wear crowns of ivy and skins of young deer. One pours libations of wine, one beats a tambourine, while others wave Bacchic wands and brandish torches because it is night; unseen in the photograph, another woman plays orgiastic music on the pipes. It is not clear how far classical Athens tolerated a real as opposed to symbolic enactment of such ecstatic practices. The City Dionysia did not exist as a festival until shortly before the emergence of democracy, and here flesh and blood women are conspicuous by their absence. We hear only of a single aristocratic maiden who carried a basket with the first fruits of the spring. Five hundred boys and five hundred men danced in the dithyramb, but no place was found for women.

Dionysos in plate 3 is represented in his traditional guise, mature and bearded. However, when Dionysos is depicted in connexion with theatre, as for example in the famous Pronomos vase (plate 11), he is normally presented as a beautiful youth. In *The Bacchae*, Euripides fixed for ever the new androgynous image. In that play Dionysos breaks down the masculinity of Pentheus, the young fascistic king of Thebes, and persuades him in a famous scene of seduction to dress as a woman in order to spy on his mother and her fellow maenads. Aristophanes parodies this image of Dionysos in *The Frogs*, specifying a woman's saffron dress as the god's costume. (Note however that the vase painter in figure 1 omits the dress and reverts to the older image of Dionysos.) The idea of androgyny was reinforced in all theatre performances by the appearance of the piper, who wore a long feminine robe. One reason for building a second temple in the theatre complex soon after the classical period must have been to house a statue that represented this new conception of the god.

Dionysos, god of theatre, is a god who dissolves identity in general, and gender in particular. Euripides makes it clear that Pentheus, in trying to suppress maenadism, also suppresses the feminine aspects of himself. When the male in Greek plays seeks absolute dominance, and absolute suppression of the female, then he ends by destroying himself. Perhaps the exclusion of women from

Plate 3 Maenads worshipping Dionysos.

the Dionysia created conditions in which men could uncover, within themselves, their own female dimension. One can explain the sexual ambivalence of Dionysos in psychoanalytic terms. Carl Jung argued that everyone has a male *animus* and a female *anima*, and countered Freudian patriarchy by arguing that every female has an Electra

complex just as every male has an Oedipus complex.[18] It may be more helpful to compare Greek thinking to Chinese ideas about the need to balance the opposed principles of *yin* and *yang*.

Whether we take a positive view of Athenian theatre, considering it a public recognition of patriarchy's deficiencies, or a negative view, considering it as an appropriation by men of women's very identity, is a matter of our politics. At all events, male cross-dressing is bound up at a fundamental level with the Greek conception of theatre. The legal–political system denied women a place in the new democratic order, and the religio-political institution of theatre addressed the resulting imbalance. The exclusion of women from public performance is in a sense the source of Greek drama's preoccupation with gender.

Despite (or because of) the androgynous conception of Dionysos, the major emblem of the Dionysia was the phallus. Colonies sent golden images of the erect male member to Athens to be paraded through the streets. The chorus of satyrs wore erect life-size phalluses, probably in memory of the festival's foundation myth (see above, p. 31). The costume of comedy gave males a long, hanging phallus. Whilst the golden phallus represents the power and fertility of Athens, the erect phallus of the satyr play and the grotesque phallus of comedy represent negatives: the male Athenian who has lost his self-control, or his well-proportioned beauty. Biological drives are at the forefront of the satyric and comic view of life; tragedy, on the other hand, effaced the human body beneath long robes, and made little verbal reference to bodily functions. Where comedy and the satyr play identify human beings in relation to their biological sex, tragedy is concerned with how human beings perform their gender. In tragedy men are shown surrendering, for better or worse, to female emotion and female behaviour.

SEXUALITY

The bodies and minds of women were generally associated with the physical qualities of cold and wet, whilst men were associated with the hot and the dry. These qualities accorded with the contrasting life-styles of women who worked indoors and men who sailed, ploughed, fought and conducted politics in the open sunshine. Women's bodies were conceived as dark, porous containers, with their genitalia indoors, so to speak. These anatomical conceptions

correlate with codes of dress. Respectable women covered their heads in public, and their cloaks concealed their bodies, while Athenian men exposed their genitalia in the gymnasium and in athletic contests. Although the female body was conceived as a container, it was a moist container, and the normal classical assumption – despite the views of Aeschylus' Apollo, and later Aristotle – was that women concocted sperm just like men and that female orgasm was needed for reproduction; though of course, it was weaker sperm that engendered females.

Differences between male and female were not seen as absolute but as differences of balance or degree, and Greek males were bisexual in their tastes. Mature Athenian men, married or unmarried, liked to establish sexual relationships with adolescent boys between the age of puberty and the growth of the beard. Sexual intercourse was approved provided the couple faced each other, and the older man took the role of active partner whilst the younger avoided giving signs of sexual pleasure. Plato idealizes young male beauty, and praises pederastic love as the highest form of love. Though his claim that the truly wise man avoids physical consummation may not have accorded with common practice, he provides valuable evidence of cultural anxieties about self-control. Athens was not a society of carefree sexual abandon. The idealization of pederastic love may have been less prominent amongst the poorer classes, who have not left their writings to posterity. It required leisure to cultivate the body beautiful in the gymnasium, and the poor probably felt that elaborate rituals of courtship had an aristocratic flavour. This is one explanation for the striking absence of homosexual love in tragedy. In a lost play by Aeschylus, Achilles recalled embracing his dead boy-friend Patroclus, but elsewhere desire is heterosexual.[19] In Aristophanic comedy homosexual love never has positive associations, but of course it was in the nature of comedy to present the body as ugly. The comic body, with its huge phallus, bulging buttocks and sagging stomach was the antithesis of the body beautiful which many Greeks spent many hours acquiring.

Normally young men are portrayed naked and respectable women clothed on classical vases. If we look at vases where prostitutes are naked, it is frequently hard to tell whether we are looking at a male or female body. The breasts are small, the hips no larger than a man's, the limbs no more or less slender. A single set of aesthetic criteria determined the qualities that made the young

Plate 4 Aristophanes, *Women at the Thesmophoria*. A relative of Euripides disguised
as a woman holds as hostage a baby which turns out to be a wineskin.
Parody of a scene from Euripides, *Telephus*.

human body beautiful. When Aristotle described the biological
difference between male and female, and decided to deny women
their equal status in reproduction as producers of sperm, he
rationalized the difference by describing women as sterile or castrated men. Their menstrual blood was sperm that had not been
properly cooked by male heat.[20] Aristotle does not speak for the
classical age, but his theories accord with an old understanding that
male and female differ in degree rather than essence.

It can plausibly be argued that the young chorus-men who

impersonated old men or women in the theatre were engaged in a rite of passage, acquiring virility through impersonating those who lacked virility. When playing a woman, a young man encountered not an opposite but an aspect of himself that had to be transcended. After all, he knew what it was to be loved by a man. Transvestism was shameful in daily life, as Pentheus is acutely aware, but was perfectly admissible in a ritual context. In an Athenian festival called the 'vine-bearing', for example, two beautiful young men processed out of one of Dionysos' temples dressed as women. The rite celebrated a ruse played by Theseus when he dressed two men as girls destined for the minotaur. Judith Butler writes that 'The performance of drag plays upon the distinction between the anatomy of the performer and the gender that is being performed.'[21] Young men playing women in a tragedy or in the vine-bearing were not engaged in anything like modern drag because the anatomical distinction was not conceived in such clear-cut terms as it is today.

The most elaborate exercise in cross-dressing in Greek drama is found in Aristophanes' *Assembly Women*. Here a group of women (played by male actors, of course) steal their husbands' cloaks, sticks and shoes, and with the further aid of false beards successfully hijack the assembly. They expose how far masculinity is a construct by tanning their skin in the sun, avoiding perfume, and declining to shave their body hair. The mannerisms of men are easily acquired, and the main giveaway is their habit of invoking the goddesses whose cults have been the focus of all social activity.

FEMINIST APPROACHES

American feminism

In a sense the feminist critique of Greek tragedy begins with Aristophanes. In *Women at the Thesmophoria*, the premise of the plot is that women gathered for their festival are determined to indict Euripides for slander. The focus of their attack is the characterization of Phaedra in Euripides' play *Hippolytus*. Phaedra is a married woman who tries to seduce her stepson, and the women allege that all husbands in Athens now suspect their wives of adultery. The debate about Euripides' misogyny has rumbled on ever since.

Sarah Pomeroy in a pioneering feminist study of 1975 spoke up for Euripides:

My subjective estimate of Euripides is favorable. I do not think it misogynistic to present women as strong, assertive, successful, and sexually demanding even if they are also selfish or villainous. Other feminists share my opinion, and British suffragists used to recite speeches from Euripides at their meetings.[22]

Pomeroy values Euripides, in comparison with Sophocles and Aeschylus, because his women are 'scaled down closer to life'.[23] The proposition that Euripides reflects Athenian social conditions is certainly one that can be defended. Consider, for example, the case of Medea, a highly educated princess from a city on the Black Sea who has migrated to Corinth. Her husband suddenly decides to divorce her because he wants to marry a Corinthian. Twenty years before Euripides' play, a change in Athenian law meant that the children of non-Athenian brides would be considered illegitimate. At the time when Euripides wrote, the first children of these unions would recently have been refused citizenship.[24] Many real-life women must have found themselves in Medea's predicament. Pomeroy admires Euripides as a realist playwright, and her views echo those of early suffragettes. Following a celebrated production by Granville Barker in 1907, members of the Actresses' Franchise League incorporated extracts into their repertoire.[25]

By 1985 the climate had changed. Sue-Ellen Case published a manifesto in which she declared that it was 'no longer possible to believe that the portrayal of women in classical plays by men relates to actual women'.[26] The key text now became the *Oresteia*, with its 'public rationalization of misogyny' effected through the judgement of Athene. Case argued that the feminist reader should avoid reading in sympathy with figures like Medea, but read against the text, and she implied that feminist actresses and directors should leave Greek tragedy to men. Her thinking was in line with that of Tony Harrison, who decided that the *Oresteia* should be 'vacuum-sealed in maleness because the play seemed to have been written to overthrow ... dynamic female images ... and to present some kind of male image liberated from this defeat of the female principle'.[27] Peter Hall adopted an all-male cast when he produced Harrison's translation in London in 1981.

Case assimilates Greek performance to drag, and argues that female roles are male stereotypes:

Though all the characters were formalised and masked, even with cross-gender casting for female characters these were distinguished in kind from

the male characters. A subtextual message was delivered about the nature of the female gender, its behaviour, appearance and formal distance from representation of the male.[28]

It is hard to find evidence to support her proposition. The male actor of forty-something who played a female character was not doing anything that differed *in kind* from the activity of representing a male youth or a slave or an old man. All were types. The long robes and full head mask prevented the audience from seeing the actor's anatomy in counterpoint to the role. Case's distinction between 'real women' and 'masks of patriarchal production' does not relate to the real masks that were a defining feature of Greek performance.[29]

A further weakness in Case's argument is her readiness to read Greek tragedy through the mediation of Aristotle's *Poetics* (see p. 180 below). She lays much stress on Aristotle's statement that female characters should not exhibit the courage or intellect of men,[30] without recognizing that the Macedonian philosopher was engaged in sanitizing Athenian tragedy. Whatever the views of Aristotle, Medea does not, on the face of it, lack either courage or intellect. I find it more helpful to start from the premise that Greek tragedy explored competing and contested values, rather than the premise that it delivered a static ideology – which is not to deny that men alone set the agenda and debated the issues.

In the same year that Case published her essay, Froma Zeitlin offered classicists a new direction, tying literary criticism to anthropology. She considers tragedy to be 'a kind of recurrent masculine initiation, for adults as well as for the young', and more broadly a mode of education for the citizen. Consequently 'the self that is really at stake is to be identified with the male, while the woman is assigned the role of the radical other'.[31] The feminization of the god Dionysos and the exclusion of women from the festival are thus highly significant. It was in the nature of the theatrical medium, Zeitlin argues, to centre on women, for theatre is the medium of the body, and women were particularly associated with the body through their role in reproduction and in burial rites. As 'the radical other' the woman served to define the true male, just as the Persian served to define the true Greek. Whilst Case reads plays as representations of Greek society skewed and falsified by the male gaze, Zeitlin sees them as authentic records of a male ritual conducted in response to flesh and blood women. Case dismisses female roles as

stereotypical masks, but Zeitlin provides a more dynamic view of those roles, opening the way for female practitioners to recolonize the 'radical other'. A recent study of Aristophanes by Lauren Taafe, owing much to Zeitlin, ends with specific proposals as to how a feminist theatre company might proceed.[32]

French feminism

French feminists have often found Greek drama relevant to their concerns. As a psychoanalyst, Luce Irigaray shares Freud's perception that Greek myths relate to fundamental psychic processes: 'Give or take a few additions and retractions, our imaginary still functions in accordance with the schema established through Greek mythologies and tragedies.' Irigaray condemns Freud for putting all his emphasis on the primal murder of the father-figure, Laius, and argues that Freud 'forgets a more archaic murder, that of the mother, necessitated by the establishment of a certain order in the polis'. The murder of Clytaemnestra seems to her particularly important because it symbolizes the suppression of the mother, a key feature of western civilization. Athene, bonded only to her father, embodies an ideal of femininity which Irigaray deplores. 'The mythology underlying patriarchy has not changed. What the *Oresteia* describes for us still takes place.'[33]

A feature of patriarchy for Irigaray is the imposition of the 'rule of language' in place of the world of the flesh which unites the mother to the child in her womb. The same distinction between language and the body has preoccupied Hélène Cixous, who develops a notion of 'feminine writing' effected through the body. 'Why so few texts?' she asks, and answers: 'Because so few women have as yet won back their body. Women must write through their bodies'.[34] The logic of this position drew her to theatre, though a theatre in which women would not like Electra and Antigone be offered as the eternal sacrificial object. 'It is high time', she wrote in 1977, 'that women gave back to the theatre its fortunate position, its *raison d'être* and what makes it different – the fact that there it is possible to get across the living, breathing, speaking body'.[35] And so began a long collaboration with the (female) French director, Ariane Mnouchkine. Cixous translated the final play of *Les Atrides*, Mnouchkine's version of the *Oresteia* presented in 1991/2. Mnouchkine's assumptions about

Plate 5 Dancers from the chorus of *Iphigeneia in Aulis*: the first part of *Les Atrides*.

gender are in line with those of Cixous and Irigaray, and inform her production at every point.

As an introduction to the three plays of Aeschylus, Mnouchkine presented Euripides' *Iphigenia at Aulis*, which tells how Agamemnon sacrificed his and Clytaemnestra's daughter in order to secure a fair wind to sail to Troy. This extension of the narrative established Clytaemnestra as the injured party, and *Les Atrides* became her story, the story of the murder of the primal mother. The production used make-up masks, formal costumes and movement reminiscent of kathakali, the classical dance-drama of India. This orientalized style turned the characters into mythic prototypes rather than members of a specific society. It placed Aeschylean theatre not as the great ancestor of 'our' western theatre but as something strange and hard to account for. It related the marginalization of women to the marginalization of the east by a male-dominated western tradition. But most important of all, it created the conditions for a kind of *écriture corporelle*, a 'writing with the body'. As Cixous writes: 'Where does the tragedy first of all take place? In the body, in the stomach, in the legs, as we know since the Greek tragedies. Aeschylus' characters tell, first and foremost, a body state.'[36] While most male

directors like Hall and Stein give first emphasis to the text, Mnouch-kine adopts the priorities of eastern theatre and thinks first of the actor's body. The masks, extraordinary costumes and ever-present percussionist fostered an acting style in which the body became more eloquent than words. The element of dance, eliminated in most contemporary performances of Greek tragedy, was allowed the dominance that it had in Athens. Another important device was the doubling of actors, where Mnouchkine reverted to and perhaps rediscovered the power of an Aeschylean practice (see pp. 159–61 below). The player of Agamemnon became Agamemnon's son Orestes; Clytaemnestra became Athene who forgives Clytaemnes-tra's murderer; and Iphigenia the victim became first her vengeful sister Electra and then leader of the Furies. The doubling disorien-tates the spectator, and suggests that the past is contained in the present, that individuality and uniqueness are a 'phallocentric' obsession. As Cixous puts it, 'Pure I, identified to I-self, does not exist.'[37]

CHAPTER 5

Space

THE GREEK WORLD

The world

The Greek world at the start of the classical period looked rather like the playing space of a Greek theatre: a flat disk with a drainage ditch around the edge and a strong focus on the point of balance at the centre. Hecataeus in around 500 BC drew a map of the world which looked like this (see figure 7).[1]

For Hecataeus the centre is his own city of Miletus, greatest of the many Greek cities on the coast of what is now Turkey. Those cities had once been economically and culturally dominant in the Greek world, but by 500 BC they were under the control of the Persian empire. Miletus was destroyed after an uprising in 494 BC, and the Greek centre of gravity shifted westwards. The sacred centre in the classical period was normally taken to be Delphi, home of Apollo's oracle, where a stone called the *omphalos* symbolized the navel of the world. Orestes in Aeschylus' *Eumenides* is shown clinging for safety to this navel stone before retreating to the law court in Athens.

To the east of the Greek world ran the road to Susa, capital of the Persian empire (in today's Iran), and to the far west were the straits that led out of the Mediterranean and beyond the normal limits of navigation; to the south were the deserts of Africa (considered part of Asia), to the north a mountainous Europe, and this whole earth was thought to be encircled by ocean. Aeschylus set his play *Prometheus* above a ravine on the extreme north. The hero is pinned to a barren rock face, and because he is on the edge of the world he is visited by Oceanus, a god symbolizing the ocean making its circuit around the earth. The classical Greeks believed that they had the ideal balance of qualities thanks to their position at the centre of the world.

89

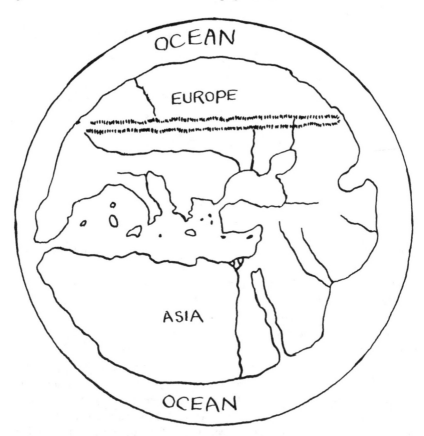

Figure 7 Map of the world according to Hecataeus, 500 BC.

In the course of the classical period Athens attained a position of dominance in the Greek world. Four years after the destruction of Miletus, Athens defeated the Persian invaders in the land battle of Marathon. Ten years later the Persians came for revenge, entered Athens and burnt its temples to the ground, but against all odds were defeated in the sea battle of Salamis. Claiming to be the protector of Greece, Athens established a league, and in the course of a generation transformed itself from being the protector of its allies to an imperial power (see above, p. 50). A later orator used a traditional metaphor to suggest what it felt like to be an Athenian. He compared the world to a round Greek shield made of five layers

of leather with a projecting boss or *omphalos* at the centre: Greece with its perfectly balanced climate was at the centre of the world, Attica at the centre of Greece, the city of Athens at the centre of Attica, the rock of the Acropolis at the centre of Athens, and the temple of Athene was the omphalos. Supporting this conception of the world, the orator goes on to compare the islands of the Aegean to a chorus dancing round the harbour of Athens. He describes Attica, the territory of Athens, as a region that is naturally autonomous because it is surrounded by mountains. Its population had never migrated from elsewhere, but some Athenians had emigrated to found cities such as Miletus.[2] These last two claims were highly contentious. Euripides' *Ion* draws upon the authority of Delphi to support an Athens-centred body of myth. The play tells how Ion, the future king of Athens, is descended from serpentine figures who emerged from the rock of the Acropolis, and how his descendants will become the 'Ionian' Greeks of the eastern Mediterranean (see above, p. 24). A propagandist element is commonly present in Athenian plays, but is not always so overt.

Greece

With its multiplicity of islands and its cities set in fertile plains penned in by sea and barren mountains, the topography of Greece lent itself to the emergence of independent city-states. The Cithaeron range, for example, separated Athens from its long-standing enemy Thebes. The unification of Greece was, to all intents and purposes, a geographical impossibility. Athens acquired an empire because it gained control of the sea, and it won control of the sea because it was a democracy. Naval warfare needed many citizens to man the three banks of oars which would propel a warship fast enough to ram the opposition. Land-based warfare required the participation of a rich elite who could equip themselves with suits of armour and food. The Peloponnesian war was partly an ideological struggle fought between an aristocratic Sparta, which had the strength on land to destroy Athenian agriculture, and a democratic Athens, which could bring in food by sea and control the islands and coastal cities of the Aegean.

The story of the Trojan war, as recounted in the *Iliad*, was found so compelling because it represented a flawed but heroic attempt by the different Greek states to unite in a common cause. Homer

Figure 8 Map of Greece showing the major settings of Greek plays.

portrays the difficulties of the Greeks in forging any kind of durable
alliance. In Homer there was no sense of the Greeks being ethnically
superior to the Trojans, but in the democratic period a sharp
demarcation line between free citizens and a slave labour force
began to encourage a different way of thinking. The Athenians
developed the myth that they had sprung from their own soil, and in
451 BC forbade the children of non-citizen mothers from acquiring
citizenship, thus fostering a notion of racial superiority and the
reality of separation. In Euripides' *Medea*, the heroine is a woman
brought to Greece years before by adventurers who reached her
homeland in modern Georgia. Medea associates as an equal with
the Greek women who form the chorus of the play, but her husband
rejects her for a local bride, and speaks of how he once rescued her
'from a barbarian land'. The word *barbarian* implies one who speaks
an incomprehensible language that sounds like 'bar! bar!', a cultural

rather than a genetic conception. Medea acts barbarically, but whether she has the birth and nature of a barbarian is left an open question. It may be that she comes from a remote Greek colony. Behind Euripides' treatment of Medea's foreignness lie conflicting and shifting notions about racial identity.

Attica and Athens

We often use the term *Athens* to embrace both the city and its hinterland. It is helpful to think of Marathon as a typical outer settlement, from where a runner ran 26 miles to bring news of victory to the city. All citizens were supposed to be equal participants in the democratic process, wherever they lived, and most could reach the city in a long day's walk. In practice many Athenians with houses in the city owned lands and were registered in the country. Each rural community functioned like the city in miniature, and the larger ones had their own performance spaces. The most famous of these is at Thorikos, rich enough in the classical period because of adjacent silver mines to build a huge stone auditorium. In such auditoria, used for multiple purposes, it seems that the local community would organize in January some kind of reperformance of plays performed in Athens, with local men dancing the chorus parts. It is unfortunate that we know so little about the theatrical culture of Attica which supported the achievements at the centre.

Athenian theatre was designed for a complete community. Men would walk in from the countryside to see twenty dithyrambic dances and seventeen plays in the space of some five days. They feasted in their democratic groupings, and would bivouac if they had no lodgings. Plato speaks impressionistically of a theatre audience of 30,000,[3] but the surviving remains indicate that 15,000–20,000 is a more sensible estimate. Some would have been visitors and foreign residents, but the great majority were citizens. The adult male population must have been in the region of 40,000 to 50,000 at the start of the Peloponnesian war, but somewhere between 15,000 and 25,000 at the end of the war.[4] If we eliminate the old, the sick, men on military service and overseers of slaves, then we may guess that perhaps half of those free to attend the plays of Aeschylus would have done so; however, with a smaller population more concentrated in the city, the vast majority would have attended the later plays of Sophocles and Aeschylus. If the last plays of Euripides seem more

intimate than those of Aeschylus, this may in some measure be explained by the fact that so many of the audience were now dead.

The procession at the start of the City Dionysia reflected the journey that so many spectators made from the periphery to the centre of the community in order to view the plays. In the 'leading-in' ceremony, the wooden statue was brought from a shrine outside the city through the gates in a journey that symbolized the god's arrival from the border town of Eleutherai. Next day, *en route* for the theatre, the main procession visited significant locations in the city such as the altar of the twelve gods in the classical agora ('marketplace'), and the symbolic 'hearth' of the city at the foot of the Acropolis in the area which served as the agora before the city was destroyed by the Persians. The procession clarified the nature of the city, and the plays which followed undertook to do the same.

The city of Athens grew up around the great natural citadel of the Acropolis. Famous today as the site of the temple of the Parthenon, the Acropolis housed many other shrines. The most sacred area contained a serpent associated with the myth of Athenian ancestry, the ruins of Athene's temple burnt by the Persians, the ancient wooden statue of Athene, and an olive tree which had survived the Persian flames. Euripides' *Ion* explored the body of myth associated with these sites, probably at a time when the Erechtheum, home of the serpent, was being rebuilt. Whilst the Acropolis remained the major religious centre in the classical period, the new agora became the centre for commercial and legal activity. Political activity was centred on the hill of the Pnyx used for the assembly (see above, p. oo) and on the council chamber in the agora. Although shrines were associated with every public building, the topography of classical Athens reflected a divide between the sphere of the gods up on the high rock and the sphere of social activity in the agora below. Many Greek plays articulate a tension between a rationalistic political approach to life and a traditionalist religious approach, and the surviving stones of Athens reflect that tension.

Athens was in a state of constant transformation through the classical period. Supported by revenues from the empire, the city was rebuilt from the rubble left by the Persians. Many migrated to set up enclaves around the Aegean, consolidating Athens' power and relieving pressure on food and land. Then in the course of the Peloponnesian war walls were built to link the city to the port. The

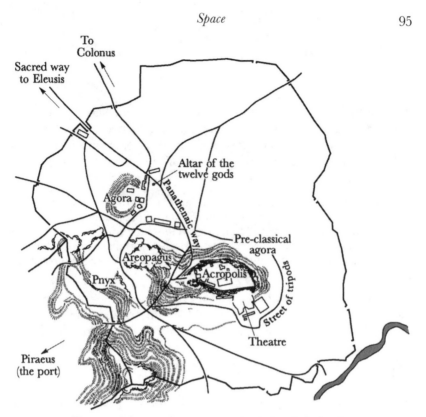

Figure 9 Athens at the end of the classical period, showing major public buildings.

rural population was forced to shelter behind these walls when the Spartans invaded Attica and built a base there, and new building was concentrated around the port. Behind Greek drama lies the experience of spatial dislocation and insecurity. When Aeschylus presented the terrors of a siege in *Seven Against Thebes* to an audience seated on the slopes of the Acropolis, he did not need to remind the audience of the fate that befell the valiant few who stayed to defend the Acropolis thirteen years earlier. Aristophanes magically fulfilled the aspirations of Athenians to escape Athens during the Peloponnesian war. A farmer in *The Acharnians* returns to his farm to celebrate a festival, worshippers in *The Frogs* process down the Sacred Way to the outlying town of Eleusis, and in *The Birds* two Athenians found a colony in the sky.

THE PLACES OF GREEK TRAGEDY

Thebes

The settings of Greek drama had associations lost to modern
audiences, and an effort of the imagination is needed to view the
plays from an Athenian perspective. In a patriotic speech the
Athenian orator Isocrates evokes some of the crimes that, according
to legend, had been committed in other powerful states:

> We encounter, oh we do, a profusion of murders! brothers, mothers, guests
> – and the slaughter of mothers, sex with her, impregnating the one who
> gave you birth; eating your children, tricked into it by relatives; abandoning
> your offspring, drowning, blinding – a score of similar atrocities, so no
> shortage has ever been faced by those whose annual task it is to present in
> the theatre the evils of yesteryear.

Not only did Athenians never commit such crimes, he continues, but
they gave proof of their virtue, and in this context he cites the
theatre again, alluding to Euripides' *Suppliants*. He evokes the tale of
how Theseus, king of Athens, came to the aid of Adrastus, king of
Argos, and fought the Thebans to secure burial for the soldiers of
Argos.

> Who does not know, who has not learned from the teachings of tragedy at
> the Dionysia, about the woes of Adrastus at Thebes?[5]

In typical Athenian fashion, Euripides' play presented its audience
with the folly of Argos, the evil machinations of Thebes and the
heroism of Athens. Euripides left it up to the audience whether they
wished to see some irony in his portrayal of Athens.

The Thebes of tragedy has been described as an 'anti-Athens',[6]
for ancient Thebes in some ways mirrors ancient Athens: a fortified
acropolis ruled by kings whose ancestors emerged from the earth of
the city – in the case of Thebes sprouting from the teeth of a dragon.
Myth told also that the god Dionysos was born in Thebes, but
brought his gift of wine to Athens, and the statue of Dionysos which
viewed the plays in the theatre was supposed to have come from a
town on the Athens–Thebes border. When the negative aspects of
Dionysos descend upon Thebes in *The Bacchae*, the politics of the
classical period seem highly significant. Athens and Thebes were
hostile neighbours, and at the end of the Peloponnesian war Thebes
wanted Athens to be destroyed, with its population enslaved, but

fortunately the Spartans were more merciful. Athenian dramatists portrayed Thebes as the site of atrocities within the ruling family: the incest of Oedipus, the burying alive of Antigone, the sons of Oedipus who kill each other, Agave tearing apart her son, Herakles killing his children. We never glimpse democracy in Thebes, only an aristocracy turned in on and destroying itself. The dominant spatial image of Thebes, fixed by Aeschylus' *Seven Against Thebes*, was of a walled city with seven gates, and walled enclosure seems an appropriate metaphor for the situations of entrapment depicted in Thebes.

Argos

Argos is mainly important as the location for the Orestes/Electra story. Orestes, heir to the Argive throne, comes to trial in Athens at the end of *The Oresteia*, and Aeschylus uses the play to bestow a sense of ancient authority upon the recent alliance sworn between Argos and Athens. In Homer, Agamemnon's capital was Mycenae, a prehistoric city built with huge stone blocks some miles from Argos, where the modern tourist can visit beehive tombs associated with Agamemnon. Aeschylus was making a contemporary point by setting his play in Argos, which had recently overrun Mycenae and taken control of the region. The Argive aristocracy had been decimated in a war with Sparta, and the city now had strong democratic tendencies, so Aeschylus represents Argos as a state in transition. In simple topographical terms, Argos resembled Athens, and during the classical period it likewise transformed itself into a coastal city by building walls down to the sea to avoid entrapment. Where Thebes tends to be the inverted opposite of Athens, Argos is rather an analogue. Euripides and Sophocles in their versions of *Electra* reverted to a setting in Mycenae to create the flavour of the epic world, but Euripides' *Orestes* is set in Argos in order to depict tensions between a confident democracy and an embattled group of aristocrats.

Troy

The ruins of Troy on the Turkish coast were excavated in the nineteenth century, and confirm that the city was attacked and destroyed some seven centuries before the classical period. Troy had no political significance at the time of the Greek tragedians, and the

relationship between Greeks and Trojans could thus be interpreted in any way the dramatist chose. Aeschylus in *Agamemnon* describes the war not from the point of view of an aristocratic hero as in Homer, but from the standpoint of a disillusioned common soldier. The lack of good reason for fighting the Trojan war is a running theme in tragedy. Despite the fine intentions of individuals, the seige ended in atrocities, and the gods ensured that the victors would in turn become victims. Sophocles' *Ajax* is set in the Greek camp, and provides an opportunity to depict a jockeying for power among the different Greek states; in Euripides' *Trojan Women*, the Greek expedition against Troy serves as a metaphor for the Peloponnesian war (see above, p. 60): in both plays the heroic milieu of Homer's *Iliad* stood as a counterpoint to the squalor of war as experienced by the audience.

Athens

The dramatist who set his play in Athens was obliged to present his city, at least overtly, in a glorious light. When Theseus agrees to rescue the bodies of Adrastus' warriors, irony can be glimpsed at the end of the play when the sons of the fallen make bloodthirsty promises to renew the war; no act of healing has taken place. When Aegeus, king of Athens, promises asylum to Medea, some in Euripides' audience may have viewed his generosity with scepticism, knowing that Medea would attempt one day to murder Aegeus' son Theseus. Critics disagree about how far knowledge of events outside the play conditioned spectators' responses. Euripides set his *Children of Herakles* in front of a temple at Marathon in order to link the rescue of young refugees to the famous battle, fought beside a temple of Herakles. Marathon was the place where Athens claimed to have rescued the Greek world, and it was the image of rescuer and protector that Athens constantly tried to project. The city justified its imperialist strategy on the grounds that it was protecting Greece from the external tyranny of Persia, and from the internal tyranny of non-democratic regimes. These claims were not entirely cynical.

A minority of plays are set in Athens for, as Isocrates pointed out, the most colourful stories are set elsewhere. In any case pure patriotism does not make for good theatre. To challenge Athenian policy, a dramatist needed a fictional guise for the Athens he knew. In *Orestes*, Euripides ascribes to Argos a style of manipulating the

democratic assembly which reflects back upon Athens (see above, pp. 58–9). The Theban plague in *Oedipus the King*, which prompts Oedipus to search out the source of the city's pollution, must reflect the Athenian plague which swept through an overcrowded Athens in 430 BC (see above, p. 20). The Athenians were penned behind the city walls, concentrating their resources upon controlling the sea, and had not anticipated the loss of manpower that would stem from disease. It may seem curious to the modern reader that the plague, evoked so powerfully by Sophocles at the start of the play, is subsequently ignored; for the Athenian spectator the epidemic could not be wished away by a playwright's magic wand, nor could it be forgotten.

It is difficult for a director to reinstate an Athenian perspective. To the modern spectator the Greek world is likely to seem homogeneous, and not divisible into 'us' and 'them'. At the end of *The Oresteia* Peter Hall asked his audience to stand in order to demonstrate their solidarity with the Athenians of the play. Peter Stein, in his second production of *The Oresteia*, stripped away the set when the scene transferred from Delphi to Athens, indicating that the world of dramatic illusion had vanished. Suzuki created a striking contrast between the heroic past and the political world of the present in his adaptation of the Orestes story called *Clytemnestra*. Orestes spoke in English and dressed in modern western clothes, while the other characters spoke Japanese and mostly dressed in the formal costumes of Noh theatre. Suzuki first explored this technique in his *Bacchae*, where Pentheus who spoke and dressed in the American style confronted a Dionysos who spoke and dressed in the Japanese style.[7] The tension characteristic of so many Greek plays between here and there, now and then, was fully realized.

THE THEATRE OF DIONYSOS

The evidence

The modern visitor to the Theatre of Dionysos can no longer approach along the Street of Tripods, the processional route once lined with monuments commemorating victorious choruses. Walking up from the main road, through a boundary wall enclosing the sanctuary, the modern visitor finds a semicircular *orchestra* (or 'dancing floor') and stage built in the Roman period, and the

crumbling remains of a stone auditorium built in approximately 330 BC. It is no easy matter to extrapolate from these traces some sense of the space in which the classical dramatists presented their plays. Today a more important tourist attraction than the theatre in Athens is the restored theatre of Epidaurus, used every summer for productions of classical plays. Epidaurus influences most people's conceptions of what the Athenian theatre was like, but its acting area was not completed until approaching 300 BC, and the upper part of the auditorium may be much later still, so that theatre proves even more unsatisfactory as evidence for classical theatre practice.

The earliest remains (probably before 500 BC) are the foundations of a temple of Dionysos, built to house the wooden statue of the god so it could face the rising sun. At festival time an altar in front of the temple would have been used for the sacrifice of bulls. The slope of the Acropolis was the natural place for a large crowd to gather and view the killing of the animals whose meat they were going to eat. Between the crowd and the sacrifice was the obvious place for dances to be performed in honour of the god, and thus the present acting space came to be defined.

The earliest sign of an acting area is an arc of seven stones, uncovered by a German archaeologist called Wilhelm Dörpfeld in 1886 (see figure 10).[8] These stones, mostly still in place, allowed him to project a large circle of about 24 metres in diameter as the orchestra of the classical period. This vision of the classical theatre as a primitive dancing circle appealed to the romantic mood of the day. The German philosopher Nietzsche had recently popularized the notion that tragedy should be associated with the wildness of Dionysos as much as the order of Apollo (see below, p. 184). The primitivist spirit of the age is epitomized by Isadora Duncan, who took up the habit of going into the ruined Theatre of Dionysos by moonlight to dance and listen to her brother reciting from Greek plays. When she heard some Greek boys singing folk songs one night, she recruited them as her choir and toured Europe, dancing solo the choruses from Aeschylus' *Suppliants*, which she took to be the earliest and most primitive Greek tragedy.[9]

After the destruction of the First World War, fashions in German archaeology changed. The taste for Dionysos and the primitive gave way to an Apolline desire for order. The polished plays of Sophocles were preferred to the raw choral plays of Aeschylus. Classical Athens was interpreted as the quintessence of European civilization, and

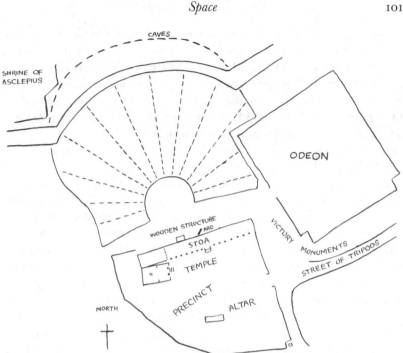

Figure 10 The Theatre of Dionysos, after the building of the Stoa at the end of the classical period.

there was a desire to find in the Theatre of Dionysos a monument comparable to the Parthenon, symmetrical, dignified and invested with the power of the state. Massive buildings were imagined that would lend Greek plays the grandeur of high opera.

After the fall of fascism, fashions changed again. In 1951 the American William Dinsmoor published an influential essay that aimed to rehabilitate the discredited Dörpfeld.[10] The taste for the primal returned. Landmark productions in 1955 include Jean-Louis Barrault's *Oresteia* in Paris, inspired by voodoo rites witnessed in Rio, and Tyrone Guthrie's *Oedipus the King* in Stratford, Ontario, inspired by Freud and by Christian passion plays. Both productions used masks to emphasize the ritual dimension. Neither, however, was willing to abandon the notion of a high stage for actors, and return completely to Dörpfeld's idea that the large primitive circle was the sole acting area. The pendulum continues to swing between those who are attached to the ritual circle as a space for dancing, and

those who emphasize the dominance of the stage façade as a wall of illusion and a backdrop intended to reinforce the power of the actor. The best defence of Dörpfeld would seem to lie in the ritual practices of the Dionysia. The primary activity was the performance at great expense of twenty dithyrambs, circular dances each performed by fifty people, and Dörpfeld's circle seems ideal for the purpose. Tragedy and comedy did not honour the god so directly. As appendages to the festival, plays would at first have accommodated themselves to the needs of the dithyramb.

Much controversy surrounds the erection of an architecturally dominant stage wall. A long colonnade (or *stoa*) was built as a place of shelter, perhaps in the late 400s BC but more probably in the century following. This building opened towards the altar and temple below, and presented a blank face to the audience. It indicates the alignment but not the form of the wooden structure placed in front of it. Wood could be painted as stone to create the sense that theatre was the space of illusion, but the main reason for using wood must have been resonance. A piece of paving set in the ground to abut the stoa fixes the alignment of the central doorway in the wooden wall, and proves that the auditorium by the time of the stoa had moved from the position it once occupied when focussed on Dörpfeld's stone circle. Because the seats and stage building were made of wood, we are left with little further useful information about the nature of the space in the classical period.

We do know that Pericles built on stage right a huge and exotic structure called the Odeon, which seems to have evoked the king of Persia's tent. The tragedians presented their choruses here before the festival, and here choruses must have gathered when preparing to perform. The reason for building the Odeon so close to the theatre must have been to create an architectural and functional relationship. At the end of the classical period, the acting space must have been configured in relation to the central door of the Odeon, allowing choruses to process from the one space to the other.

The theatre at Athens was not planned from the outset but evolved, and a natural hollow in the hillside was gradually transformed into a roughly semicircular form. The obvious advantage of the semicircular bowl is that it creates the best possible sightlines and acoustics, in addition to a feeling of democratic equality – so this form probably emerged at an early date. Only a limited amount of earth-moving was possible, so the majority of spectators remained in

Plate 6 The restored theatre at Epidaurus.

front of the performers, necessitating a frontal mode of performance. The audience sat on wooden planks throughout the classical period, so there was no question of a pure semicircular line. Because of the Odeon, it was impossible to make the two sides of the auditorium symmetrical, and it is clear from four small theatres which survive in the demes of Attica that the Athenians did not make architectural symmetry a priority.

Epidaurus is a misleading guide to the practice of the classical period. The perfect geometric form bears little relationship in its mood and symbolism to Athenian texts that invariably demonstrate how Dionysiac disorder undermines the best human attempts at rational forward planning. The stone theatres that we visit today belong to a period when the plays familiar to us had themselves become monuments frozen in time. For the classical period we must visualize a performance space that was temporary, disorderly and constantly changing. On-going experimentation with space, at a time when the rules of the theatrical medium were being worked out from first principles, helped to generate the creative energy that later generations have sensed in the surviving texts.

The stage?

It seems that the first plays were given in the pre-classical agora used for all types of assembly, and the audience sat on the north-east slope of the Acropolis.[11] Around the time of the Persian invasion, an area on the south side of the Acropolis was dedicated to the performance of dithyrambs and plays in honour of Dionysos – a simple space for dancing between the sacrificial altar and the hillside. Amongst the surviving plays of Aeschylus, it is only *The Oresteia* at the end of his career which requires a stage building, but all subsequent Greek plays require a building with a door. It is a reasonable inference that the circle used for the dithyramb on the first day of the festival was transformed on subsequent days by the erection within the performance space of the wooden building called the *skênê*, literally a 'tent'. Aeschylus would most likely have set his wooden building with its central door *within* the dancing circle. Epidaurus offers a misleading model when it defines a small acting circle at a tangent to the stage building. If we look at earlier stone theatres like the one at Megalopolis, a new model city erected in the 360s BC, we see that the stage building was sited within the circle. Megalopolis is a particularly interesting example because we can see the foundations of a scene dock from which the original wooden building was slid into place.[12]

Whether or not there was a stage is one of the most controversial questions surrounding the performance of plays in the classical period.[13] The surviving theatres of the Greek world have stages on which the 'actors' performed, whilst the chorus danced in the orchestra below, but they are all of later date. The important exception is the 'theatre' surviving from classical times at Thorikos, where there is no stage or room to erect one, and the space must have been built for assemblies as much as for performances. Other surviving theatres were built after actors had become international stars touring the festival circuit. It was not feasible for a team of fifteen dancers to tour the world, and if the local community was able to provide choral dancers, those dancers would not have a chance to rehearse with the actors, so the physical separation of actors and chorus became an inevitability. The simplest way to understand the process of evolution is to assume that the acting area on the roof of the stage building, formerly used for gods or figures like Antigone in *Phoenician Women* (see above, p. 21), came to be used

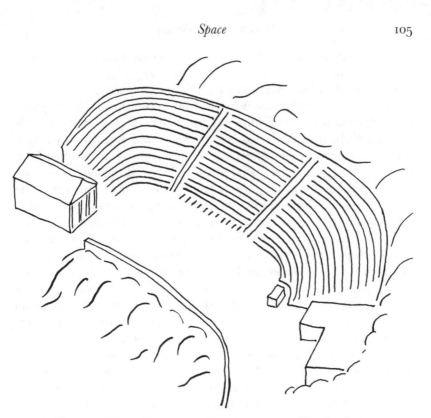

Figure 11 The multipurpose performance space at Thorikos in the classical period.

by all the 'actors'. The roof was found to offer acoustical advantages, since the voice was reflected off the floor of the orchestra.

Tracing the evolution of Greek theatre is a hazardous business. The only hard information we have about theatre before Aeschylus is Aristotle's statement that the leader of the chorus entered into dialogue with his fellow-dancers, and there was thus in the beginning only a single actor.[14] If the story is one of actors progressively separating themselves from the chorus, then the task of the theatre historian is to determine the exact extent of that separation in the classical period. Actors were funded by the state, at least from 449 BC when a competition was introduced for best tragic actor, whilst the chorus were recruited and paid by the choregos, but this institutional division was probably intended to prevent the buying up of talent, and does not imply separate rehearsal (see above, p. 35). There was

no international circuit and the actors were available to work with the chorus under the supervision of the playwright. The internal evidence of the plays makes any kind of spatial separation seem most unlikely. In the *Suppliants* and *Eumenides* of Aeschylus or *The Suppliants* of Euripides, the chorus functions as if it was one of the central characters. In *The Libation Bearers*, Orestes and Electra dance with the chorus around the tomb over which the libations have been poured. In a comedy like *Lysistrata* it would be a nonsense to separate the half-chorus of women from their leader Lysistrata who leads them into the Acropolis. Physical interaction is constant in Greek drama. It does not take much experimentation to realize that in a space like the Theatre of Dionysos the actor who comes too far forward within the orchestral circle will have less power to command the back of the auditorium; he will be too close to the spectators, there will be less empty space around him to frame his form, and the line of his voice will travel less clearly across the heads of the front spectators as it approaches what acousticians call 'grazing incidence'.[15] It is reasonable, therefore, to think of the 'up-stage' space as a privileged or stronger area. There is not, however, any obvious advantage in defining a stage – though a few steps to the door may be a different matter. It is crucial to remember that the audience faced south. The later stage building put a high wall behind the high stage so the actors would be in permanent shadow and the spectators' eyes could adjust accordingly, picking out more easily details of mask and costume. So long as the stage building was a low wooden hut, there was a danger that the actor could be placed unsatisfactorily half in shadow half in sun if he stood too close to the building. A stage required a monumental building behind it if it was to serve a useful function in terms of focus.

Back in the nineteenth century, when the idea of performing any play without a stage seemed unthinkable, no one questioned the assumption that the actors and chorus performed on different levels; this accorded with an operatic view of Greek tragedy, the chorus being regarded primarily as singers. In the course of the twentieth century, following the excavations of Dörpfeld, the dominant assumption has been that a low stage (for which we have no archaeological evidence) stood in front of the stage building and was the favoured location of the actors, though free movement between stage and orchestra remained possible. Hall and Stein, in their versions of *The Oresteia* which aimed at a high degree of spatial

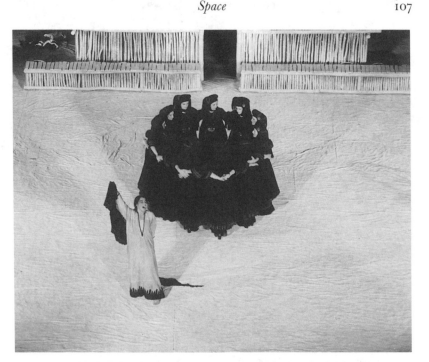

Plate 7 The relationship of actor and chorus: exclusion. Euripides, *Electra*
directed by Costas Tsianos for the Thessaliko Theatro, with L. Korniordou
as Electra. 1989.

authenticity, adopted this solution and used two levels. The majority
of recent professional directors with no such aspirations seem to
have considered that a single level allows maximum flexibility when
exploring the relationship of actors and chorus.

Academics and practitioners have become increasingly interested
in the actor–chorus relationship, and it seems today rather perverse
to postulate a structure which limits that flexibility. Today, in a more
or less democratic age, what seems unique and particularly fascinating in the Greek dramatic form is its ability to explore the shifting
relationship between an individual and a group. In *Medea* the chorus
initially show solidarity with Medea, and they distance themselves
emotionally when she announces her plan to kill her children, but
decline to betray her. By using a single wide acting space, Ninagawa
was able to depict a series of different relationships between the
protagonist and the sixteen women of his chorus:[16] sometimes

Figure 12 The crowd of suppliants approaches Oedipus in Max Reinhardt's
production in the Zircus Schumann, Berlin.

Medea stood with them, sometimes apart, sometimes in confronta-
tion. No such effects were possible in the proscenium theatre
production starring Diana Rigg in 1993/4, for here the narrow space
prevented the chorus of three from being more than an emotional
and musical backing to the central performance. The relationship
between the individual and her society was lost. One of the strengths
of Brecht's *Antigone*, which set all the characters within a primitive
place of sacrifice, was the way it explored Creon's dependence on
the chorus of Theban elders, and the moral turpitude of those men
who would never voice their opposition to a proto-fascist leader (see
above, p. 63). This sociopolitical dimension is lost when the play
becomes a vehicle for the two star performers.

   Reinhardt back in 1910–12 used three levels in his production of
Oedipus the King: Oedipus stood before his palace on the highest
rostrum; below and around him were a chorus of Theban elders,
and below them was a proletariat of 500 or more Thebans (only 300

in the London production).[17] Reinhardt made an important political statement when Oedipus abandoned his status as a heroic figure at the end of the play and walked down to the level of the pit to join the mass of humanity. The chorus on their intermediate level provided vocal orchestration, voicing the thoughts of the dramatist or feelings appropriate to an audience, but they could not offer serious political advice. Reinhardt was interested in primitive impulses within crowds and powerful men rather than the workings of Greek democracy. Peter Hall's production of *Oedipus the King* at the Olivier Theatre in 1996, which aspired to a kind of classical formalism, demonstrates the perils of vertical separation today (see above, p. 61). Reinhardt's Nietzschean vision of superhuman individuals subject to primal drives was by 1996 the stuff of history. In large measure the failure of Hall's design concept, which isolated the characters on a high red ramp, can be attributed to assumptions about space rooted in nineteenth century scholarship. At the end of the twentieth century the human being can no longer be regarded as an entity isolated from its social environment. Greek tragedy cannot any longer be conceived as the tale of a hero. It was and is the spatial correlative of democracy that all individuals should be placed on the same level.

PERFORMING IN THE THEATRE OF DIONYSOS

The effects of scale

The scale of Athenian theatre, played to an audience of 15,000 or more, makes it more akin to pop concerts or sporting events than any modern form of theatre. From the central door in the stage wall to the furthest spectator the distance was over 100 metres in Athens, as opposed to 70 metres in the fuller semicircle at Epidaurus and some 25 metres in Shakespeare's Globe. To speak or sing audibly required formidable training if the voice was to carry over such a distance. Men probably had better hearing than today, and there was less ambient noise, but wind was always a danger. There were no side walls to reflect the sound, and a frontal delivery was therefore essential. The presence of the chorus underpinned the convention, essential if the text was to reach its audience, that every speech was a mode of public address. The long speeches of Greek tragedy fit the requirements of the space. Quick-fire has the formality of a cross-examination in court (see above, p. 57). Antigone and Creon, for

example, do not talk to each other, but talk to the chorus and by extension the audience in a bid for moral approval. Tragedy could not permit interpersonal dialogue because intimacy simply is not interesting to a spectator 100 metres distant. One can of course create intimacy when performing Greek plays today in intimate spaces, but the risk of such transposition is that the speeches will seem unnaturally long, and the chorus irrelevant.

Considerations of distance are fundamental if we want to analyze the visual image and use of the body. All movements had to be simple, clear and bold. The costumes of tragedy were long and bright to create strong tableaux; the costumes of men in comedy were exceptionally short to allow energetic movement and a sense of the whole anatomy. Masks covered the whole head, requiring the spectator to project emotion on to the face and imagine movement in the few simple features that the mask rendered visible. The actor brought the mask to life through configurations of the whole body. Later Greek theatre was able to use subtle densely coded masks because the actors stood in shadow, but in the classical period the actors in Athens stood in the circle of the orchestra with the sun behind them. To see the face in these silhouetted figures was almost impossible, and Greek theatre relied rather upon the patterns which bodies made on the ground. It would be wrong to commiserate with such a theatre for its limitations. We should think of the passions and depth of meaning which fifteen distant bodies on a cricket pitch or twenty-three bodies on a football pitch can offer a packed crowd, and recall that Greek theatre was, amongst other things, a hard-fought contest in physical skills.

In lieu of the single body which the eye fixes upon in proscenium or studio theatre, it was the collective body that held the attention in Greek theatre. Inspired by his work in the large Greek theatre at Syracuse, Jacques Lecoq writes:

The chorus is the essential element which uniquely allows the release of a true tragic space. A chorus is not geometric, it is organic. As a collective body, it possesses a centre of gravity, extensions, breath. It is a sort of organism that can take different shapes according to the situation in which it finds itself.

In a vivid metaphor, Silviu Purcarete describes the chorus as 'a single organism made up of dozens of heads and arms, like a sort of giant squid'.[18] The blocking of the chorus is a subtle instrument for

Plate 8 The relationship of mask and body. Classical masks designed and made by Thanos Vovolis, used in a production of *The Dibbuk*. Stockholm, 1994.

directing attention to different sections of an empty space, and has a similar function to modern stage lighting. Lecoq continues:

A chorus arrives on stage, to the sound of percussion which through rhythm creates collectivity. It occupies the whole space, then withdraws to one part of the arena. In so doing it frees a new space and offers a kind of invitation to the hero. But who will come and fill this space? What equilibrium can be found today between a chorus and a hero?[19]

As Lecoq discerns, the Greek use of performance space differed from today in its constant positioning of the individual in relation to the group. In a small performance space, the shifting relationship of an individual body to a collective body cannot be reproduced. The ability of the play to engage with political issues is reduced. Modern performance space reflects a reluctance to understand individual identity as a function of social identity.

Many modern performers feel that performance in a huge space is a constraint upon subtle delivery and the development of an actor–audience relationship. Peter Brook, for example, regards 1,000 as a sensible threshold.[20] This is to miss what lent Greek theatre its power. The spectator 100 metres away was part of a single crowd, bonded by a space that created no vertical or horizontal boundaries, and concealed no group from all the rest. If all 15,000-plus tightly packed people were listening to the same words at the same time, and shared the same broad response, the power of emotion generated would have been quite unlike that created today in a studio theatre. Communication was effected not simply via light and sound waves but via an osmosis passing through the bodies of the spectators.

Patsy Rodenburg, voice coach at the National Theatre in London, laments the dead acoustics of the Olivier auditorium, used for the Greek productions of Peter Hall. The actor gets no sense of feedback from the auditorium and has to reconstruct the audience's perception. Another major drawback is the division of circle from stalls, leaving the actors tempted always to play to the stalls below. 'In the original Greek theatre ... the space's perspective pulls the actor up to make full contact with the whole house ... The design of the Greek theatre centres the actor's body rather than suppressing it.'[21] In the pseudo-Greek Olivier, inspired by Epidaurus, the commercial logic which divides cheaper seats from dearer ones undermines the power of the performance. The audience are not bonded because comfortable seats divide shoulders from shoulders and knees from backs, creating an individualized mode of viewing. Stage lighting

and an acoustic destroyed by the roof prevent the actor sensing the audience and therefore interacting with it in the moment of performance.

The natural world

Roland Barthes, in an essay on Greek theatre, attempts to develop an aesthetic of open air performance: 'In the open air, the spectacle cannot be a habit, it is vulnerable, perhaps irreplaceable: the spectator's immersion in the complex polyphony of the open air (shifting sun, rising wind, flying birds, noises of the city) restores to the drama the singularity of the event.' The spectator has an acute sense of being in the present, the passing day of the festival. He shares the same sense of space as the characters of the play, placed on the threshold of tombs and palaces. The theatre is open to the sky in order 'to amplify the news (i.e., fate) and not to smother the plot'.[22] Viewed in the open, the play will thus be seen as a treatment not of interpersonal relationships but of the relationship between human beings and their environment, an environment which for the Greeks necessarily included the gods. An event at Delphi, where *Prometheus* was performed in 1927 (see below, pp. 183–9), illustrates these principles. As Prometheus referred to his liver being pecked by eagles, two eagles flew down from the mountain, creating a sense in the audience that Zeus was at work. Three years later, when Aeschylus' *Suppliants* was performed in Delphi, rain coincided with the crisis of the plot, and sunshine accompanied the triumphant conclusion, again creating the sense that the performance was part of a larger cosmic process.[23] Performances at Epidaurus in high summer under stage lighting do not provide the same opportunities for divine intervention.

Greek theatres were modifications of the landscape rather than impositions, and Greek architects always built their theatres with attention to the view, unlike the Romans who enclosed the audience within high walls. The audience on the slopes of the Athenian Acropolis had a fine view of the hills to the south-east, and a few at the top could also see the sea. Greek plays dealt with the limits of the human ability to control the world. Spectators sat inside the city they had created and looked at the wilderness beyond. From the security of their seats, they contemplated a world where nothing was secure. In tragedy the city was viewed in its relation to the wilderness

Figure 13 The theatre of Athens in relation to its environment: from a coin
of the Roman period.

beyond. Violent women like Phaedra, Medea or Electra seek to
escape from the confinement of the city. Men like Oedipus, Creon
and Pentheus are destroyed by events that take place in the
mountains, where they cannot impose rationality and the gods seem
to be in control. The topography of the theatre shaped the meaning
of the plays. In the modern theatre, because Zen is attuned to the
idea that energies link humans to their environment, Suzuki has
been the major practitioner to experiment with this aspect of Greek
theatre. He built his open-air theatre at Toga facing a lake and
mountains, which are selectively illuminated in accordance with the
needs of the play.

Sacred space

Western practitioners like Grotowski and Brook have pursued the ideal of a 'holy' theatre which rejects the façades of orthodox commercial theatre and adopts the condition of a 'poor' theatre.[24] Many have been impressed by the practices of the east. The *Natya Sastra*, for example, describes a complex of rituals performed when laying out a temporary theatre in ancient India, and in the Noh theatre elaborate rules govern the preparation of the polished cypress-wood floor. The theatre of the classical period meets the physical conditions of a Grotowskian poor theatre, with its wooden seating arranged around a hillside, an earth floor, and a painted wooden hut for its set. Actors working in 1992 on a trilogy in the Greek-style theatre of Minneapolis found it helpful to conceive that they were working in a circle which was somehow 'sacred',[25] and this is a common experience in productions that attend to the ritual dimension. It is important, therefore, to clarify how far the 'poor' space was also a 'sacred' space.

The whole of Athens was experienced as a sacred place, and more particularly the rock of the Acropolis since the origins of the Athenian people were traced to that spot. The procession led the audience on a journey to the ritual centre of their community, and the actors performed on the earth of a city protected by Athene. The performance circle lay inside the sanctuary of the god Dionysos, while the audience sat on the slope outside the precinct, and this helped to define the nature of the actor–audience divide. Performers would dress as gods, engage in obscene behaviour and slander fellow-citizens in a way that was only acceptable in a time and space dedicated to a god. Behind the wooden stage building, the stone temple was a visible reminder of the divine reality behind the illusion of the play. The sacredness of the performance space was emphasized by rituals in the same way as other public events: the blood of a young pig was sprinkled around the orchestra to ward off evil, and libations were poured into the earth.[26] The performance space was not contaminated by the blood and smell of slaughtered oxen, whose place of sacrifice was lower down the slope. Religious taboos may explain why in plays the act of killing is never accomplished in front of the audience, though non-violent death may occur. After the classical period, the new stoa, followed by the move of the actors on to a high stage, effectively separated the temple from the playing

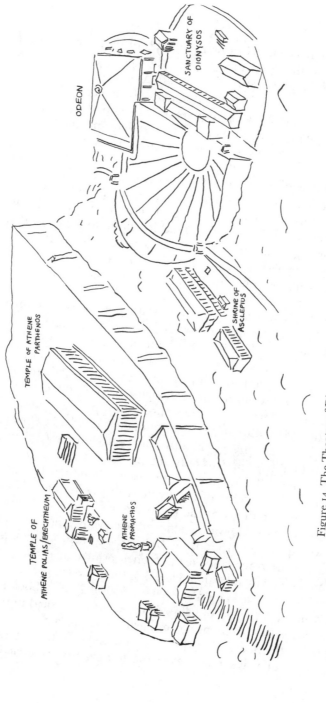

ODEON

SANCTUARY OF DIONYSOS

SHRINE OF ASCLEPIUS

TEMPLE OF ATHENE PARTHENOS

TEMPLE OF ATHENE POLIAS/ERECHTHEUM

ATHENE PROMACHOS

Figure 14 The Theatre of Dionysos after the rebuilding by Lycurgus in about 330 BC.

area, and this must have weakened the sense that the playing space was a sacred space.

Entering the space

From the side

Greek plays were written for specific spatial requirements, and I shall focus on one example. Euripides' *Hippolytus* tells how Hippolytus learns that his stepmother Phaedra has fallen in love with him. He rejects Phaedra and all women, whilst Phaedra commits suicide, leaving a message to incriminate Hippolytus. Theseus, Phaedra's husband and Hippolytus' father, returns and calls a curse upon his son.

As Oliver Taplin recognized in a book which transformed the study of ancient theatre, the most important dramatic effects in a huge theatre were achieved through control of entries and exits.[27] There were three main points of entry: through the single central door of the skênê, or through the side approaches known as *eisodoi*. To enter through an eisodos took a large amount of stage time and the actor could be seen by some spectators long before others (see plate 6). It is a rather exceptional moment when Theseus arrives unannounced because the chorus are focussed on the suicide within the skênê. Normally text is required to cover entries. This is a typical example, which I translate rather literally:

> Well now, a servant of Hippolytus here I see
> Urgently dark-faced to the house hastening.   (1151–2)

Only two lines are allocated because the messenger is moving quickly. The angle of the eisodos directs the actor towards the 'house' rather than the centre of the orchestra. The chorus halt their dance ('well now') and point in order to change the focus ('here'); they identify for the audience who the new character is, and help them to interpret his gait and project an emotion upon the distant mask. The first entry of the chorus was always a special moment of spectacle, created in *Hippolytus* through the mime of washing long robes. Hippolytus makes two imposing processional entries through an eisodos: first of all with a group of hunters chanting and bearing a garland to crown the statue of Artemis, and at the end, again to music, when his wrecked body is carried on and he cries out in agony.

Because there were two more or less symmetrical eisodoi, Greek

theatre commonly set up a contrast, both geographical and symbolic, between the two sides. Like many Greek cities, Troizen where the play is set was built on the coast, protected by an impenetrable hinterland. Accordingly one exit in *Hippolytus* leads to the sea and one to the mountains. The mountains symbolize the wilderness and state of virginity which Hippolytus loves, whilst the sea symbolizes both access to the civilized world of Athens and the passions of sexual desire. This contrast was fixed by visual icons in the post-classical period, but in the time of Euripides the audience simply used its imagination, attaching different connotations to the two eisodoi as the play developed. The massive presence of the exotic Odeon on the audience's left (built after the time of Aeschylus) and the more modest presence of the temple on the audience's right must in practice have given a very different feel to the two sides.

From the house

Tragedy used only a single doorway in the stage wall, apparently in the form of a double door opening inwards.[28] This doorway created a powerful point of focus, and is used for a long section of the play to keep attention fixed on Phaedra's non-verbal reactions, as she listens to the servant within telling Hippolytus of her love whilst the chorus sing of love. She hears Hippolytus' violent response, and is still beside the door when Hippolytus bursts out and delivers a long anti-feminist diatribe. The audience watch the silent mounting agony that will culminate in suicide.

Phaedra's first entrance from the house is slow and imposing: she is carried on a couch, the picture of an invalid, her body and head covered. When Phaedra appears for the second time, it is as a corpse on the '*eccyclema*', a wheeled platform rolled forward through the doorway. A dummy dressed as Phaedra lay upon it, with an incriminating letter displayed in the hand, and the costume doubtless disposed to suggest the victim of a rape. The house in Greek tragedy is regularly associated with death, and the eccyclema was often required to display a scene of horror. It should be understood as a formal convention rather than a primitive attempt to depict an inner room. As the corpse lies before the audience, Theseus speaks of his wife as the best beneath the sun and stars, and delivers a public address to the city. Only an imagination conditioned by naturalism bothers to ask whether the corpse is supposed to be indoors or outdoors.

Plate 9 The power of the doorway. Euripides, *Electra*, directed by
Costas Tsianos. 1989.

On a symbolic level, the themes of the play are bound up with a
tension between two spaces: the unseen world behind the skênê, and
the public world of the orchestra. The world indoors is, sociologically speaking, the world of women, and Phaedra, daughter of an
Amazon, rejects her forced seclusion. The statue of Aphrodite,
goddess of sex, is placed by the doors, whilst the statue of Artemis,
goddess of chastity, stands in the orchestra, for the first goddess is
associated with the bedroom, the second with hunting in the wilderness. Aphrodite by the doorway represents a body space with an
interior, a body space that can be penetrated, while Artemis, virgin
goddess of the open spaces, admits no one. As in most plays, death is
conceived as a farewell to the sun, and the death of the heroine takes
place indoors in the space of darkness. Repeated images of light and
dark which seem monotonous to the modern reader had a different
force for an audience warmed by the sun in early spring.

From above
Entry could also be effected by using the roof of the skênê, and gods
may have been given further elevation by a structure called the

theologeion. Another possibility was the crane which swung an actor out over the *orchestra*, whence the familiar Latin term *deus ex machina*, 'god from the machine'. At the start of *Hippolytus* it is clear that the goddess Aphrodite appears at ground level, for no human beings share the space with her, and she has come to involve herself in human affairs. At the end of the play, however, the goddess Artemis is obviously airborne when she comes to visit Theseus and the dying Hippolytus. She mocks Theseus for his inability to fly, and Hippolytus seems able to sense her but not to see her. The relationship between gods and humans was a flexible one in the Greek world. The spirit of Aphrodite enters the earthbound Phaedra at the start of the play, but Artemis at the end separates her immortal self from the mortal Hippolytus. The crane and theologeion were useful devices when the dramatist wanted to emphasize the separateness of Olympian gods from mortals.

Unlike many plays, *Hippolytus* is not concerned with gods who live below the earth. In a play like *Libation Bearers*, it is of great symbolic importance that the actors play on a floor of beaten earth because a strong relationship is established with a figure imagined to be in the underworld beneath the earth. Tunnels were constructed in a few later theatres to allow an entrance from below, but this was not attempted in Athens.

The centre

The focal point of the orchestra was the centre. Polished flagstones at Delphi bear witness to the millions of tourist feet that have been drawn irresistibly to this central spot, where lines of force defined by the gangways seem to converge and echoes return to create a strange acoustical experience. In a few theatres like Epidaurus, a small stone called a *thymele* marks the centre. Just as Delphi was conceived as the sacred centre of the world, and within Delphi the most sacred spot was the navel stone at the centre of the temple in the midst of the sanctuary, so likewise in the theatre a sense of the sacred tends to pervade the centre of the space. In many plays the thymelê evidently becomes the site of a tomb or an altar, a place for offerings, or for suppliants to take refuge. Directors of the *Oresteia* rarely hesitate to put the tomb of Agamemnon in this position. In *Hippolytus* the sacred centre must belong to the statue of Artemis,

Plate 10 The command position in the centre of the circle. K. Paxinou in the
role of Electra. Sophocles, *Electra*, directed by D. Rondiris in 1938, was the
first modern production at Epidaurus.

formally crowned in an opening ceremony and then left as a
reminder of what Hippolytus represents. The play can be seen as a
battle between centre and doorway, two focal points in the theatre
competing for dominance. Phaedra leaves the private female space
of the house and invades the public, male space in the centre,
destroying both.

OPEN AND CLOSED SPACES

Location

Whilst the world of tragedy seems closed and sealed, comedy is open
and has no sharp boundaries. This principle applies first of all to
location. Greek tragedies are set in a single place, with only two
clear exceptions.[29] Typically, the characters of tragedy are trapped
in a situation from which no physical escape is possible. There are
three points of exit, and none offers release from a trap that will
culminate in death. In *Hippolytus*, for example, the house is Phaedra's
prison and death chamber, and the place where Hippolytus is
ensnared. One eisodos leads to the impenetrable mountains, the
other to the sea and thus the forbidden city of Athens. Hippolytus
attempts to break from his trap by creeping along the shoreline, but
a bull emerges from the sea to destroy him. In *Antigone*, Creon is the
man entrapped. One eisodos leads to the city, and thus symbolically
to the political imperatives that constrain him; the other leads to the
wilderness outside the city, where a corpse lies unburied, Antigone is
buried alive, and the gods assert their will. The third exit leads into
Creon's house, where at the end of the play his wife commits suicide.
Creon does not die but is caught in agony beneath the gaze of the
audience, with no moral or physical route of escape. It was always a
symbolic topography that tragedy tried to establish, not a 'real'
location in the naturalist mode.

Comedy, by contrast, allows the action to melt from one location
to another. Journeys are frequent: in *The Frogs* a boat is rowed to the
Underworld and in *Peace* a dung-beetle flies to Mount Olympus.
Whilst the skênê of tragedy displays a single ominous doorway, the
skênê of comedy is permeable. In *Wasps* an old man is locked in his
house to prevent him from voting for Cleon, but he knocks a hole in
the roof and climbs through a window. Comedy was a utopian form
in which escape from the problems of contemporary Athens became
possible.

Time/space

In tragedy the chorus use mimetic dance to enter a world of mythic
time and infinite space, breaking the closed frame. Before Phaedra
dies, the chorus of *Hippolytus* imagine themselves flying to the

marriage chamber of Zeus in the far west; they return from this wishful fantasy to imagine and simulate Phaedra's historic journey from Crete to her marriage in Athens, and the harsh reality of her suicide. The first chorus of *Antigone* recreates the battle that took place before the formal action of the play begins; the elders take a kind of aerial view of Thebes, portraying the invading army as an eagle soaring around the city. The tight control of dramatic space in the formal action of the play gives a special force to these other times and spaces created by dancers. The messenger likewise opens a kind of window when he or she describes another world to which the hero has tried to escape.

Bakhtin's term *chronotope* usefully captures the notion that a single 'time/space' characterizes any given historical genre.[30] Time in Euripides and Sophocles is closed in just the same way as space, and Aristotle notes that tragedy usually keeps to 'a single revolution of the sun'.[31] The dramatic action echoes the way the spectators experience time, with the sun rising and sinking as they sit in the theatre, and many plays start the action at dawn. The real time taken by a messenger to cross the specified mountains or consult an oracle has no bearing upon the illusion that no delay has occurred and the story has gone full circle. However, in an Aeschylean trilogy such as *The Oresteia* a sequence of closed narratives creates an epic sense of time, and the time span of the play extends into the world of the audience.

The time setting of tragedy is the Homeric world, modified in certain ways by the present (see above, pp. 10–11). Comedy, on the other hand, is set in the here and now of the audience. *The Frogs* poses the question very directly: what political course of action should be taken *now* to save the city *here* from destruction? In tragedy the issues of the present were transposed into an entirely separate space/time in order that they could be judged with some measure of objectivity.

The body

Besides introducing the notion of the chronotope, Bakhtin has popularized the notion that we can distinguish between a 'classical' body which is closed and sealed and a 'grotesque' body which is permeable and characterized by protruberances and orifices.[32] The former implies the separateness of the human being from the surrounding cosmos, the latter implies a biological merging with the

natural world. This notion of the body as a space can usefully be applied to Greek drama. In tragedy the body beautiful was enclosed within long robes, whereas in comedy grotesque bodies were put on display in an illusion of nakedness. The human characters of tragedy are trapped within their bodies, isolated from the collective mass of the chorus, and unable to touch the gods who destroy them. Comedy signals that all males are identical whether slave or rich, human or divine; the same sexual and excretory functions characterize all those whom society divides, and link them to the earth. Even distinctions of sex dissolve in the world of comedy. In *Assembly Women*, when the husband of the heroine is forced to appear in his wife's delicate dress and attempts to defecate, in the pain of his constipation he invokes Artemis, goddess of childbirth.

In tragedy the domestic space of the house is associated with women, both sociologically and physiologically. The female body like the house is considered to be a container, concealing its hidden secrets, and the skênê can be viewed as an embodiment of the woman within. The male who enters through the door of the skênê often seems doomed by his action, for tragedy is a hermetic form. Hippolytus, Agamemnon, Oedipus and many others are destroyed by the sexuality of the woman inside the house.

The audience

Tragedy is also enclosed in the sense that it makes no formal acknowledgement of the audience. Comedy reverses tragedy and plays on the permeability of the actor–audience boundary. Named individuals in the audience are constantly mentioned or portrayed. 'Now,' says a slave at the start of *Wasps*, 'I'll give an explanation to the spectators, present them with a few initial points' (54–5). The spectators thus cease to be passive onlookers and are caught up in the action. The slave goes on to deny that he will throw nuts at the audience, a traditional gag which crossed the actor–audience boundary in too literal a way. He denies too that he will make mincemeat of Cleon, who would have been sitting rather prominently in the audience, and became through this reference part of the performance. The comic audience were made participants in a shared Dionysiac ceremony. The actors of comedy would inevitably have adjusted their timing in response to bursts of laughter, making their interaction with the audience very clear. For the tragic actor,

responding overtly to expressions of audience emotion was a more delicate matter.

Notionally, the tragic audience remained outside the action. The reality of course was that the text had to be delivered directly to the audience if it was to be understood. In *Antigone* two women in the prologue claim that they have come out of the house to speak privately together, but the audience do not remain long in this unusual relationship of eavesdroppers. Because the chorus represented old men of Thebes, it was easy for the audience of Athenian men to consider themselves extensions of that chorus. The case is a little more complex in a play which deploys a chorus of female confidantes. In the prologue to *Hippolytus* the goddess Aphrodite describes, as she gazes at the spectators, her temple only yards from the theatre, which she claims to see across the gulf in Athens, and a rather complex relationship to the dramatic fiction is established. When Theseus declares publicly that Hippolytus has raped his wife, he addresses himself to the 'city' (884). The audience are implicitly cast as citizens, quite separate from the low-status female chorus. In the oratorical contest that follows, Hippolytus says that he dislikes speaking in front of the masses (986), a phrase which continues to locate the audience as a kind of public assembly. The illusion of the fully detached spectator is only sustainable in a proscenium theatre, where the auditorium is placed in darkness, physically separated by the proscenium arch from the fictional universe of the play. The performers of Greek drama never pretended that their encircling audience was invisible, and had to find a mode of address that made sense of the relationship.

CONCLUSION

The proscenium arch negates the form of Greek tragedy because it places so much focus on the protagonist. The chorus retreats inconspicuously to the wings or backdrop, or else takes over the stage for choral 'interludes'. What the proscenium theatre cannot represent is a continuing dynamic between the actor and a large choral group. In the Greek theatre the chorus functioned variously as a physical extension of the audience, as the narrator of ancient myth, as an objective arbiter, as the extension of a particular character with whom it expresses solidarity, or else as a fragmented group with diverse views. The Greek form gains its interest from

constant shifts of function as the chorus morally and physically relocates itself. The two-way relationship established by a proscenium arch is incompatible with the triangular relationship of audience/actor/chorus upon which Greek tragedy depends.

The spectator in proscenium theatre is an eavesdropper peering through an invisible fourth wall at people living out their private lives, and this premise is incompatible with a genre in which all utterances are public. Greek plays have of course succeeded in proscenium theatres, with Oedipus or Medea standing in a small pool of light, confiding their inner agonies to an audience which may feel deeply touched by the experience. Missing here, however, are the qualities which make Greek drama different from any other form. Major productions of Greek tragedy in the modern period have, time and again, started by reconfiguring the performance space.

The story can be traced back to 1841, and the first attempt in the modern period to play Greek tragedy as it was written. A circular dancing area was constructed amidst the seats of the Prussian auditorium, so that the chorus of *Antigone* could play in an appropriate relationship to the audience (see p. 63 above). Another important landmark is 1910 when Max Reinhardt took over a circus in Berlin for his production of *Oedipus* (Figure 12).[33] This allowed him to exploit the power of long entrances, and to develop the relationship of Oedipus to the Theban masses. The lighting and percussion techniques of circus helped him to break with naturalism, and the social diversity of the audience did more to redefine the nature of the performance event. Reinhardt demonstrated successfully that the scale of Greek theatre performance was not a problem but rather its greatest asset. A Russian observer described how the amphitheatre created continuity from one end of the building to the other so that 'the audience, drawn into the whirl of action in the Arena, is lifted, so to speak, to the state of potential actors', stopping just before the state of 'religious actuality' supposed to characterize early Greek theatre.[34]

Many directors have used Greek tragedy to test out the possibilities of new performance spaces. When Reinhardt in Berlin opened the Grosses Schauspielhaus with *The Oresteia* in 1919, and Gémier in the same year played *Oedipus* in a Parisian circus, when Tyrone Guthrie in 1955 played *Oedipus* on the Elizabethan thrust stage in Stratford, Ontario, and Peter Hall in 1981 played *The Oresteia*

in the new Olivier Theatre, a running theme was the democratic nature of these new spaces. The audience, it appeared, was not disposed hierarchically as in nineteenth-century proscenium theatres but as a community. At other times, practitioners have invoked Greek theatre as the archetypal place of ceremony, a place where a ritual is enacted. Ninagawa has built a theatre that simulates a ruin with grass growing between the stones, where memories of the past are preserved for ever. Richard Schechner in 1969 turned a disorderly garage into a space for the ritual re-enactment of Dionysos' birth, with the aim of creating an 'environmental' theatre in which all would participate.[35] Ariane Mnouchkine, in her converted gunpowder factory in Paris, sent the spectators on a journey past effigies of dead warriors, food, and actors completing their make-up in order to create a sense of ceremony.[36] The ritual space, the democratic space: these are the two aspects which practitioners will carry on seeking to reconcile.

A recent writer on modern theatre architecture has criticized the 'nostalgic unitarism' that, through the twentieth century, has interpreted Greek theatres as the scene of consensus. He challenges the empty myth of the ideal city 'for which the model is the Greek city, its crucible the theatre space'.[37] Athens fell to Sparta because of internal divisions. The performance space in the classical period was not the model of architectural harmony that we see in Epidaurus but a site of imbalance, conflict and continuous change. After the initial joy of discovery in the first years of the festival at Epidaurus, the limitations of the space are now becoming apparent. The grandeur and beauty of the scenery and architecture all too easily dwarf the performance. The location of that theatre in an ancient shrine of healing is consistent with its social function as a place where modern Greece annually reasserts its links with its classical past.[38] This modern imposition of sacredness constrains the process of renewal which alone makes theatre live.

CHAPTER 6

The performer

THE CHORUS

The Pronomos vase

The complete personnel of an Athenian theatre performance at the end of the classical period are depicted on a pot used for mixing wine. The pot commemorated a victory in the competition, as we see from a monument on the right. The actors and chorus are dressed for the satyr play, and not for one of the tragedies that preceded it in the contest, because it was here that drama made explicit its links with the god of wine. The chorus at the end of the satyr play emerged from their long period of training and testing day of performance, drank their fill of wine to celebrate, and returned to everyday life.

In addition to the chorus, the pot depicts three trios. At the centre of the upper level is the divine group: Dionysos, his spouse Ariadne, and an enigmatic figure who might be the Muse of tragedy or the heroine of the play transformed by the spectator's erotic desire into a real woman. On the lower level we see the playwright with his scroll, the chorus trainer with his lyre and the piper dressed in the costume he wore in the theatre. Pronomos, the player of the pipe or 'aulos' depicted here, was the most famous of all Greek aulos-players, and his central position in the vase emphasizes the role of music in creating a Dionysiac experience. On the upper level, framing the divine group, we see the three actors of the play, mature men with beards, one dressed as a king, one as Herakles with his club, and one in shaggy skins as Silenus, leader of the satyrs. Around these figures are eleven young men dressed as satyrs in furry shorts to which a small erect phallus is attached. Like the actors, the young men carry their masks. The one nearest the music has donned his mask and

Plate 11 The 'Pronomos' vase.

started to dance; another close to the victory monument has put over his obscene costume the formal robes that he perhaps wore in the victory procession.

The painter emphasizes the ritual aspect of Greek drama. The performance is seen to be dedicated to Dionysos, even though the god ignores the mortals around him. The three mature men who shared the 'acting' roles are quite distinct from the idealized youths who play the chorus. One of the mature actors is labelled with the name of his character, Herakles, and perhaps this actor also took the role of the heroine whose mask is held close to his head. Nine of the chorus-men are labelled with their real extra-theatrical names, as are Pronomos the musician, Demetrios the dramatist and Charinos the trainer. Whilst the identities of the actors were of no consequence for the main competition, so long as they numbered only three, the chorus-men had to be citizens. It was they who honoured the god on behalf of the city, and their performance was perhaps in some sense a rite of passage, an important encounter with the divine in the course of their journey to manhood. On the reverse of the pot, not shown in the photograph, Dionysos runs free in a natural environment, having seized the lyre which symbolizes creative control. Around him are four satyrs who have lost their theatrical accoutrements and become creatures of myth, but serve to make up the proper complement of fifteen dancers. One of the four holds a pot, a miniature version of the Pronomos vase itself, over the heads of the two figures bottom right on the photo, the pair who have no name labels. The wine has washed away their civic identity as they become creatures of pure imagination. The theme of the vase is the way Dionysos, through music, wine, dance and masked impersonation effects a psychic transition. The playwright with his script occupies a physically low and marginal status. The lyre beside him is a reminder that his role was to invent rhythms as well as words.

The choral dancers of tragedy

Aristotle records the historical consensus that drama originated in improvizations by the leaders of choral dances dedicated to Dionysos (see above, p. 30). However, the classical historian Herodotus mentions that 'tragic choruses' in the town of Sikyon were transferred in pre-classical times from the worship of the hero Adrastus to the god Dionysos,[1] so we should beware of postulating an *essence* of tragedy

identified with the spirit of a single god. Only one thing is entirely clear: tragedy is a logical extension of choral dance, which was the most important form of cultural expression in the pre-classical period. Choral dances honoured the gods, they demarcated and drew together the component groups of the community such as unmarried girls or warriors, and they had an educational function in physical training, in transmitting the traditions of the community, and in teaching individuals to subordinate self to the collective. Plato famously declared that a person who cannot dance is a person with no education.[2] In Greek choral dance, the relationship of a chorus leader to his or her chorus was fundamental. The earliest fragments of dramatic dialogue from the Greek world (see above, p. oo) were probably written to be performed as an interchange between Sappho as chorus leader and the chorus of girls for whom she bore responsibility. The circular dance around the altar allowed the leader either to lead and set movements for the procession, or else to stand in the centre and establish her or his difference.[3] The function of playwright only slowly differentiated itself from the function of chorus leader.

The ritual and educational traditions of choral dance explain why the tragic chorus-men in our images are always young. The state paid the actors, but the choregos had to pay and house the chorus in accordance with the ancient principle that the old should instruct the young, and the new democratic principle that the rich should support the poor (see above, p. oo). A mosaic based on an earlier painting captures the sense that performance was a transitional rite. Two young chorus-men in satyr costume gaze reluctantly at two masks offered them by an aged trainer or playwright. A third youth tries on the costume of Herakles. In one interpretation, the youths are being offered promotion to the adult role of actor. In another we see youth happy to assume the role of rough combatant, but dismayed by masks which symbolize the suffering and aging that lie ahead of them.

The choregos was appointed in the summer, and thus had about eight months in which to gather and train his chorus.[4] The scale of the task made time essential. The chorus had to perform four plays in succession, and each dance arrangement was new and original. The chorus members had to sing and dance in precise unison, articulating so clearly that complex language could be heard by spectators 100 metres away. Though the chorus could be split in half,

Plate 12 Dressing-room scene: a mosaic from Pompeii.

the emphasis of the form was always upon collective behaviour.[5] The necessary unison was only possible because these young men had practised choral dance and song from an early age in the context of different religious festivals. Expertise was also a feature of the audience, who seem to have been able to commit much of what they heard to memory. It is said that when the Athenians were routed in Sicily many common soldiers and sailors were spared because they were able to repeat choruses from the plays of Euripides.[6] For the modern performer, the task of performing a Greek chorus seems superhuman. The repetitive rhythms and easy language of the musical offer little help. Most directors opt for speech without movement in order to ensure that the audience grasps the language, and they divide the text amongst different speakers to ensure clarity and vivacity. A few take the operatic route and use song to emphasize feeling. Those who opt for dance generally find either that the text is obscured, or that dance in

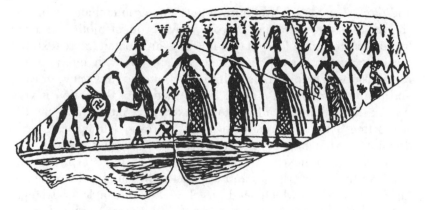

Figure 15 An early portrayal of actor/leader and chorus.
Vase of the late 700's from Argos.

service of the words becomes slow and mechanical. The dance-
dramas of the east offer fruitful ways of integrating chant with
symbolic movement, but the best-known forms like Noh and Kathakali are not based on the principle of choral unison. Balinese and
African traditions offer more scope. In the fragmented modern
societies of the west, the collective ideal has no cultural roots.
Purcarete's success with the chorus derives from the collectivist
traditions of communist Romania, which gave him insight into the
behaviour of crowds, though not any musical tradition within which
to work. One of the most successful choral experiments in recent
years was Lee Breuer's adaptation of Sophocles' *Oedipus at Colonus*,
which drew on the African-inspired music of a Pentecostal service to
find a mode of collective singing where song shades into dance.[7]

In the time of Aeschylus there were twelve in the tragic chorus,
the number twelve signifying the complete cosmic circle,[8] and the
function of chorus leader still belonged, effectively, to the lead actor.
In Aeschylus' earliest play, *The Persians*, the lead actor – presumably
Aeschylus himself – must have taken the two major tragic roles of
the Persian Queen and her son Xerxes. First the chorus instruct the
Queen in a ritual she must perform to expel her dream; then she
and the chorus learn of the Persian defeat, so she performs the ritual
and raises the ghost of her husband; and finally, her son returns. The
lead actor is the focus of the chorus' attention throughout: as Queen
he silently performs the act of raising the dead whilst the chorus sing

and dance; as Xerxes his entire role is a sung interchange with the chorus. Most later dramatists would have brought mother and son together at the end of the play, a meeting anticipated in the text, but the concerns of early Greek tragedy were not with interpersonal relationships. The play bats a shifting set of emotions between ruler and people, leader and chorus. The structure of the action is very simple: a sustained leader–chorus exchange interrupted by the supporting actor who recites two epic narratives; the messenger's account of what happened in the past; and the ghost's account of what will happen next.

In the time of Euripides and Sophocles the number increased to fifteen, a number which lends itself to the rectangle or triangle rather than the circle, and generates a strategic position for the leader, now known as the *coryphaeus* (indicated below by x).

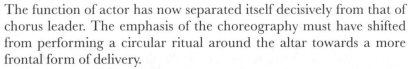

Or:

```
    *  *  *  *  *
    *  *  *  *  *
    *  *  X  *  *
```

```
    *  *  *  *  *
      *  *  *  *
       *  *  *
        *  *
         x
```

The function of actor has now separated itself decisively from that of chorus leader. The emphasis of the choreography must have shifted from performing a circular ritual around the altar towards a more frontal form of delivery.

In the twentieth century, Jacques Lecoq has been the most systematic researcher into choral movement. He stresses the importance of flexibility in the chorus:

> It can be a bearer of contradictions: its members can sometimes oppose each other in sub-groups, or alternatively unite to address the audience together. I cannot imagine a tragedy without a chorus. But how do we group these figures? How do we bring life to this collective body? How to make it breathe, and move like a living organism, while avoiding aestheticized choreography and militarist geometry?[9]

In later times, when chorus and actors occupied different spaces, the militaristic rectangle became established as the standard formation, but in the classical period the choreography would have been more fluid.[10] Though opposed to regimentation, Lecoq personally finds

more flexibility in the rectangle than in the ritual circle, and the Greeks of the classical period must have gone through similar processes of experimentation.

An inscription from the classical period relating to a tragedy by Euripides lists fourteen members of a chorus by name, and it may well be that the 'Socrates' who set up the monument took on both the financial role of choregos and the performance role of cory-phaeus in order to maximize his prestige.[11] This may have been quite common (see above, p. 51). Post-classical references to the famous 'chorus-trainer' Sannio indicate that his role extended to performing and thus taking the coryphaeus role.[12] The coryphaeus was both leader and teacher, and in performance played a crucial role in setting the time that the other dancers followed. However, there is no evidence to support the common idea that the cory-phaeus alone spoke the short passages of dialogue which are allocated to the chorus but not designated for dancing. Because the actors were masked, a single anonymous voice emanating from the crowd would not have been identifiable as the speech of any one individual; but unison speech is equally plausible, even though this seems an alien convention to individualistic modern performers.

The dancers of comedy

The organizational basis of the comic chorus was rather different. The first comedies were performed by volunteers, and the state assumed control at a much later date, eventually passing responsi-bility over to the ten tribes just like the dithyramb.[13] Since there were five comedies each with a chorus of twenty-four, it seems likely that each tribe provided a half-chorus of twelve. To dance in the tragic chorus was an exceptional honour, for the dancer represented the state as a whole, but comedy was a lesser responsibility. The rehearsal period did not need to be so long, since the actors had only one play to rehearse, so the dramatist had time to make his play as topical as possible.

To dance in a tragic chorus was regarded as part of a young man's education, and the generic name given to tragic dance was *emmeleia*, a dance 'in harmony'. It was not so easy to regard dancing in a comedy as educational, for the body had to appear ugly and distorted. Plato believed strongly that dance should remain at the core of Greek education, and was exercised by the problem that

people who enact negative behaviour will gradually acquire those negative characteristics. He accepted tragic dancing on the basis that tragedy is the representation of a noble life, but regarded comic performers as people with misshapen bodies and a degraded outlook, and he urged that the performance of comedy should be left to slaves and foreigners.[14] Comic actors at the Dionysia were not honoured with a prize. The feeling that dancing in comedy was a morally ambivalent affair may explain why there was no tradition in the visual arts of representing half-costumed comic actors. There are many images of masked comic performers but none of adults with their comic masks removed.[15] Demosthenes illustrates the shameful character of an Athenian by mentioning that he removed his mask in a Dionysiac procession.[16] The dancers of comedy were most probably mature men who could not so easily as youth be corrupted by grotesque body movements. Their persons were not on display in the same manner as those finest representatives of the city who danced the tragedy and satyr play.

The tragic chorus of fifteen functioned as a single organism, projecting a single emotion, but the comic chorus of twenty-four created a more chaotic impression, filling the space with disparate figures. In *The Birds* each of the chorus-men was dressed as a different species to create the effect of anarchy, but order could instantly be restored when the birds drew themselves up into battle lines. In *Lysistrata* some have individual names (see below, p. 207); twelve are dressed as men and twelve as women, and they unite only at the end. All comedies incorporated a long setpiece address to the audience half way through the play (called the *parabasis*), and in *Lysistrata* the two groups alternate, which probably indicates the normal practice. Twelve bodies can function as a single body, but twenty-four becomes a crowd or a regiment.

The choreography

When we try to imagine Greek performance, the hardest thing of all is to picture the dancing, and grasp what the medium of dance communicated to the audience. Two principles set out by Plato are a helpful starting point. First, dance is agreed to be a matter of *mimesis* or 'imitation';[17] in other words, it is not simply expressive, or the making of an abstract pattern, but represents a visible event out in the world. To take two very simple examples: a dance that involved

Figure 16 A stage tradition records that the characters of Superior Argument and Inferior Argument in Aristophanes, *Clouds*, were played by fighting cocks in a cage. This vase from the classical period may depict the contest between those figures.

kicking the feet together on a jump was called 'the tongs'; and the dance of the 'horned owl' involved staring and holding the hands as horns, simulating the movements an owl makes when stalked by a human.[18] Dances of the latter kind inspired the animal choruses of Aristophanes. Ritual dances commonly imitated the actions or attributes of specific gods: a woman with shield and spear, for example, might dance in front of a statue of Artemis, honouring the goddess by imitating her war-like qualities.[19] Theatrical dances were in a sense second-order imitations of imitations, quoting, recontex-tualizing and synthesizing dance movements drawn from ritual practices. Plato disliked tragic dancing for this reason, and in the interests of a stable society wanted to restrict dances to their traditional contexts.[20] The modern choreographer has no substitute for the rich vocabulary of movement available in the ancient world.

Figure 17 Characteristic dance poses of tragedy in about 450 BC.

The modern dancer can arrange her or his body like an ancient Greek through the study of vase paintings, but the meaning of those movements is substantially lost.

Plato states that dance took two forms: either acting out the words of the composer, or physical training, the second being a means to achieve the first as dancers limbered up different parts of their bodies. He distinguishes from dance a second form of choral performance that we might liken to eastern martial arts such as *tai chi*.[21] These martial arts trained men for warfare, honoured the gods, and constituted a performance art at festivals like the Panathenaia. True dance as distinct from martial arts, Plato implies, was bound up with words, and should not be allowed to exist as an autonomous art form. The Greek intertwining of dance and song is a difficult ideal for modern western performers to assimilate, because they are used to being led by the musical accompaniment.

It was the words which lent the dances of tragedy their rhythm. There was no percussion, only the stamp of feet on the earth. The piper was not supposed to change the rhythm embedded in the words, but only to enhance the words through his melody. The job of the dramatist, at least in the earlier part of the period, was to compose the dances at the same time as the words. The metres in which the choruses were written presupposed specific dance steps. Greek metre was based upon the precise length of time taken to utter a syllable, and not upon stress or pitch, and this feature of the language allowed the two rhythms of word and movement to be

precisely aligned. The 'spoken' sections of Greek tragedy are all written in an iambic metre (the metre of Shakespearean blank verse) with the basic form:

ᵛ—ᵛ— ᵛ—ᵛ— ᵛ—ᵛ—

A common marching rhythm is the anapaest, with a heavy falling rhythm based on the unit:

ᵛ ᵛ—

The main dance rhythms display a bewildering variety, and I shall cite just one example, the 'dochmiac' metre used at moments of high emotion. The basic unit here is:

ᵛ——ᵛ—

A short syllable occupies half the time of a long syllable, so the metre seems to establish a 3:5 time ratio, given that the first di-dum = 3, and the dum-di-dum = 5, and this fixes the underlying beat established by the dancer's feet. When Clytaemnestra is led off to be killed by her son in the *Libation Bearers*, the chorus sing and dance an ode that is almost entirely in dochmiacs (935–71). One can translate to clarify the underlying form:

> A just   fate arrived
> At last   Trojan sons
> Your just   doom is come
> Has found   out the house ...   (935–7)

But such a monotonous rendering belies the fact that the dochmiac in its pure form arrives only at the end of each verse of the ode to mark the climax. Until that point the text works a series of variants on the underlying rhythm which English verse cannot replicate.

Greek odes are divided into pairs of verses called *strophe* and *antistrophe* ('turning' and 'turning back'). Each strophe has exactly the same metrical structure as the balancing antistrophe, but is otherwise unique, different from any other strophe in Greek literature. Greek dramatists would not have gone to such trouble if they had not wanted in each case to create an original dance that was precisely mirrored, for the precise symmetry would otherwise have been lost on the spectator. If we attend to the formal structure of a Greek ode, which some translations make clear while many do not (see below, p. 206), we can make inferences about the mimetic actions envisaged by the dramatist. Rather than competing for the audience's attention, the physical action made it possible to grasp the complex words, and the words in turn made it possible to read the action.

Let us continue with the same example, the dochmiac ode from *Libation Bearers*. Whilst the ode is being performed, Clytaemnestra is being killed off-stage. The normal pattern used by Sophocles and Euripides is:

STROPHE A
ANTISTROPHE A
STROPHE B
ANTISTROPHE B

In this instance Aeschylus enhances the sense of a ritual enactment by adding a refrain.

STROPHE A + refrain A
ANTISTROPHE A + refrain A
STROPHE B + refrain B
ANTISTROPHE B + refrain B

Strophe and Antistrophe A both start with someone coming: 'Justice' *coming* to Troy, and Orestes *coming* to kill his mother. In the fourth line (emphasized by a brief change of metre) the someone becomes two people: Orestes and his friend Pylades; Orestes and Justice. The climax suggests a lunging movement: the blow struck by Orestes; the invisible blow of Justice. Two very simple movements, a single procession becoming a double procession and an aggressive lunge, fix the key ideas in the spectator's mind. Agamemnon's journey to Troy anticipates Orestes' journey to Argos, and both journeys of revenge are morally problematic. Pylades has just gone out beside Orestes, as the voice of reassurance that the killing is an act of justice. The linking of two opposite ideas to a single dance movement clarifies the patterning of the trilogy.

The lunging movement at the climax of the first strophe and antistrophe substitutes for the stabbing of Clytaemnestra, which happens unseen behind the skênê. Instead of some sleight of hand using stage blood, Aeschylus made his audience imagine the horror of the killing, and fired their imagination through the concerted movement of twelve bodies, an effect more powerful than words alone. The refrain which follows shifts the emphasis from language and movement to the power of sound, for it opens with the ritual ululation uttered by women as a cry of victory.

The first strophe and antistrophe develop from the preceding exit, when Orestes and Pylades go indoors to kill. The second half of the

ode sets up the entry which follows, when Orestes appears on the *eccyclema* (see above, p. 118), over the bodies of Clytaemnestra and Aegisthus. The first image in the second half joins the oracle of Apollo issuing from a cave (strophe) to the evil which is about to be expelled through the doors of the skênê (antistrophe): just as the oracle rights the wrong, so the house is cleared and purified. The dominant gesture must be one of expulsion. The dancers focus the attention of the audience on the skênê, and make them see a double image, at once the oracle at Delphi and the palace here and now at Argos. The last line in strophe and antistrophe B implies a movement of falling to the ground, the first time in obeisance to the power of the gods, and the second time to demonstrate that the residents of the house have fallen. The phrase 'residents of the house' hints not only at Clytaemnestra but also at the demonic Furies, whose presence Orestes will soon imagine in the black-clad chorus when they rise to their feet and gather round him. The refrain which follows is a direct address to the house calling upon it to arise; the principal movement in the refrain comes not from the dancers but from the skênê as the doors open and the platform rolls forward.

This kind of formal analysis, which can be performed on any choral ode, shows how the Greek dramatists integrated sound, language, the design of the space and choreography to create a total art form, rooted in the capacities of the human body.

The function of the chorus

The function of the chorus can be understood in many different ways, and any modern production has to make difficult choices. At the end of the nineteenth century the director of the civic theatre in Vienna, responsible for reviving many Greek plays, was clear that the Greek chorus 'lies as if an enchanted castle to which one can no longer find an entrance. Its *form* is petrified: it only remains to be asked: how can its *content* be rescued again?'[22] With the decline of naturalism in the twentieth century, ways into the castle have been found, and the old form no longer has to be discarded as a relic. In order to suggest some of the entrances available to the modern practitioner, I shall consider different functions of the tragic chorus, and show how they can be related to Lecoq's programme of training.

The surrogate spectator   The romantic critic Schlegel early in the nineteenth century saw the chorus as the 'ideal spectator', offering back to the spectator 'a lyrical and musical expression of his own emotions'.[23] This conception was related both to the tradition of the operatic chorus and to the spatial assumption that the chorus stood as intermediary between the audience and the actors. Though critics have rejected the idea that there is always a right way to feel about a play, the fact remains that the chorus are in large measure spectators. Lecoq asks his students to simulate the watching of an event in order that the audience may, simply by looking at the watchers, reconstruct what is seen, and the students discover how watching involves taking on the physical properties of that which is watched. Dynamic watching of this kind requires huge physical concentration. When the audience is able to view both the action and the dynamic watching of the action, its response becomes more complex and more intense.

The character   Aristotle, who showed little interest in the choral aspect of drama, urged that the chorus should be treated as one of the actors, and thus integrated with the whole.[24] Although to an extent the chorus is involved in the action, giving advice and being sworn to silence, Aristotle's advice plays down the ritual and political aspects of tragedy in order to focus on moral decisions made by individuals. His approach is that of the reader, who tends to find song–dance sequences opaque on the page, and not that of the spectator whose visual field is dominated by the ever-present choral group. Lecoq's focus of concern is the coryphaeus, and he has developed techniques for making the single spokesperson emerge spontaneously from the group so as to interact with the hero like a character and yet remain part of a non-personal mass.

The voice of myth   The chorus embody the collective wisdom of the community, for they refer allusively in their odes to a body of mythology familiar to the ancient audience. Many productions reduce the chorus to three or even one speaker, whilst translations simplify and clarify the myths in order to ensure that the modern audience follows the narrative thread. Unfortunately Lecoq shows no interest in this storytelling aspect, for his concern is with the body.

Worshippers of Dionysos   The choral dancers had a double identity, (a) as citizens honouring Dionysos on behalf of their community, and (b)

as characters within a dramatic fiction. Some recent critics therefore attribute a metatheatrical dimension to the chorus, and discern slippage between performer and role.[25] The ritual aspect of tragedy was brought to the fore by Nietzsche, who pointed to a link between the god Dionysos and the loss of individuality in collective behaviour. Lecoq finds this ritual aspect problematic in a secular age which severs the individual from society and the cosmos. He describes the unaccustomed sense of transpersonal linkage experienced by an actor in a chorus who feels that he or she is mouthing words that stem from other voices. Lecoq's goal is a form of unison speaking that avoids being mechanical.

The body politic   There are no private conversations in Greek tragedy because the chorus is present as a kind of assembly or jury to judge the rights and wrongs of what is said. Lecoq captures this aspect of the chorus through the 'Hyde Park exercise'. A student stands on a soapbox as if at London's Hyde Park Corner and argues for a belief, trying to sustain the attention of a milling crowd. After improvized speeches have been tried, and a speaker on a second soapbox has competed for attention, real pieces of political rhetoric are introduced. The chorus is then orchestrated until the random crowd is transformed into a chorus.

The feminized other   Although the chorus are constantly being invited to make judgements, they cannot be seen in any direct way as the voice of the political community, for in most plays they are cast as marginal figures – as men too old for physical intervention, or more often as women. Greek tragedy also favoured a female chorus because women's relationship to the community was established through ritual rather than politics. Lecoq avoids mixing the sexes in his choral work, but confines his comments to the psychological plane, commenting on the relative sense of wisdom in choruses of old men, the deep sense of cohesion and solidarity in female choruses. We should not assume with Schlegel that the emotions of the chorus were shared by the audience, for the gender gap between the male audience and the female chorus created a degree of critical distance. It was a commonplace in Greek male thinking that women lacked control over their emotions. In European opera the audience are normally expected to submerge themselves in the emotions expressed by the orchestra and chorus, but Greek theatre encouraged more complex responses.

Counter-weight to the actor Lecoq's most important exercise is called 'balancing the stage'. He invites his students to imagine that the acting space is a rectangular plate balanced on one central pivot. A single actor at the centre point leaves the centre, creating an imbalance, and a second actor restores equilibrium by entering on the opposite side and going to the same distance from the centre. Further actors arrive and increasingly complex geometric problems have to be solved if equilibrium is to be preserved. Then the rules are changed so that one actor as hero is the counter-weight to a complete chorus, and is deemed to have fifteen times the weight of each individual in the chorus. The exercise interprets Greek tragedy as being in essence a relationship between the exceptional individual and the force of the collective. It teaches the students to work organically as a group, and sense intuitively the patterns that their bodies create on the ground. Given the scale of Greek tragedy, which made it impossible to discern small individual movements, and the lack of stage lighting to focus attention, Lecoq's exercise is a valuable tool for directing attention and creating strong visual forms. Though Lecoq is no devotee of the ritual circle, intense concentration on the centre creates a mood which invites the label 'ritualistic'.

THE AULOS-PLAYER

The player

The aulos was a double pipe made of wood or bone. It was a reed instrument like the modern oboe, but the fixed diameter of the borehole created a droning effect which recalls the shawm. In plate 12 we can see the two finger positions which allowed the player to create one tune overlaying another, and the headband which secured the two mouthpieces, allowing the player complete freedom of movement. This was important because the aulos-player was not a static figure but, being in origin part of the same procession as the chorus, took up whatever position best allowed him to interact. Aristotle criticized players who distracted the audience by participating in the dance.[26]

Aristotle's discussion of the aulos is extremely revealing.[27] He links together the aulos, the music of Dionysos, and the 'Phrygian (Asiatic) mode'. He describes the aulos as an orgiastic rather than educational instrument, and argues that it should be used when the aim is not to

stimulate thought but to release emotions. The aulos was widely used in Greek life to accompany and energize collective actions, like dancing at a sacrifice, marching into battle or rowing a warship. The antithesis of the aulos was the lyre, the instrument of Apollo associated with order and thought. The lyre is associated with the individual because one person can play and sing simultaneously, and it is orderly since only one note can be played at a time. In the Pronomos vase the chorus trainer holds a lyre so he can teach while marking the rhythm, and the playwright has one by his head because the instrument allows him to compose words and tune simultaneously. Greek music was divided into a series of modes or moods, and the exotic 'Phrygian' mode was contrasted with the plain 'Dorian' mode of the earliest Greeks. Aristotle considered the Dorian mode the most educative since it created neither wild excitement nor relaxed inertia, but proper manliness.

Historical developments

Aristotle goes on to discuss the history of aulos-playing. In the Aeschylean period the leisured classes took to the instrument with enthusiasm, evidently because the instrument was a symbol of being Greek rather than Persian, but by the end of the classical period this attitude had changed. The release of feelings associated with the aulos no longer seemed conducive to the formation of a good character, and mastery of the instrument was no longer part of being an upper-class Athenian. Aristotle cites in this connexion the popular story that Athene invented the instrument, but threw it away because it distorted her face, whereupon it was appropriated by one of Dionysos' ugly satyrs. Thebes, the birthplace of Dionysos, tends to be associated with the god in his wilder aspects, and the city was particularly noted for its devotion to the instrument. The Pronomos vase portrays the most famous Theban aulos-player surrounded by Athenian performers. The aulos came to be associated with a complex of 'non-Athenian' values that lay at the heart of the festival of Dionysos – the Theban, the foreign, the feminine, the emotional, the collective, the non-verbal and the non-rational.

The first nineteenth-century attempt at playing the authentic text of a Greek tragedy in 1841 is usually known as the 'Mendelssohn *Antigone*'. The German translation attempted to replicate the metres of the Greek, and Mendelssohn paid close attention to metre when

he composed his orchestral settings. The director felt in retrospect that the elaborate instrumentation made the singing difficult to grasp, isolating the choral sections from the play as a whole, and destroying the sense of aesthetic unity.[28] The relationship between music and text has always proved problematic. In recent times the power of a single musician to co-ordinate and energize the actors has best been demonstrated by Mnouchkine's *Les Atrides*. Jean-Jacques Lemêtre drew upon a huge array of instruments in order to sustain a rhythm that never wavered, interacting with the actors as an equal, and he has been described as the 'second lung' of the performance.[29] Even in this production, however, speech and dance alternated rather than merged. The text of the chorus was given to three leaders in order to make it comprehensible and sustain a single tempo. The Greek synthesis of dance, song and instrumental accompaniment remains elusive.

Clearly this synthesis was not easily achieved in the classical period. In an early satyr play the chorus, dancing faster and faster to simulate a competition with the musician, deliver a diatribe against the aulos. 'Dionysos belongs to me!' they cry. 'The aulos must follow, for he is only a servant . . . with the breath of a motley toad.' They end by urging their god Dionysos: 'Listen to my Dorian dance!' The term *motley* suggests that the instrument is less pure than the voice because it mixes notes, and the claim that the dance is Dorian whilst the music is Asiatic emphasizes the absurdity of splitting music from action. The immediate humour of the passage related to controversy about money paid to hire prestigious players, who were no doubt foreign.[30] Yet in the joke lay the seeds of an idea which would later help to separate literature from theatre, the idea that language is properly master and music a servant.

The classical period was marked by controversy and continual change. One comic poet brought on 'Music' as a wronged woman, battered and raped by a sequence of musical innovators.[31] By the end of the period Euripides was starting to break down the strict correlation of word and rhythm, and Aristophanes parodies this tendency in *The Frogs*. First Euripides is made to burlesque the ponderous rhythms of Aeschylus, with a series of heavy beats apparently represented by beatings on the breast. Then Aeschylus is made to parody one of Euripides' light choral dances in which the chorus evoke the world of nature to escape the cruel present – a mood piece rather than a narrative. The parody includes a notable

piece of coloratura to evoke the spider's feet whir-ir-ir-irring as they weave,[32] pointing to an important new gap between the time values of a spoken syllable and the time values imparted by music. We see hints of this technique in a fragment of music which survives from a late play by Euripides.[33] Music had begun to assert its autonomy.

Aeschylus goes on to parody one of Euripides' arias, and performs the lament of a woman for her stolen cock, using a bewildering variety of metres. This is the second major musical change associated with Euripides, a shift of emphasis from choral dances to solo pieces delivered by the leading actor. A later source maintains that choruses used strophe and antistrophe and a single musical mode because the performers were mere amateurs, whereas professional soloists could deploy much more modulation.[34] The demand for increasing musical sophistication and innovation went hand in hand with the cult of the individual performer and the decline of the collective ideal embodied by the chorus.

THE ACTOR

The mask

Ritual interpretations
The mask is the defining convention of Greek theatre performance. In the mosaic that we examined at the start of this chapter, a young man reacts to the power of a mask's gaze – though the tears on the face of the female mask are a post-classical feature, limiting the mask's power to express a full emotional range. Several of the performers on the Pronomos vase are studying the features of their masks as a preliminary to losing themselves within the person that the mask represents. The masks were made of glued rags and covered the whole head. They were not permanent objects like Balinese or Noh masks, but were dedicated after the performance to Dionysos in his temple.[35] Dionysos was god of the mask, and vases depict his worshippers gathered around a mask set in a basket, or a mask and costume set on a pole as in plate 3.[36]

In Greek cult Dionysos was associated both with natural fertility – the phallus – and with the grave. An influential essay of 1933 portrayed the mask as 'the symbol and manifestation of that which is simultaneously there and not there ... It excites with a nearness which is at the same time a remoteness. The final secrets of existence

and non-existence transfix mankind with monstrous eyes.'[37] Inspired by such thinking, two influential productions of 1955 placed the mask at the core of a ritualist interpretation of Greek tragedy (see above, p. 101). Tyrone Guthrie in Stratford, Ontario, wanted to portray Oedipus as a mixture of Christ figure, god of light, and pagan sacrificial beast, so gave his actors masks in order to achieve a quality of 'universality' and obliterate the personalities of the performers. In accordance with a heroic conception of Greek drama, he gave huge masks to the actors and life-size masks to the ordinary mortals in the chorus.[38] Jean-Louis Barrault in Paris, in his 'voodoo' *Oresteia*, looked for inspiration to African uses of the mask. 'A mask', wrote Barrault, 'confers upon a given expression the maximum of intensity together with an impression of absence. A mask expresses at the same time the maximum of life and the maximum of death.'[39] The emptiness of the classical mask is undoubtedly one of its aspects.

Neutrality

Tragic masks of the classical period are characterized by a lack of expression. Pale skin colour signifies a woman, and dark a man; a beard symbolizes mature manhood, and white hair age; but no indication is given of character or feeling. The 'neutral' mask has been much used in actor training, notably by the French teachers Michel Saint-Denis and Jacques Lecoq. Saint-Denis showed how the immobilizing of the face made the body more expressive. The mask, he argued 'can only be animated by controlled, strong and utterly simple actions',[40] and his demand that the masked body be calm and balanced helped inspire the classicism of Peter Hall. Lecoq stresses that all masks must create the illusion of mobile features if they are to succeed in the theatre, and he distinguishes the death mask of 'ritual' theatre from the true neutral mask which places the actor in a state of discovery, open to the space around him and seeing it as if for the first time. The impression of death is created by a mask that is precisely life size, Lecoq maintains, and a proper theatrical mask needs to be slightly larger than life. Lecoq's neutral mask has no character, so can never communicate with another person, and to this end students go on to work with expressive masks. The wearer is now guided by the form implicit in the structure of the mask, which 'becomes like a vehicle, drawing the whole body into the space, into specific movements that reveal the character'.[41]

The principles of the expressive mask are directly relevant to comedy, where distortions of the face encourage the actor to develop distorted patterns of movement, and it is a general truth that masks determine how the body will move. The tragic mask at once was and was not 'neutral'. An Oedipus, an Orestes or a chorus-woman in a sense see the world as for the first time from a position of naïve neutrality, for they encounter situations that no one has encountered before. However, Richard Hornby urges caution in a review of Hall's *Oedipus Plays* at Epidaurus. 'A neutral mask can have a stage potency when seen *up close* (as in classes, or in most avant-garde theatres), and when the actor animates the mask with dynamic poses, along with meaningful gestures of both head and body. But when the theatre is huge and the actors are still as sticks, the masks just look like pallid blobs.'[42] Classical masks, Hornby assumes, were varied and highly coloured in order to make the features as visible as possible. It is a fact that spectators listen more effectively when they focus on the face of the speaker. Neutrality remains an important principle so long as it is not contaminated by the idea that classical acting should be statuesque.

The alienating mask

It is a common conception, related most obviously to Brecht's development of masked acting within the Berliner Ensemble, that the mask creates a relationship of distance. Tony Harrison, translator of Hall's *Oresteia*, argues that masks, like the formality of verse, create the detachment necessary if we are to contemplate horror. Like the visor worn by a welder so he can look into the flame, the 'mask keeps its eyes wide open when the axe blade falls, when the babies burn'.[43] The argument that the mask allows the actor to present a situation and not wallow in emotion is a compelling one. In relation to the processes of the spectator, however, Hall perhaps generalizes too much when he claims: 'The screaming, naked, actual face repels you. The screaming face of the mask does not.'[44] Although masks create distance in a modern theatre with stage lighting, in a large open-air theatre the effect of classical masks was to bring the face closer to the spectator and thus create intimacy. Hall is nevertheless right to indicate that emotion is most powerful when it is created and placed on the mask by the spectator's imagination.

In Greece a series of successful masked productions emerged from

Plate 13 G. Lazanis as Dikaiopolis sitting in the Assembly: Aristophanes, *Acharnians*, directed by Karolos Koun, with masks by Dionysis Fotopoulos. Athens, 1976.

the partnership between the director Karolos Koun and mask-maker Dionysis Fotopoulos established in 1976. With a clear political agenda, Koun drew from Brecht the notion that masks destroy illusion and put the actors at a distance. Masks, he argued, should be given to characters in performance 'to help maintain their scale, and their impersonal nature'.[45] To describe character portrayal in Greek tragedies, he took as his reference point the lack of physical contact between Romeo and Juliet in the balcony scene. 'Their existence depends on the effort to touch, but never being embraced.' For Koun, the tragic mask eliminated the carnal aspect of the human being. This conception of the mask as a negative lies behind the half-masks of Koun's *Oresteia*, which define a break between the visible part of the face and the hidden (plate 1). In the carnal mode of comedy, the false noses of Koun's *Acharnians* were inspired by Greek folk tradition, and suggested continuity between Greece ancient and

modern. The persons of the actors remain visible in Koun's productions, whereas in the ancient theatre the mask covered the whole head like a helmet. What Koun fails to recognize is the fundamental difference between half-masks, which are devices to *conceal,* and classical head masks, which were devices to *reveal.* The Dionysiac head mask encouraged fresh identities to emerge. The classical world was populated by countless gods thought to act through people, and people impersonated gods in many rituals. They also engaged in many forms of collective behaviour. The idea of letting go one's individual self in order to become Dionysos, or a character in one of his plays, was therefore neither threatening nor problematic. In the classical world actors did not go into trance, but belonged to a culture which defined personal identity in different terms. In the Christian and post-Christian world, the idea of abandoning responsibility for one's own individual soul or self became intolerable. Both Stanislavski and Brecht required the actor's self to remain intact, not vanish in the otherness of the mask.

The acoustical mask
The orator Demosthenes, who learned from an actor the technique of holding a mass audience, trained his voice by speaking with stones in his mouth or while running up-hill.[46] Because of the size of the audience, the first requirement of the Greek actor was audibility. Masks in the modern theatre have often impeded the voice, and Hall in his *Oedipus Plays* resorted to hiding microphones within the mask. However, an authority in the Roman period assures us that the actor's voice, because it passes through a single aperture becomes concentrated and directed, and thus clearer, more tuneful and more resonant.[47] Recently the Greek mask-maker Thanos Vovolis has worked with an opera director to explore the acoustical benefits of the mask. The point is not that the mouth functions as a megaphone but that the mask as a whole works as a resonator for the head.[48] Patsy Rodenburg, observes that the head resonator is generally underused by modern actors, who are trained to concentrate on the throat and chest.[49]

Vovolis argues that the Greek mask, like eastern masks, created 'a body/mind state of panic-free emptiness'. The restricted vision of the actor increased his awareness of the architecture of his own body, but also helped him sense the presence of others beside and behind him, and thus function as part of a chorus. The sound of the

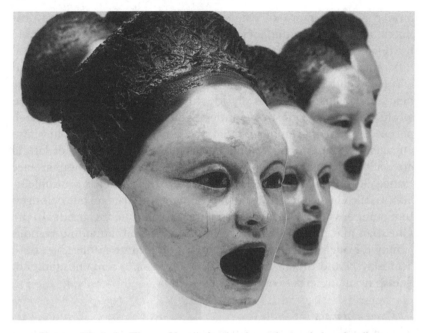

Plate 14 Masks by Thanos Vovolis for the chorus in Aeschylus, *Suppliants*: Epidaurus, 1994.

voice is maximized when the body functions as a unity, and tensions are eliminated. When working on a classical text, Vovolis starts with the ritual cries which appear frequently in Aeschylus and at moments of extreme crisis in Sophocles and Euripides. Sounds like *iou, oimoi* and *eleleu* are untranslatable because modern western culture has no ritualized channels for the vocal and collective expression of pure emotion, yet they are crucial markers in Greek tragedy of points when words reach their limit, and the playwright hands all responsibility to the actor. The search for these ancient sounds leads the actor to assume postures that maximize the production and direction of sound, and when the right postures are found in rehearsal, Vovolis sees in the face of the actor the emptiness of the classical mask. Total emptiness is thus total presence. Vovolis identifies the classical mask as part of a ceremonial theatre devoted not to the delineation of character but to the narrating of myths, and the spectators supplement the work of the actors by projecting different emotions upon the mask as they listen to the words of the

playwright. A major aim of his work is to extend the principles of the classical mask to more modern forms of theatre (plate 8).

Mind and body

Socrates, in one of Plato's dialogues, encounters Ion of Ephesus, a professional rhapsode (see above, p. 15). Ion maintains that he is inspired by the gods when performing Homer, but contradicts himself by claiming a rational understanding of his material. He describes the intensity of his possession by the gods as he performs passages of high emotion with tears in his eyes, heart beating and hair standing on end, but goes on to say that he can observe simultaneously whether or not his performance is succeeding with the audience.[50] Ion did not perform in a mask and that made it much easier for him to keep an eye on the audience. It was a function of the Dionysiac mask not only to prevent the audience seeing actor against role, but also to increase the concentration of the actor by restricting his external vision.

Plato's fascination with Ion stems from his obsession with dualism: the separation of mind from body, and thought from feeling. A dualist position leads Plato to dismiss the performer as a second-order creative force, portraying Ion as interpreter of the poet, who is in turn interpreter of the gods. In Plato's philosophical system, Homer is equivalent to mind, and Ion to body. Platonic dualism helped shape Christianity, and influenced western thinking about theatre in two fundamental ways. First, the performer became subordinate to the playwright, and second the body became subordinate to a mind located in the head. Because the head, since Plato, has been regarded as the home of mind and soul, the mask in the western tradition since Plato has functioned as a mode of concealment. The anonymity of the renaissance mask legitimated taboo behaviour, and the Brechtian mask was made a barrier to audience identification. The classical world before Plato, like the eastern tradition, took a holistic view of the human being, and found in the mask not a negative mode of concealment but a positive mode of embodiment. Rather than conceal the most important part of the human being, the mask helped the body to function as a totality.

For eastern performers the focus of the body is not the head but the area at the root of the navel, the *hara* of Japanese theatre or *nabhi mula* of Indian theatre.[51] In classical Greece the psychê or breath of

life was assumed to reside in the head, but had no effect on everyday behaviour. The body, like the theatre itself, was a centred space. It is very clear in the language of Aeschylus that thought and feeling are associated with the physical processes of the lower body, and four terms in Aeschylus' psycho-physical vocabulary are particularly important.[52] The *phrên* (or plural *phrenes*) somewhere around the diaphragm is particularly associated with thinking and engendering words via the breath, and is vulnerable to attack from other parts of the system. The *êpar* or liver is a place where deep emotions form slowly, transmitted to the system via the blood and bile. The *kardia* is the heart, which throbs in different ways in a wide variety of emotions. The *thumos* responds more quickly, powerfully and indiscriminately than the *kardia*, and has the function of adrenalin, being conceived as a kind of vapour from the blood. There is no concept of an independent mind functioning outside these psycho-physical processes. The implications for the actor are clear. There can be no question of fixing and defining character, as if the self can be separated from the body that acts. There can be no question of searching out motives in the Stanislavskian manner, as if the will can be separated from the action that stems from the will. It is fruitless to debate whether Agamemnon did or did not *choose* to sacrifice his daughter. In a world where multiple gods regularly operate through humans, it made no sense to think of actions being rooted in an autonomous ego.

Sophocles and Euripides bring us one step towards dualism with the portrayal of personal decision-making. New ideas afoot among the intelligentsia are mocked by Aristophanes when he makes the servant of Euripides declare that his master is at home writing but Euripides' mind is elsewhere seeking inspiration.[53] One of the most famous decisions in Greek drama is that of Euripides' Medea as she resolves to kill her children.[54] She speaks as though there was a single decision-making 'I' behind her voice, but on the one hand addresses her violent thumos and complains of its power to work evil, and on the other complains when soft words penetrate to her phrên. Her kardia is said to vanish in a moment of indecision. Medea's voice is thus multiple rather than single, until at the end of the speech an 'I' that knows right from wrong seems to separate itself from a thumos that governs her action. For the actor, the climaxes are the inarticulate words *aiai*, *pheu* and finally a sustained *a a*, when language breaks down and one voice starts to replace another.

Figure 18 The interior made exterior: in Ninagawa's production Medea and
the chorus draw red ribbons from their mouths in a sign of pain taken from
Japanese puppet theatre. *Medea* 409ff.

Although Euripides is exploring here the implications of a split
between thought and emotion, the conflict remains rooted in the
body. The mask is of the essence here. The instinct of the modern
western actor is to transmit the pain of a unique individual called
Medea through the face. The masked Greek actor used the body to
demonstrate a set of impulses, so the 'I' which articulates an
intention does not represent the true Medea any more than the
thumos governing the character's actions. When Tokusaburo Arashi

played the decision-making speech in Ninagawa's production,[55] his face was masked by kabuki make-up and tear-beads hanging below the eyes, whilst a sinuous red dress made a unity of head and body, and contracted legs energized the spine. Such techniques made it possible for the actor's throbbing hands to interact with the centre of energy in the torso, where we might imagine the thumos to be located. In this production the intense and involved gaze of the chorus furthered the idea that Medea's body was not the casing for a self but a field where social, physical and divine forces interact.

Costume

The movement of the actor was shaped not only by his mask but also by his costume. The dancing satyr in the Pronomos vase makes high leaps, the verticality suggested by the erect phallus sewn to the satyr pants. Whilst satyrs strive to be airborne, the costume of comedy kept ordinary mortals tied to the earth. The actors of comedy wore flesh-coloured tights to simulate nakedness, and a large phallus was sewn on the tights of males, worn either loose or strung up in a coil after the manner of athletes. Other features of the male body in comedy include breasts, a padded stomach and padded buttocks, and the shoulders are hunched, eliminating the divide between body and mask. The human being becomes a single organism, for comedy regards people as creatures who gratify themselves through talking (large mouth), eating (stomach), sex (phallus) and excreting, often in fear (buttocks).

In the 'choregos' vase, a middle-aged choregos looks up admiringly at a slave who represents the essence of comedy, whilst an elderly rival choregos brings on the effeminate Aegisthus to embody tragedy. In this scene from a lost comedy, the two genres are in competition. The players of the two choregoi establish presence by placing their huge buttocks in opposition to their masks, so the upper part of the body aspires to honour while the lower part sags. The slave stands with his arm raised like an orator, but the lines of his beard and phallus point earthwards. Aegisthus, on the other hand, represents the idealized body beautiful, although the body as always in tragedy is concealed by clothing. It is interesting that the vase painter did not depict the tragic mask of Aegisthus because no pictorial convention allowed him to do so: once worn, the mask ceased to be viewed as a separable object. The convention of the

Plate 15 The choregos vase: about 350 BC.

phallus, which is notoriously difficult to replicate in the modern
theatre, must be understood as the expression of a society which did
not regard the flesh as sinful or corrupt, but celebrated the naked
body in the gymnasium and on the athletics track. Comedy portrayed the neglected or aging body that Athenian men trained hard
to escape, whilst tragedy allowed the heroic body to be imagined.
The satyr play finally allowed the torsos of the best young citizens to
be glimpsed.

The costume of tragedy was highly ornate, and doubtless colourful, emphasizing the status of the performance as a ceremony.
Upper-class male characters in tragedy wore a chiton (a basic slip) to
the ankle in the old-fashioned Ionian style, whilst in comedy they
wore the plain, short, Dorian *chiton* preferred by the age of democracy, shortened further to allow constant glimpses of the genitalia.
Whilst tragic costume has eastern and feminine overtones, comic
costume mocks Greek aspirations to masculinity. In our vase, each
choregos wears a cloak (the 'himation') gathered in the left arm,

Plate 16 The 'Oedipus' vase: figures on a stage wearing tragic costume but
not masks. About 330 BC.

though these are of minimal size in comedy to allow energetic
movement. Aegisthus is dressed as a warrior, so has a military cloak
pinned at the neck to allow him to use his spears.

A standard himation, with the ornamentation characteristic of
tragedy, is worn by the actor left of Dionysos on the Pronomos vase
(plate 11), and much less elegantly by the central character in the
'Oedipus' vase.[56] Greek women spent their lives weaving, not
sewing, and the Greek himation was nothing but a rectangle of
woollen cloth held in place by the arms, neither sewn up nor secured
with pins. It was the garment of leisure that made work and fighting
impossible, immobilizing the left arm but leaving the right free to
pass the wine cup and make rhetorical gestures. The shepherd in the
'Oedipus' vase is a working man, so his cloak is pinned and his arms

and legs are free. In tragedy as in everyday life, the wearing of the himation imposed a bodily discipline involving stillness, balance and restricted gesture. Just as the himation forced Greeks in daily life to talk rather than fight, so the garment in the theatre pushed actors to maximize the potential of speech. There remained, always, a tension between the social code which governed the wearing of the himation, and the force of emotion which in a dramatic situation caused the rules to be broken. The Aeschylus of Aristophanes attacks Euripides saying that his own plays showed how the himation could be worn with dignity, but Euripides dressed his characters in rags.[57] In costume as in so many other aspects, Euripides challenged Aeschylus' ceremonial conception of theatre.

The woman in the 'Oedipus' vase uses her himation to cover her hair with the modesty of a woman in public, and her face in shame. The inwardness of the gesture holds the attention because the audience knows that the himation can be cast aside and the character may throw herself to the earth when social controls prove insufficient. The lower-class women who appear in so many tragic choruses probably wore chitons only, and danced without constriction. In Athens, women continued to wear the long Ionian chiton in the classical period, when men had changed to the short chiton, amplifying the sense of gender difference in democratic society. In comedy, since costume was based on contemporary life, the genital area of women was not under scrutiny in the same way as the masculinity of the male.

Doubling

Tragedy began as an interchange between a chorus and a poet/chorus leader, and the tradition remained that only one individual was properly speaking the 'actor' of the play. Though the earlier plays of Aeschylus seem to require two actors, and most of the plays of Euripides and Sophocles require three, only one man was the 'protagonist' whose name appeared in the records. After the playwright had withdrawn from the role of actor, the 'protagonist' competed for a separate acting prize, and the other two performers were regarded as his assistants.[58] Three actors was a sensible maximum because the audience could not see mouths moving, but had to know at every point who was speaking.

The doubling convention drew strength from the traditions of

Homeric performance, which required a single storyteller to adopt the voices of one character after another. The convention of the head mask did not simply make doubling possible; rather, it created the opportunity for the protagonist to display his versatility. Since the chiton and himation were garments of extreme simplicity, a complete change of identity could be effected within seconds. Stanislavskian theatre celebrates the fusion of actor and role, and thus abhors doubling, but Greek theatre celebrated the ability of the actor to change his identity completely. Stanislavskian theatre assumes that people are locked into and fixed by their characters, but Greek democratic theatre respected the idea that people could transform themselves and their world.

Plutarch comments on the irony that the protagonist often played low-status characters in performance, and kow-towed to the man playing the monarch who was in actuality his employee; the main prestige, he says, often belonged to the man playing the messenger part, not the man playing the king.[59] Demosthenes makes some snide remarks about a political opponent who once as third actor performed the opening speech of Creon in *Antigone*, the speech in question being a rather static piece of political rhetoric full of high sentiments.[60] The protagonist presumably played Antigone in the earlier part of the play, and then took over the role of Creon after Antigone's death, when Creon recognizes his errors, and song replaces speech as the dominant mode for expressing the character's feelings. In Creon's opening scene the second actor might well have regarded the semi-comic part of the guard as a more attractive role, leaving Creon to the luckless third actor. The division of Creon's part between two or three actors would have seemed an entirely natural procedure in the classical period, helping to mark the different emotional phases through which the character passes. The mask established Creon as a particular type of ruler rather than a unique individual, and any competent actor could impersonate the type. There would have been conventional ways of modifying the voice to signify youth and age, male and female, because there were shared assumptions about the physiological basis of age and gender distinctions, and voice was part of the bodily whole. The actor's skill lay not in building a character but in holding the audience, projecting emotions, and transmitting twists of thought.

In a modern performance, doubling can be used to create specific echoes. Purcarete, for example, doubled Agamemnon with Apollo,

defender of patriarchy, in his *Oresteia* of 1998. Mnouchkine used doubling more systematically, and the actors' physiques in her multi-ethnic company were unmistakable (see above, p. 88). In the classical theatre, although the bodies of the actors vanished behind the mask and himation, the emergence of an acting competition soon after the death of Aeschylus presupposes recognition by the audience. Perhaps doubling was used strategically in the patterned trilogies of Aeschylus, when the author still had control over casting. In the single plays of Euripides and Sophocles, the allocation of actors by the state, and the status of the actor as independent competitor, prompted a new awareness of the actor's skills. What came to matter was the creation of entirely diverse roles in three different tragedies. There was no competitive advantage for the actor in creating performances that were idiosyncratic, or characters that were other than types.

The doubling convention affected perceptions of aesthetic unity. It is not uncommon for a figure like Antigone to be the centre of tragic interest and then vanish from the play. In *The Persians* the Queen is replaced by her son (see above, p. 133). Herakles' wife kills herself in the course of Sophocles' *Women of Trachis*, allowing the protagonist to reappear as the dying Herakles. When Pentheus dies in *The Bacchae*, the protagonist is free to assume the role of Pentheus' mother Agave, who arrives with her son's head to perform a wild dance and poignant lament. When Phaedra dies, the protagonist probably assumed the role of her husband Theseus who arrives to discover the corpse. All these plays allowed the protagonist to demonstrate his versatility by playing contrasted male and female roles. The perform-ance is unified not through the way it traces the story of a single figure but through the way a single actor creates a build-up towards an emotional climax. In comedy, because of its looser structure, the rules were more relaxed. In *The Frogs*, when Dionysos adjudicates between Aeschylus and Euripides, a fourth speaking actor was permitted to play the god of the underworld, though Aristophanes avoids setting up a confusing four-way conversation. Aristophanes eliminates the engaging slave Xanthias so the actor is free to double as one of the playwrights. The doubling of Xanthias with Euripides would have clarified thematic links between the two halves of what appears to be a split play. Audiences accustomed to the Shake-spearean model, which brings all major characters together at the end, often find the disappearance of Xanthias a disappointment.

Song

One of the greatest difficulties when reading Greek plays in translation is to tell which parts of the text were spoken and which sung.
The protagonist who switched to the role of Xerxes, Creon,
Herakles, Agave or Theseus used the medium of song, supported by
the dance of the chorus, to bring the play to a powerful climax, yet
translators very rarely signal shifts of metre which tell us the actors
are singing and the aulos is playing.

Kenneth McLeish's translation of Sophocles' *Electra*, prepared for
the Royal Shakespeare Company in 1989, assumes that the whole
text will be spoken, and the language seemed well adapted to the
psychological self-exploration sought by the production.[61] Yet the
first ninety lines of Electra's part were actually written by Sophocles
to be sung. Fiona Shaw, who took the role of Electra, professed
herself terrified by the opening because the emotion was so direct
without any layer of irony. It is plainly the lack of music which
caused the actress this problem, which she could only overcome
through a courageous and remarkable process of self-exposure. If
Shaw's almost psychopathic Electra had burst into song when
Clytaemnestra was being killed, or when Orestes emerged bloodstained from the house, the production would have seemed tainted
by the falsity of high opera or the triviality of the musical. Modern
western culture has no tradition of collective female lamentation
that might have provided McLeish and Shaw with an appropriate
musical idiom. As Shaw remarks, 'in England there are no rituals
left except putting on the telly and making a cup of tea'.[62]

Timberlake Wertenbaker's translation of *Oedipus the King*, prepared
two years later for a more formalist production by the Royal
Shakespeare Company, does not homogenize the language but
rather creates a binary divide between sections marked 'chorus' and
sections marked 'episode'.[63] There are no pointers in Wertenbaker's
text to the two moments in Sophocles when chorus and actor come
together in accordance with the ancient function of actor as chorus
leader. The first of these moments occurs when the chorus use the
power of music to calm Oedipus after his confrontations with
Teiresias and Creon (lines 649–67, 678–96), changing the mood in
preparation for the devastating revelations of Jocasta. The second is
the climax when Oedipus appears at the door with bloodstained eye-
holes on his mask. A non-strophic lament covers the period of

Plate 17 Oedipus enters with a blindfold to signify bloodstained eyes, in a tableau modelled on the pediment of a temple. From the first production of a Greek play in the People's Republic of China: *Oedipus*, directed by Luo Jinlin & Du Haiou. Central Academy of Drama, Peking. 1986.

stillness while he stands in the doorway, and a choreographed strophic section covers his attempt to relate to the chorus. Wertenbaker heightens the language generally at this point in the play, but makes no distinction between the factual, spoken delivery of Sophocles' messenger and direct expressions of emotion which originally had the support of music and dance. Performance techniques at the disposal of the company did not allow them any means of flowing between the realism of spoken drama and the formalism of opera or ballet. Faced with Greek drama, but rooted in traditions of Shakespearean performance, the RSC appear to have only two options: to give the language a single texture, or create a binary division, almost an exercise in alienation technique, by dividing off the important spoken parts of the play from opaque choral 'interludes'.

When the actors sing strophic sections of text, it is obvious that the chorus participate as dancers, for there would otherwise be no possibility of creating the necessary visual repetition, and no purpose in giving strophic verses to bed-ridden invalids. The case is different with arias or monodies, virtuoso displays of song and movement by

individual actors. Monodies were a particular feature of the later plays of Euripides, as the parody in *The Frogs* makes clear. The finale of *Phoenician Women* offers a good example. The demure virgin Antigone casts off her veil, loosens her robes and engages in a Dionysiac dance, lamenting that not even a bird joins in with her. The character's isolation from the chorus, who are in any case foreigners, is the whole point of the monody. Antigone calls her ancient father from the house, as the music continues, describing the death of Jocasta not in the deadpan tones of a messenger but in the mode of song and dance which allows her to act out her narrative; the only role of the chorus is to call the dance to a final halt. The music starts again at the end, allowing Antigone and her father to simulate their long, solitary journey into exile. The convention of the monody offered new opportunities to the actor which later generations would exploit, but marked at the same time the separation of the individual from his or her roots in a collective culture. It may be no coincidence that Sophocles stayed in his community when the enemy started to close in, but Euripides fled north into exile.

CHAPTER 7

The writer

The emergence of the writer

The Greeks cannot be said to have invented theatrical performance; they do, however, seem to have invented the western playwright, the dramatic poet whose written output stands in its own right as creative work. The divorce between text and performance was a gradual process. Early Greek poets like Sappho, Alcman and Pindar composed words, music and dance for specific performance events, and the word *poet* simply meant 'maker'. Writing (without any markers of rhythm such as line and punctuation) existed to preserve the words alone, but the totality of words, music and dance were preserved into the classical period through memorization and reperformance. Of course, each reperformance would have modified the original, but the sense remained that Sappho or Pindar was the *maker* of a performance, not a set of words. This was the tradition into which Aeschylus and Sophocles stepped.

The dramatist had to go through the process of 'seeking a chorus' from the newly appointed magistrate, the *archon*. Plato speaks of poets 'demonstrating their songs to the archons'.[1] Although there was clearly no question of the archon taking a script away for silent reading, the writing process had become formally separate from the rehearsal process. In the course of time the writer withdrew from acting, and then passed the job of training the chorus to a specialist, whilst new competitive rules deprived him of the right to select his own actors. Continuity of the performance tradition was helped for a while by the tendency of dramatists, as in the Noh theatre, to pass their scripts and knowledge on to their sons. However, when the

state decided to revive plays by Aeschylus in the classical period, and plays of Euripides and Sophocles some twenty years after their deaths, the scripts entered the public domain. It was in the interests of actors competing for prizes to update their material. Aeschylus' *Seven Against Thebes*, for example, has come down to us with an added final scene; the play written as part three of a trilogy has been revamped to work as a free-standing piece. Fortunately for us, a law was passed in about the 330s BC to ensure that an official text would be kept in perpetuity to check against the scripts of the actors.[2] The scripts now became objects of respect, timeless, and separated entirely from the men who 'made' them.

Aristophanes' relationship to his text was rather different. His plays were probably written closer in time to the performance, since he only wrote one play per festival, and dealt with topical matters such as recent productions or the death of Euripides. He also seems to have kept more distance from the production process. As the voice of obscenity and personal insult, his role in Athenian society had a certain ambivalence. Vase painters , as we have seen, do not portray comic actors with their masks removed (see above, p. 136), and we hear only of tragic actors coming unmasked to the proagon (see above, p. 31). It seems that most of Aristophanes' plays were performed under the mask of anonymity.[3] His first three were directed by a man called Kallistratos, who was probably the leading actor.[4] Aristophanes' early plays pursue a vendetta against Cleon, and it was probably Kallistratos whom Cleon tried to prosecute for slandering Athens. In *Knights* Aristophanes seems to have abandoned his incognito, perhaps because his identity had become too well known, and his rival playwrights, Cratinus and Eupolis, promptly claimed that the play had actually been written by Eupolis.[5] Kallistratos later took responsibility for *Lysistrata* and a minor comic dramatist called Philonides directed at least four other plays of Aristophanes, while the last two went to Aristophanes' son. It is unclear how many comedies Aristophanes presented in his own name, and whether he ever performed in them. Tragedians wrote farcical satyr plays, but never comedies, because their role as teachers of the community was incompatible with the role of licensed slanderer and voice of obscenity.

An oral culture

Greek culture was predominantly oral in the classical period. The dramatists taught the roles to their actors face to face, with the correct intonations, movement and music, and there is no evidence that actors ever received a script. Memories were quick in a culture that did not rely on written records, whilst scripts were expensive to produce and clumsy to manipulate. In the original script of *Oedipus the King*, Jocasta's final exit would (if written in English) have looked something like this:

HURRYFETCHMETHEHERDSMANNOWLEAVEHERTOGLORYINHERROYAL
BIRTHAIEEEEEEMANOFAGONYTHATISTHEONLYNAMEIHAVEFORYOU
THATNOOTHEREVEREVEREVERWHERESSHEGONEOEDIPUSRUSHINGOFF
SUCHWILDGRIEF[6]

a convenient *aide-mémoire* for those who had seen the performance, but not a substitute for those who had not. The audience had no basis for conceptualizing the text as something separable from performance.

This was a culture that accorded low status to the written word. The teacher Alcidamas explained the principles of good public speaking as follows. Writing is easy, he says, because one has infinite time to think, but success in public depends on spontaneity and quick repartee. Many good writers do not know how to speak, but any good speaker can write. Speakers who read their speeches or memorize them word for word never manage to persuade an audience; a speech that is written may be admired as an 'imitation' or aesthetic object, but it does not convince.[7] There was a rather complex relationship between the art of public speaking and the art of performing plays. Aristotle approves the principle that language cast in verse should seem like a foreigner, someone who astonishes us, and remarks that Euripides was the first who attempted to conceal his poetic art. He compares Euripides' writing technique to the acting technique of Theodoros, a famous performer of Euripides' plays who created the illusion that in any role he spoke with his own personal voice.[8] Euripides, in other words, created the impression of spontaneity, just like a skilled speaker in a law court. This technique conflicted with the older assumption that the dramatist wrote a choral poem designed for a ritual context.

Plato, Aristotle and the critical tradition

In one of Plato's dialogues a youth reads out to Socrates a speech about love, and Plato uses the occasion to satirize the falsity of written language. Socrates explains to the youth that one cannot persuade a person of the truth without understanding their particular soul. The written word is inert, it cannot control who reads it, cannot distinguish appropriate from inappropriate readers, and cannot answer back when misunderstood.[9] Plato himself wrote in dialogue form to prevent any text from fixing definitive views of what he thought. When Plato writes about drama, he always thinks of it as a performance in a specific social and ritual context. Even when he writes about Homer, he (or his fictitious mouthpiece Socrates) discusses what the poet 'says', and the notion of speaking leads him directly into consideration of the voice and bodily movements that are part of Homer.[10]

Plato was an Athenian and grew up within the performance culture of the classical period, so it was natural that he should think of tragedy as a social practice. In the course of his youth, like other Athenians, he would have seen new plays, memorized some of the songs, dances and aphorisms, and absorbed theatrical performance as part of an Athenian way of life. When Aristotle came to Athens as a foreigner, it was equally inevitable that he should find in the written texts the real *Oedipus* and the real *Medea*, for the versions revived in the theatre of his day had been modified. One of his important contributions to theatre was to sort out the records of which play was performed by whom in which year, laying the foundations for theatre history.

Aristotle's *Poetics* is a set of lecture notes comparing tragedy and Homer as two classes of text. The book transmitted to the future a mode of reading and understanding Greek tragedy, and more importantly a mode of writing serious plays. A manual written in 1996 continues to advise would-be playwrights that Aristotle's 'blueprint for a play is as useful now as it was then'.[11] However, inspired by Brecht, Augusto Boal in 1974 mounted an influential attack on the politics of the Aristotelian tradition.[12] More recently, the playwright and translator Timberlake Wertenbaker addressed herself vigorously to an audience of playwrights on the subject of over-prescriptive criticism:

I think that the *Poetics* wrecked theatre for the next two thousand years. It's my own belief. I'm quite serious. There are few good plays by the Romans and it's not just because they were building lavatories. It's because they had all read Aristotle, and it had a deadening impact. And I think that what we are getting now . . . is a proliferation of Aristotles, and the reduction of playwriting. And I think this is the problem of the '90s.[13]

The aim of the *Poetics* is to define a *technê* (an 'art' or 'technique') of dramatic writing. skills. In Aristotle's various works which discuss performance, we find value judgements that would have made little sense in the classical period.

The seen is subordinate to what is heard. Of all the elements, Aristotle says, 'the visual inveigles the soul but is hardly a technê and belongs least to poetry. The power of tragedy is separate from the contest or the actors. The main responsibility for manufacturing the visual lies with the art of the property man and not with poets.' He adds that the plot should be constructed so it can arouse pity and fear in one who does not see the play but simply hears the story. Tragedy 'has its brilliance both in a reading and in a production'.[14]

Performance is subordinate to language, and it is basically a matter of instinct. 'No technê', says Aristotle, 'has yet been composed on performance, since even the study of language is recent, and performance is a vulgar affair, when rightly considered . . . but potent because of the baseness of the listener . . . To perform is in one's nature and is not a matter of technê – except in regard to the composition of words.' The lack of any analytic treatise on acting is explained by the fact that poets originally performed their own tragedies, so did not need to set down their techniques.[15]

Theatre and politics belong to separate worlds. Aristotle writes with approval of characters 'speaking politically' within tragedies, but only considers tragedy as a genre in relation to the pleasurable emotions felt by individual readers or spectators. In his *Politics* he distinguishes the elite from manual workers with warped souls, and argues that public performance debases the performer, who corrupts his own mind and body through seeking to please the vulgar spectator. Aristotle concedes that appropriate performances should be provided in the theatre for these manual workers. He states disdainfully that theatre in this case may be considered an extension of music, and that the corruption of traditional musical forms must be tolerated.[16]

Aristotle's dislike of performance and isolation of the written text from its performance context is bound up with his deep dislike of the Athenian democratic system. The theatre of words was for the elite, the theatre of sound and spectacle for the masses. It was part and parcel of Aristotle's elitist thinking to identify a certain type of script as the aesthetic ideal.

Transmission

The rolls of papyrus on which the first scripts were written were manufactured from reeds that grew in the Nile, and it was in Alexandria on the mouth of the Nile that the world's greatest library was established in the early 300s BC. The librarians secured by dubious means the official Athenian script, and embarked on the task of editing and annotating the works of the great Athenian dramatists. Whilst Greek actors in the Roman period concentrated on performing extracts, particularly musical numbers from Euripides, scholars in Egypt set up literary scholarship as an independent exercise. Over the centuries a certain social cachet became attached to the Greek once spoken in classical Athens, and the study of classic texts entered the educational system. Seven plays by Aeschylus, seven by Sophocles and ten by Euripides were bound up in book form and widely circulated, and our knowledge of Greek drama is thus largely based on the literary tastes of the second century AD. The eleven surviving plays of Aristophanes also reflect the choice of this period. Happily we have a better perspective on Euripides because of the chance survival of a volume of his complete works (titles E–K), together with many fragments of papyrus that reveal his popularity in the later Greek world.

How far we would agree today with the taste of the second century AD is largely unknowable. It is clear from *The Frogs* that Aeschylus, Sophocles and Euripides were already recognized as the great three in the classical period – though there is little correlation between the plays most often quoted and the ten that were later selected. The 'alphabetic' plays of Euripides – texts like *Ion* and *Herakles' Children* – tend to be much more specific in their reference to an Athenian context, and the selected plays must in part have been chosen because they can be read as universal stories. Our access to ancient theatre has been mediated before we can ever begin to study it. Our reading of *The Oresteia* is irrevocably affected by the fact that the satyr

play, the fourth part of the whole, was not thought worthy of preservation, and it is only thanks to the alphabetic collection of Euripides that one satyr play, *The Cyclops* (*Kyklôps*) has come down to us. We have no means of evaluating the view of later antiquity that original texts written after the classical period were greatly inferior. It is now generally held that *Rhesus*, included among the ten selected plays of Euripides is (a) written by a later dramatist, and (b) a good yarn with little moral substance – but an unfortunate circularity enters the argument about dating here. The comedies of Menander, who wrote between 321 BC and 292 BC offer a better control. These adhere rigorously to Aristotelian rules of dramatic construction, with the chorus reduced to the status of musical interlude, and they represent individuals as victims of rather than potential makers of a sociopolitical system. There is no obvious reason to reject the ancient view that the classical period was a golden age of playwriting, whilst the following century was the golden age of the actor. Everything was new in the classical period: the audience was in the process of building a political system, and the playwrights were exploring and developing a new medium. Within this new medium, the writing process was not cut off from the performance process. Aeschylus and Sophocles were actors just like Shakespeare and Molière.

THE WRITERS

The career of dramatist

We know rather little about the men who wrote Greek plays, since the biographies that have come down to us consist largely of fanciful anecdotes and humourless inferences based on jokes in comedy.[17] At the risk of stating the obvious, it is worth noting first of all that the Greek dramatists wrote masterpieces at an age when the average Renaissance writer was in his grave. Aeschylus was about sixty-six when he wrote *The Oresteia*, Euripides about seventy-four when he wrote *The Bacchae*, and Sophocles probably ninety when he wrote *Oedipus at Colonus*. Athens was a culture that placed a premium on care of the body, and the major centre for philosophical discussion was the gymnasium. The history of Greek theatre must be understood as the history of bodies, not as the history of words emanating from great but disembodied minds.

The Greek dramatists were not 'artists' living on the Bohemian

fringe of society; there was indeed no term in the Greek language to isolate 'the arts' from other activities of a political and ritual nature. To write was to engage publicly in shaping the past, present and future of the community. Though Aeschylus undertook a commission in Sicily and Euripides in Macedonia, the plays we possess were written for Athens,[18] and the lives of the four authors were shaped by the fact that they were Athenians. This meant that they had to risk their lives for their city. We hear of Aeschylus fighting the Persians at Marathon and Salamis; Sophocles was twice elected as general, and was involved in putting down a major revolt in Samos. The dramatists had to contribute their wealth in acts of public service like putting on plays, and we hear of Euripides going to court because of such an obligation. The holding of public offices was sometimes voluntary, sometimes compulsory; Sophocles was chosen, probably by election, as treasurer of revenues from the empire. The dramatists had also to participate in the rituals of the city. As a beautiful adolescent boy, Sophocles is supposed to have been chosen, because of his noble birth and excellent musical education, to lead the chorus in the victory celebrations after the battle of Salamis, keeping the chorus in time by playing his lyre. Some accounts said that he wore his himation, others that he danced naked.[19] Like Sophocles in this story (which suggests the kind of activity later Greeks thought plausible), Euripides also is supposed to have been involved in a cult of Apollo, bearing a torch and pouring libations.[20] The negative treatment of Apollo in many of Euripides' plays needs to be seen in the context of such public demonstrations of piety. These chance biographical details indicate why there was no perceived separation between the public and private, political and artistic lives of dramatists.

We can calculate from their total output that each of the three tragedians normally completed a tetralogy of plays every alternate year. One year would thus be given over to writing, the next to directing the newly completed work. They obviously wrote in confidence that their plays would be accepted – though a comic playwright complains about one occasion when Sophocles was turned down.[21] The Lenaian festival in January would have been an occasion when newcomers could try out a pair of tragedies, and seek to enter the system. Aristophanes averaged one play a year, but his work could be seen either at the great Dionysia or at the Lenaian festival two months earlier, and sometimes he wrote for both.

The writers of Greek theatre enjoyed an unusually close relation-ship with their audience. The same politically active members of the male citizen community came in huge numbers to every festival and followed the work of the dramatists over a long period (see above, p. 93). By parodying tragedy and constructing caricature personas for writers, comedy increased the level of audience involvement. The exceptional quality of dramatic writing in the classical period owes more to these social conditions than to an accident of the gene pool. The playwrights wrote complex plays because they had an audience capable of complex viewing. Outside the theatre, the playwrights, performers and spectators were caught up in the same collective emotions, the same moral dilemmas, the same responsibility of decision-making.

Whilst Athens may be described as a community, that community was always a fractured one, and the dramatists were members of the small elite which in practice captained ships and took the rostrum in the assembly. Sophocles served as general alongside two of the greatest statesmen of the age, Pericles and Nikias, and Aeschylus is said to have been of ancient family. Plato in his *Symposium* pictures an exclusive dinner party thrown by the young tragedian Agathon to celebrate his victory in the Lenaia, with guests including Aristophanes and the charismatic military and political leader Alcibiades. Coteries of this kind made radical democrats suspicious. We cannot therefore sidestep the question of whether the plays embody an elitist view-point. At the time of Aeschylus' *Eumenides*, the ugly political divide in Athens was symbolized by the assassination of the democratic leader responsible for the reform of the aristocratic Areopagus (see above, p. 58). How explicitly Aeschylus presents himself in his text as a pro-democrat in favour of the reform has prompted much critical debate, leading to no firm conclusion. All we can say with confidence is that, in a festival which belonged to the whole community, the tragic dramatist was obliged to articulate divergent views in a manner that allowed for divergent interpretations. It was easier in classical Athens to offer partisan opinions under cover of laughter. The argument that Aristophanes in his vendetta against Cleon represented the views of the landowning classes (including peasantry) is relatively persuasive. Cleon is the butt of the comedy and he clearly did represent the interests of the urban poor who gained most from policies of imperial expansion. Aristophanes could attack Cleon provided he made enough of Cleon's supporters laugh (see above, p. 60).

Sophocles and the dictatorship

To judge from Aristophanes, Euripides was a more controversial figure than Sophocles. Unfortunately, the historical Euripides rapidly became obscured by a mythical persona. In later times, visitors to the island of Salamis were able to inspect the miserable cave in which a misanthropic Euripides was supposed to have composed his plays.[22] Sophocles in his lifetime won at least eighteen victories at the Dionysia, as against four for Euripides, which seems to confirm that Sophocles was respected, Euripides loved for being outrageous. However, Sophocles' career began in political controversy. As a young man he vanquished Aeschylus at the Dionysia thanks to a political fix. The voting was transferred from a panel of common citizens to the panel of generals, dominated by the controversial and conservative figure of Kimon.[23] Sophocles was a politically active figure throughout his career, and information about the last years of his life gives us a glimpse of the interface between life and art in the classical period. Though it is no longer the critical fashion to seek out the 'intention' of a playwright beneath the ironies and multiple voices of a play, the attempt still has to be made if we are to understand how writing functioned as a social practice within a social context.

In 413 BC the Athenians lost an enormous number of men and ships in their failed assault on Syracuse. The Spartans had an occupying force installed in Athenian territory, and received money from the king of Persia. The empire was starting to disintegrate, and everyone expected a combined attack on Athens. The democrats had lost all credibility because of the disastrous decision to invade Sicily. In this dire emergency changes to the democratic system seemed necessary – to save expenditure, to mollify the Persians and to produce a better decision-making structure. A committee of ten elder statesmen was elected to decide on appropriate measures, and one member was Sophocles. His age made him a living link to the heroic days of Salamis, and his plays had earned him respect as a man of wisdom. It was in Sophocles' own deme of Colonus, the site of a shrine sacred to the aristocratic Knights, that a coup took place, with the support of the committee, and power passed effectively to a clique of 400 men. These men implemented a rule of terror, until a rebellion in the navy forced them out, and members of the regime were executed, exiled or deprived of their civil rights. Aristotle

records an exchange which took place between Sophocles and the leader of the dictatorship:

Asked if he, like the rest of the Committee, approved the setting up of the
Four Hundred, Sophocles said 'yes'.
'Why? Did you not think it was shoddy?'
'Yes,' he said.
'So were you not doing a shoddy deed?'
'Yes,' he said. 'There was no better alternative.'[24]

Tragedies frequently portray powerful men choosing between the lesser of two evils, and Sophocles wrote about such experiences from a position of personal knowledge.

Sophocles became not only a political elder statesman but also a religious leader. He held a priesthood related to Asclepius, god of healing, and was in some way involved in admitting the sacred serpent of the god to Athens a few years before the coup.[25] After his death a cult was set up to venerate him as the 'Receiver' of the god. It says something about the cult of Asclepius that his shrine abutted the theatre, and one of his major festivals coincided with the proagon before the Dionysia. Sophocles' association with the god of healing relates in rather obvious ways to his last two plays.

Philoctetes was presumably being written as the dictatorship crumbled, and it was performed in 409 BC when the new democratic regime was engaged in reprisals. It is a play about healing, both medical and social. Philoctetes has been abandoned on the island of Lemnos (where Sophocles himself once dumped a boat-load of hostages) because he is suffering from a festering snakebite. The Greeks cannot take Troy without the help of Philoctetes and his magical bow, so Odysseus and the young son of Achilles try to persuade or trick him into forgiveness. They want him to come to Troy to receive medical attention and bring about the fall of the city. In the context of 409 BC, the unwinnable war against Troy was a metaphor for the war against Sparta. A celebrated production in 1990, adapted by the poet Seamus Heaney, interpreted *Philoctetes* in terms of Northern Ireland.[26] The intransigent Philoctetes could be seen as a metaphor either for the republican cause or for the Ulsterman endlessly saying 'no' to compromise, and Heaney's strategy as the voice of reconciliation was to leave this ambiguity open. Likewise in the conditions of 409 BC Philoctetes could either stand for the ousted elite whose military skills were needed by the democracy, or for common democrats who needed to be brought

back into the political community. Sophocles' devotion to the god of healing is plainly relevant to his purpose as a playwright. It has also been suggested that Philoctetes stood for Sophocles himself, a man who felt he had been betrayed by his peers on the committee, but this autobiographical interpretation risks limiting the complexities of the play.[27]

The social divisions of Athens were far from healed when Sophocles wrote *Oedipus at Colonus* in 407/6 BC. In this play the body of the aged Oedipus vanishes at Colonus a few miles outside the walls of Athens, bestowing magical protection upon the city. The setting of the play in Sophocles' own deme of Colonus would have offered a much more direct encouragement to the audience to project on to the central character the person of the dramatist, whose own death was imminent. Sophocles in 407/6 BC would have been painfully aware that he might never be buried out in the countryside with his ancestors because of the Spartan occupation.[28] He boldly set his play in the cult centre of the elite group of Knights, the place where the dictatorship of the 400 had been established, and idealized the place as a symbol of spring and harmony. The equilibrium set up in the text between horses (symbol of the Knights) and ships (the democratic power-base) shows that he was again concerned with healing divisions.[29] Aristophanes states explicitly in *The Frogs* (performed in 405) that the elite must be given back their civic rights for the sake of unity, and Sophocles urges reconciliation in much the same way, evoking his own accumulated charisma in order to reinforce his message.

The writing process

In Aristophanes' *Women at the Thesmophoria* the aged Euripides goes to visit the young Agathon, who is engaged in the act of composition, and the scene introduces us to Greek thinking about the creative process. First comes the idea of writing as a craft. A song by Agathon's servant likens the playwright to a shipwright: setting up supports, bending the verbal framework, gluing songs together, stamping aphorisms, changing terms, making the joins watertight.[30] The servant goes on to explain how Agathon is now softening his strophes by exposing them to the sun so he can bend them into shape. Creating the symmetry of strophe and antistrophe was probably the most technically demanding task faced by a dramatist,

and the skill was an ancient one. What Aristophanes offers us in this parody is the materialist explanation of creative writing. Words have substance, and the poet is their 'maker'. The writer is not concerned with producing original ideas but with reshaping a series of formal elements. The same material view of words is found in *The Frogs*, where extracts of Aeschylus are weighed and found heavier than those of Euripides.

The shapeless strophes of Agathon are duly exposed when the playwright is wheeled out on the eccyclema, breastless but dressed as a woman, singing alternately the parts of chorus-leader and chorus of Trojan women. In this costume he was a visual reminder of Dionysos, as portrayed in a play by Aeschylus. Agathon/Dionysos is surrounded by musical instruments and the costumes and props of both men and women, but there is no indication that writing materials are involved in the creative process. Much of the humour turns on Agathon's effeminacy, based on the premise that Agathon needs to experience the life of a woman in order to write a woman's part. Through Aristophanes' humour we see a gap opening between the old concept, that the playwright devises material for himself to perform, and the new concept that the poet writes words which are entirely separate from his own physical person and belong to actors. The absence of writing materials is part of the comic time warp in this scene. In *The Frogs*, Dionysos declares that he was 'reading' a play by Euripides, a play about the need for rescue when on board ship at the recent desperate battle of Arginusae.[31] This fantasy points the way to the future, with the work of the dead dramatist reduced to reading-matter for the leisured classes.

Aristotle ventures a few remarks about the creative process. His premise is that the poet should in the first instance be a maker of storylines and not verses, attaching to the story language and movements. Aristotle writes also of how the key tragic emotion of pity is aroused in an audience when the writer attaches movement, voice, costume and acting to make the story more immediate.[32] He assumes, in other words, a separation of content and dramatic form. The implications of the Aristotelian method are clear in a story told about the later playwright Menander. Asked if he had finished his comedy for the Dionysia, Menander replied: 'Yes indeed, I have finished the comedy. The plot has been worked out. I have only to add the accompaniment of the verses.'[33]

In the classical period a new attitude to language slowly emerges.

Aristophanes develops at length in *The Frogs* a contest between the bombastic or noble language of Aeschylus and the trivial or democratic language of Euripides. In Aeschylus, words had texture; their sound and rhythm were as important as their meaning. In Clytaemnestra's first speech in *Agamemnon*, for example, she describes a flame racing from one beacon to the next to bring news from Troy. Take away the evocative names of the mountains and the energetic rhythm of the speech and Clytaemnestra's character becomes inert, the speech becomes empty. Euripides anticipates Menander in using an everyday language that calls little attention to itself, so that words seem transparent, and the content seems distinct from the familiar dramatic form. The change had important implications for actors like Theodoros. The power of the actor's personal presence became less important than his ability to create, like Agathon with his feminine props, the illusion of being someone else.

Plato presents with cutting irony the traditionalist view of Homer as the blind mouthpiece of Apollo. The rhapsode is asked an impossible question: is he a man of skill, or does he just transmit a magnetic charge from the gods?[34] Aristotle too examines the nature of inspiration. 'Poetry must be created by talent or by a maniac', he says. 'The first type have adaptability, the second are in ecstatic trance.'[35] Both Plato and Aristotle were committed to the view that art was a form of mimesis or 'imitation', understanding the artist as a skilled copyist, and repudiating the idea of the visionary possessed by a god. Aristotle compares two forms of mimesis when he reports Sophocles' claim to have created people as they ought to be whilst Euripides created them as they are. Missing as usual from this comparison is the figure of Aeschylus, and the theory of mimesis in the *Poetics* fails conspicuously to deal with Aeschylean theatre. Aristotle ponders how one 'imitates' the gods and advances the rationalist theory that the gods are constructed by humans in human likeness.[36] It would be rash to assume that such thinking represents the norm in the classical period. Sophocles' role as priest, and the way he was venerated after his death, suggest some kind of recognized relationship between inspired poets and the gods. When Aristophanes brings on Agathon in the image of Dionysos, the joke is a pointed one. The poet was once the teacher of his community, a position reinforced by his association with the gods. Now he is nothing but a writer, a mere copyist of reality.

CHAPTER 8

Reception

REVIVING GREEK TRAGEDY

Oedipus in 1585

We can only understand what Greek theatre was like in the past by looking through the eyes of the present. Conversely, our view of the present is shaped by the past, thanks to assumptions about 'theatre' that we have inherited. An objective view of the ancient world is impossible. However, by seeing how different generations have reinterpreted Greek tragedy, we can gain some sort of perspective on the complex relationship of past and present. Most directors who engage with Greek drama feel (a) that they have touched on something *authentically* Greek which is worth bringing to the present, and (b) that there is something in the present which they would like to bring to the ancient text. The element of *authenticity* keeps shifting: the circular auditorium, the use of the mask, uncensored Aristophanic obscenity, the message about war. What seems authentic to one generation seems stilted, ill-researched and irrelevant to the next. I shall concentrate on three well documented productions in order to illustrate the way the past is constantly being rediscovered, and clarify some major issues facing anyone who stages a Greek play today.

The plays of Sophocles and Aeschylus, long lost to the western world, were brought from Constantinople to Venice in 1423. In 1585, in the Venetian town of Vicenza, on the Sunday before Lent, the first Greek tragedy was performed in modern translation.[1] The occasion was the grand opening of a classical theatre, built in accordance with the writings of the Roman architect Vitruvius. The director of the production consulted, amongst other sources, the late Greek dictionary by Pollux on choreography, the Roman orator

179

Quintilian on acting, and the Roman poet Horace on dramatic structure. The major inspiration, however, came from Aristotle's *Poetics*. *Oedipus the King* was the chosen play because Aristotle identified it as the most perfect of tragedies. The Aristotelian approach to Greek tragedy implied a preoccupation with the emotions, in particular pity and horror, and the director was interested in how the actor's voice could be modulated to play the full emotional repertoire.

The director did not aim at authenticity in everything. The costumes were of a mixed ancient and modern style, and the most important design decision was the rejection of masks. Masks were widely worn in this period by gentry seeking anonymity at carnival time, and by mountebanks and comic actors, but they could not be reconciled with the spirit of tragedy. Feeling that masks would create 'talking statues',[2] the director followed the advice of classical orators rather than the practice of classical actors, and relied upon the face in order to transmit the desired emotions. The use of the face caused a particular problem with the character of Jocasta. Although the director had envisaged a woman of about fifty-five alongside her son/husband of some thirty-five years old, when it came to casting, the role was given to a younger woman of striking beauty; her performance was duly admired, but the problem was noted that she was much too young to be Oedipus' mother.[3] In the Greek theatre masks of middle-aged women were unlined and relatively ageless, and this issue of plausibility would never have been raised. The Renaissance desire to create a realist visual image caused a similar problem with costuming. The splendour and wealth of the courtly display seemed incompatible with the plight of a city gripped by plague. The author of a long and poisonous critique of the production also complained about the translation, which seemed to him too informal. It was not realistic, he pointed out, that people speaking everyday language should talk loudly enough to be over-heard by an audience. This is, of course, the fundamental problem of naturalism. We see why Italians came to prefer the theory that Greek tragedies were chanted from start to finish, a theory which fostered the development of Italian opera.

Aristotle pointedly ignores the chorus along with the whole civic dimension of Greek theatre, and he seems to value *Oedipus* so highly because of the single tragic hero who unifies the story. The director in 1585 duly explained that the pity and horror of the play stem

Figure 19 The opening scene of *Oedipus the King* in 1585 (from a fresco in the theatre at *Vicenza*).

exclusively from the character of Oedipus, who should be a fine figure of a man: 'The nobility of his aspect is caused by his noble blood, but far more by his innermost soul.'[4] In plague-ridden Athens it would have been natural to see the city as the emotional focus, but in Vicenza there was to be no representation of the suffering masses. This was a play about a hero. The director kept the common men of the chorus on stage throughout so that their emotions could relate to what they had witnessed, but they were only allowed them to sing their madrigals when they had the stage completely to themselves, creating musical breaks in what became a five-act drama. The sung interchange with Oedipus and the lament when Oedipus appears blinded were both spoken (see above, p. 162), and all spoken sections of chorus were allocated to the coryphaeus, who appeared to be of higher social status and thus able to talk to a king. Though there was no attempt to make the chorus dance, the mixing of unaccompanied voices shows that every effort was made to render the text comprehensible. The priority of the text was an Aristotelian principle.

The performance of 1585 was mounted by and for the aristocracy. The performers were gentlemen amateurs, the translator was a member of the Venetian senate, and the audience were aristocrats drawn from a wide area. The theatre was built and the performance mounted by the Olympian Academy, a club of upper-class intellectuals. The mayor of the town did not attend, and the poisonous review was obviously written for his delectation. Though Renaissance Italy was dominated by hereditary dukes, in Venice the aristocracy elected its head of state, and this egalitarian tradition amongst the elite explains why a democratic classical auditorium could be built, with no hierarchical division of the seating. The theatre itself is a remarkable hybrid. The famous architect, Palladio, a member of the Academy, designed the building, which gave everyone an equal view of the stage. He died before completion, and his successor, Scamozzi, built three-dimensional sets behind the five doorways, using the latest Renaissance techniques including hidden lighting to create the illusion of perspective. From most parts of the house one had a view through one of the doorways, but the idea was not altogether successful because actors walking through these sets destroyed the illusion of perspective. The theatre embodies a contradiction between the classical principle of collective viewing and the Renaissance principle that space should be organized in

relation to a single eye. Scamozzi quickly went on to design a second 'Olympian Theatre' in Sabbioneta, a town built as a pastiche of ancient Rome. In Sabbioneta the duke had a walkway from his house to the centre of the balcony, from which point he had an optimum view of the perspective, and a gangway allowed him to descend to dance in the orchestra. In the baroque period, the ideal of Roman imperialism quickly obliterated all thought of democratic Greece. Back in Vicenza, the theatre became a fossil, its temporary set preserved indefinitely, and it was rarely used again for theatre performance until the twentieth century.[5] The idea of performing Greek plays authentically was suspended until the French revolution created in Europe a new political environment.

Prometheus in 1927

My second case-study is the production of Aeschylus' *Prometheus* directed by Eva Palmer-Sikelianos in the ancient theatre of Delphi. Eva Palmer was a wealthy American who married the young Greek poet Anghelos Sikelianos, and together they conceived the dream of a spiritual university in Delphi. This was in one sense a political scheme. They were dismayed by the failure of the League of Nations, the rise of fascism in Italy and the plight of Greek refugees in Turkey, and they wanted to make Delphi once again a place that transcended national divisions. Central to their vision was the power of theatre to unite an audience in a single emotion. Theatre was seen as the total art form which 'harmonizes all the faculties of man, Poetry, Music, Dancing, Acting, Architecture, Painting, Sculpture.'[6] The academicians of 1585 enclosed their Greek play within four walls, isolating art from the streets of Vicenza, but Eva and her husband rejected Aristotle's way of dividing life into compartments. For them, the play belonged to a bigger whole: a festival in the short term, and an international institution thereafter. The festival included a banquet with folk music and an exhibition of folk art to signal links between ancient Greece and pre-industrial Greek culture. In the ancient stadium they organized classical military dancing and a competition in the pentathlon. The festival ended with a ritual performance, based on Delphic tradition, in which Apollo killed the sacred python with his bow. An American woman and her Greek husband played the roles of serpent and Apollo. Eva interpreted the python as Dionysos, and, having recently collabo-

Plate 18   *Prometheus*: 1927.

rated with a female musicologist from India, she wanted the performer to find a style drawn from oriental dancing.[7]

The tension between these two principles – the woman, the foreigner and the Dionysiac versus the male, the Greek and the Apolline – is a key to Eva's understanding of Greek tragedy, and indeed a key to her own role as a female director in patriarchal Greece. The major intellectual influence on her work was Nietzsche's *The Birth of Tragedy out of the Spirit of Music*, published in 1872 as a manifesto for the music-drama of Wagner. The book anticipates Artaud's *The Theatre and its Double* in its passionate rejection of language-based theatre and its romantic celebration of collective emotion. Nietzsche saw Greek tragedy as the marriage of Dionysos and Apollo, and gave new status to the chorus as the embodiment of the collective Dionysian principle.

Where Aristotle admired Sophocles, Nietzsche preferred Aeschylus, and in particular *Prometheus*. Aeschylus' play depicts the Titan Prometheus pinned to a rock so Zeus can punish him for giving humankind the gift of fire, symbol of enlightenment. Prometheus is visited by the innocent daughters of Ocean, and by the experienced Io, a woman with the head of a cow fleeing Zeus the rapist. Nietzsche saw Prometheus as an embodiment of Apollo in his rational desire for justice, but also as 'a Dionysiac mask'. In the 1920s *Prometheus* was considered among the greatest Greek tragedies, and it was indeed the only Greek tragedy attempted by Stanislavski, though his methods proved inadequate and he eventually abandoned the project.[8] In the late twentieth century, no longer an age of revolution, the play has been increasingly marginalized. Changing historical tastes have fostered scholarly doubts about Aeschylus' authorship of the play.[9]

The production placed Prometheus high on an artificial mountain, his hands splayed like Christ on the cross to create a figure of universal myth: part Christ, part Dionysos, part Titan and part human rebel, a figure awaiting the chance to redeem and regenerate humankind. Prometheus also represented Aeschylus himself, interpreted as the artist from Eleusis, home of Athenian mystery religions, the artist who endured a kind of crucifixion when the Athenians turned to Sophocles.[10] The decision to give masks to the actors and set them at a distance helped bond the audience to the chorus. A French critic reports that the most emotional effects were created by the female chorus, whose tender expressions of pity spread a feeling of gentleness through the packed amphitheatre.[11] The production in one sense reproduced the support relationship that Eva offered her husband the poet, but it did succeed in turning the female chorus into the central character. In contrast to the Nietzschean productions of Reinhardt, Eva's was a feminine vision of the Greek world.

Coming to Greek tragedy as a dancer, Eva saw Greek theatre not as an extension of the text but as an extension of the body. She may have known about Appia's Swiss production of *Prometheus* in 1925, with the chorus interpreted by students of eurhythmics, a system for tying music to movement.[12] An important influence was Isadora Duncan, whose dancing was driven by the Greek ideal. Eva was devoted to Anghelos' sister, who was married to Isadora's brother. But though she admired Isadora, Eva regretted Isadora's failure to realize socialist ideals by moving from solo performance to success

with a chorus (see above, p. 100). Eva's understanding of Greece as a world where body and mind were in harmony accounts for her revival of Greek athletics, and her passion for Greek costume. Hostile to mass production, she wove the costumes for her plays on traditional looms, so costume became an overt ideological statement. Eva's failure ever to recruit a male chorus indicates how far her approach to Greek theatre was related to being a woman. Gender was central to the Sikelianos project, for Anghelos believed that the maternal principle had been distorted by the artificial masculinity of scientific and industrial society. Though *Prometheus* celebrates a male superhero, Nietzsche saw in the play a radical pagan alternative to the Jewish–Christian creation myth of Adam and Eve.[13] The woman in *Prometheus* is not the corrupter of the male but his victim.

Though the body was central to her thinking, Eva was not anti text. Despite her admiration for Nietzsche, she regarded Wagner as 'an unsurpassed torment in the history of tragic art' because of the way he combined voices with a full western orchestra.[14] She knew that Greek drama used only the aulos, and she had experienced the natural music found in the laments of a Greek peasant. Knowing how the chanting of Orthodox monks clarifies the words, and believing that there must be continuity between ancient and liturgical Greek traditions, she turned to a specialist in church music. Alas, when it came to performance, her professor insisted on burdening the production with a full hidden orchestra, and it was only in the revival of 1930 that she was able to achieve simplicity, with a few musicians placed where they could see the dancers. While Nietzsche as a German wanted to push tragedy in the direction of Beethoven, Eva insisted that the music of the play should be found within the language of Aeschylus, and not imposed.

The production of 1927 reclaimed ruined Greek theatres as the natural place in which to perform Greek plays, inspiring the festivals that take place today in Delphi, Epidaurus, Syracuse and elsewhere. Place became a component of theatrical meaning. At the Delphic shrine which Apollo shared with Dionysos, where the nations of Greece once came together to seek wisdom, it was easy for the performance space to seem sacred, and Greek tragedy which once celebrated Athens now started to celebrate the nation-state of Greece. The production also began to uncover an aesthetic of open-air performance, as Eva discovered how voice and movement expanded in response to the environment (see above, p. 113). She

Plate 19 Io the cow-woman pursued by Zeus in the 1927 *Prometheus.*

also reintroduced the convention of the mask. In England at this time, Terence Gray was starting to use expressionist masks in dance-based productions of Aeschylus, but in a 400-seat theatre with stage lighting it was inevitable that Gray's masks should function in a different way.[15] In Delphi the masks called no attention to themselves, and were merely simplified faces.

Wilhelm Dörpfeld, who found the evidence for a primitive

dancing circle in Athens (see above, p. 100), lectured in the theatre on the second day of the festival. The circle had great symbolic importance for the Sikelianos couple in relation to their holistic view of the world, and their idea that Delphi should again become the world's centre. The masked actors played on a raised area behind the circle, and Nietzsche's theory that the Greek stage represented a kind of Apollo mask, a vision of light thrown up by the chorus like an image thrown on to a screen,[16] helps explain the Hollywood over-tones of the artificial mountain. The circle derived from a peasant threshing floor was thought to be the essence of the Greek theatre, and Eva wrote enthusiastically of how the 'concentration of attention in a circular form, around action which includes meaning, melody and rhythm, generates magnetic currents which are totally unknown wherever the audience is spatially divided from the stage'. The circular form, she went on, dissolves enmities and fears, and creates the sweeping emotion that is the 'be-all and end-all of Theatre'.[17]

Commitment to the circle was bound up with the idea that Greek theatre was a ritual, a cosmic liturgy. The choreography was based on movements around the circle, and there was no bunching in a mass. Eva wanted each member to be conscious both of general harmony and of her own soul. She also wanted to avoid the vulgarity of commercial theatre, with its cult of character, its direct appeal to the spectators and its two-dimensional resemblance to cinema. The Broadway musical, she felt, did nothing but 'tickle them with infectious imbecility'.[18] The chorus members therefore presented themselves in profile so that the audience would look down on women privately worshipping Dionysos, and become part of a greater unity. Masks prevented the actors playing to the gallery, and enhanced the sense of 'unity realized outside of themselves'. Eva criticized Isadora Duncan for playing frontally to the audience instead of turning her head aside in the manner of archaic Greek art.[19] Beneath these remarks, we sense a tension between the assumed demands of ritual and the instinctual demands of theatricality.

It was a common notion at the time that classical Greek dances could be reconstructed from vase paintings and sculptures.[20] Eva followed Isadora and Isadora's more uncompromising brother in recreating movements from Greek images. She felt that her own originality lay in challenging a widespread 'disbelief in the possibility of the human organism doing more than one thing at once', in other words both singing and dancing.[21] In Greek folk dance, she claimed,

this double ability survived, and the Greek peasantry thus provided Eva with her second source of authenticity. She felt that the most powerful performance was not the one given to tourists and intellectuals, but the second given to a huge audience of villagers. Like Reinhardt, she believed that Greek theatre required the right social relationships as well as the right spatial relationships. The search for the true Greek theatre is thus a highly complex one in Eva's work, embracing psychological, social, material and spatial aspects. In his speech after the performance, Anghelos described the venture not as a 'return' to the past but as a 'resurrection'.[22] Eva records her response to a sceptical German archaeologist unexpectedly impressed by the insights of the production: 'it was emotionally true, or almost true – and that was sufficient to make even you feel that it was correct archaeologically. But there is no such thing as archaeological correctness. There is nothing in Greek drama except the emotional truth and consistency of the performers, and the immense responding emotion of those who are present.'[23] She recognized that the goal of what we might term 'archaeological' productions, the goal of recreating the past for its own sake, is doomed to failure; the only useful and intellectually valid activity is to create a performance that engages an audience in the present.

Eva Palmer-Sikelianos attempted to buck the economic logic of the twentieth century, the logic which decrees that theatre-going is as an activity undertaken in the evening by affluent urban couples. She sank her fortune in the production, paying for all tickets and transport, and incurred debts she could not repay. The art collector Antoine Benaki sponsored a revival in 1930, but the relationship ended because he was only interested in plays as art and not in the Delphic project as a whole. Sponsorship from the Greek government was considered unacceptable. Though Eva became a Greek folk heroine, her resurrection of Greek theatre in the context of a religio-political festival was doomed to go no further; it was only the notion of a *theatre* festival that survived. The search to understand Greek theatre as a medium of the body continues.

Electra in 1986 (1966, 1971)

My final case-study is a production of Sophocles' *Electra* by the French director Antoine Vitez. Vitez had already directed the play twice when he undertook it again in 1986 as artistic director of the

large Théâtre National de Chaillot in Paris, and his three versions allow us to trace a path, however rudimentary, through the post-war period. Vitez translated the play himself, and his proposition that 'the director is the ultimate translator' is an important contribution to the theory of translation.[24] Vitez' devotion to the classic text is broadly representative of post-war 'director's theatre', which requires the director to assert his or her dominant role in the creative process by setting up a dialogue between some well-known text and a new directorial interpretation. The spatial and other formal conventions of Greek theatre were of no interest to Vitez: all that mattered to him were the 'traces' of the past that could be found in the written text. He saw his productions as a kind of rewriting.

As a Marxist, Vitez was interested in the political rather than spiritual dimension of Greek tragedy. From Meyerhold and Brecht, he derived the notion that the text should be defamiliarized and made to seem strange, both modern and ancient at the same time. The productions in Vicenza and Delphi were concerned to stress continuity, and draw moral sustenance from the classical roots of European culture, but for Vitez it was the differentness of the ancient world that needed to be emphasized. Though passionate about writing, Vitez also taught in Lecoq's school of acting. He wanted to distance himself from the pseudo-classical plays of Racine, and to find an acting style rooted in the body, not in the speaking of verse. English theatre is not burdened like French theatre by a neoclassical tradition, but Peter Hall's *Oedipus Plays* illustrate the danger when Greek theatre is interpreted through a received manner of Shakespearean verse speaking.

In 1966 there were three approaches that Vitez was determined to avoid. First was the academic option, the idea that you could reconstruct the past and do the plays as they were intended. This, he felt, merely created pleasure in the exotic, rather like the second option of primitivism, the belief that ancient Greece was less developed than the modern world, and its plays more primal. Barrault's voodoo *Oresteia* seemed to Vitez racialist in its ideology (see above, p. 101). The third unacceptable strategy was to make Greek plays contemporary and overtly 'relevant', pointing up their relevance: a recent example was Sartre's moralistic rewriting of *Trojan Women* in relation to nuclear weapons and Algeria (see above, p. 60).[25] None of these options seemed to Vitez to acknowledge that the road to the past is a broken one.

Though Vitez developed a passion for Sophocles' *Electra* at school, his choice of text reflects more than his education. While Aeschylus was the taste of romantic primitivists, Euripides in the early twentieth century was the choice of progressive-minded modernists. A representative British modernist is Gilbert Murray, editor of Oxford Greek texts, campaigner for the League of Nations, friend of Bernard Shaw, and successful translator for the professional theatre. Murray's *Trojan Women* was widely performed as a radical peace play around the time of the First World War.[26] When Eva Palmer-Sikelianos decided to follow up *Prometheus* with Aeschylus' *Suppliants*, Murray wrote to her expressing complete bafflement at her theatrical taste.[27] For Murray, Euripides was the quintessential playwright of ideas, the writer with a political agenda, a lyrical predecessor of Ibsen and Shaw. Vitez was no less politically minded than Murray, and he too believed in a 'theatre of ideas', but the social realism and overt radicalism of Euripides were not to his post-modern taste. Sophocles' plays had been approved since the Renaissance for their proportion and perfection of form. Vitez wanted a classic text that he could set at a critical distance, a fragment of the past that he could 'rewrite' through his direction, and his obvious choice was therefore Sophocles. 'Elitism for all' was a favourite motto, and he made no apologies for the proposition that *Electra* is 'a good play ... a perfect work of art'.[28] Though the play had a bearing on colonialism and political power, it embodied no obvious message. For Vitez, the killing of Clytaemnestra related to Brecht's idea that it is impossible to be moral in an immoral society. The return of Orestes related to a perception that the past is always caught up in the present. Vitez declared that a great play resembled the famous riddle of the Sphinx,[29] and the notorious open-endedness of *The Electra*, devoid of any emotional resolution or moral statement, added to the play's attraction.

The 1966 production was in a Brechtian mode, with the actors presenting an ancient story to the audience. The delivery was frontal on a shallow stage. Since it seemed impossible to Vitez to recreate the gestures, verbal registers and musical conventions of the classical age, three women in alternation spoke the text into an imaginary microphone aiming simply at clarity. As in Brecht's *Antigone*, all the actors remained in view throughout to emphasize the gap between actor and role. Vitez himself played Orestes' tutor, so the teacher of the actors was also the teacher of Orestes. The spatial arrangements

of the Greek theatre were not reproduced but demonstrated through the device of setting a circle in front of steps. This circle belonged not to the chorus but to Electra, and symbolized the space of her imprisonment. The climax for the actors came when the play was performed in a Roman theatre in newly independent Algeria: 'The miracle of Babel was accomplished. The whole audience recognized in the *Electra* their nation humiliated for twenty-five years, subjected to colonial rule, restored to life when hope seemed lost.' Vitez did not adapt the play to fit the Algerian situation, but simply offered the audience what he called Sophocles' 'theorem'.[30] The production reflects the optimistic mood of the sixties, when liberation from the past seemed possible. The style was posited on the assumption that the audience could understand every word spoken by the actors.

The collapse of the revolution on the streets of Paris in 1968 led to a change of mood in France, and the production of 1971 reflects the influence of Grotowski as much as Brecht. This was an intimate touring production in keeping with Grotowski's ideal of a 'poor theatre'. The acting space was arranged in the form of a cross, and the audience sat in four blocks. The actors were liberated from their static, storytelling role, to perform ceremoniously. They wore golden, vaguely Asiatic make-up masks, linking them to pre-classical death masks excavated at Mycenae where *Electra* is set. Any of the seven actors not performing at a given moment stood at the edge of the space to become the chorus. Modern poems by Yannis Ritsos were woven into the performance, and words in ancient and modern Greek were heard on a voice-over. The primary political reference was no longer to Algeria but to the regime of the 'colonels' who had seized power in Greece, and the poems invited the audience to compare the Greek past with the Greek present. The major change between 1966 and 1971 was that Greek tragedy had become something mysterious, an enactment rather than a story. The spectator had no physical viewpoint from which to judge objectively, and was not able to understand some of the language, nor to tell exactly when Sophocles turned into Ritsos, and then became now.

In the huge Chaillot theatre in Paris, home for many years to the Théâtre National Populaire, Vitez created in 1986 what appears a more conservative production. Having absorbed the 'political theatre' and 'holy theatre' impulses of the sixties and seventies, his work became in significant ways post-modern. The 1980s was not a period of political ideals or hope, and Vitez was no longer a member

of the French Communist Party. The set was a neoclassical façade placed in the middle of empty space as a kind of quotation from the past, playing on the artificiality of perspective viewing. The façade was no abstraction, but represented the wall of a solid modern Greek building. The costumes, backdrop, furniture and sound effects suggested a setting in the Peiraeus, the port of modern Athens. The bed and dressing-table implied that the façade should be an interior wall, yet it might also have been an exterior. This ambiguity of inside and outside raised questions about characterization. Vitez in 1986 was undoubtedly influenced by the passion of the day for radical psychoanalysis. He now saw a parallel between the Electra myth and the Hamlet myth, and he invested the relationship

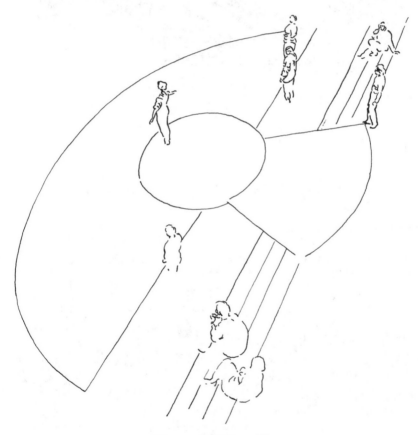

Figure 20a *Electra*: 1966.

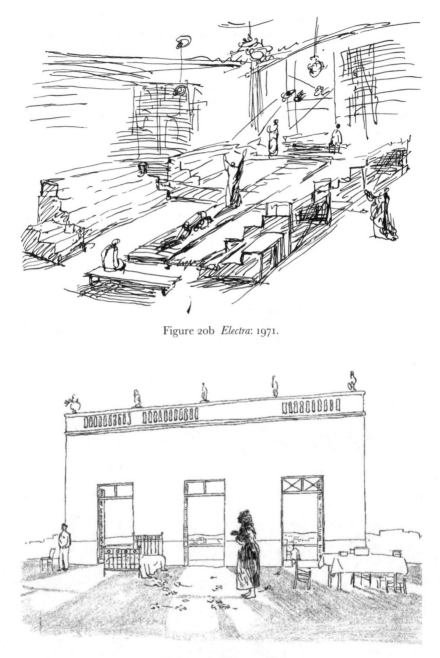

Figure 20b *Electra*: 1971.

Figure 20c *Electra*: 1986.

of Electra and her mother with a strong sexual charge, wanting the actors to create a fusion at all times between public and private modes of playing.

In 1966 an assertive chorus refracted the characters in multiple ways; in 1971 the voice of the chorus created a sense of community, emerging from the edge of the space so it seemed at once the voice of the audience and the voice of the collective actors. Now in 1986 the chorus no longer seemed to be the defining feature of the Greek form. The role of chorus was split between a group of female neighbours administering coffee, and a blind, garlanded coryphaeus, the naturalistic function of the chorus thus being split off from the religious or mythic function. This solved the difficulty of playing a Greek chorus in an end-staged theatre, where the audience itself has no sense of community. The energy of the production now lay not in its politics but in the relationships of the three female characters. Vitez decided to cast as Electra the actress who had played the role in his two previous productions. In 1585 it was a problem for some spectators that Jocasta seemed younger than Oedipus, but in 1986 the fact that Clytaemnestra was played by a younger actress than Electra was a deliberate device. Vitez' production embodied memories of its previous versions. Electra became an eternal figure who might have been waiting 2,500 years for her liberation.

In 1966, Vitez viewed the past as distant and alien, but in the end comprehensible. In 1971, the past was viewed through the eyes of a contemporary Greek poet, making it further removed and ultimately mysterious. By 1986, past and present have become inseparable. The historical past and the modern poet's view of the past have merged, for history has become a set of signs or traces that are part of the present. The classical statues on top of the façade represented at once a frozen antiquity that can never be brought to life, and the fantasy of a post-modern architect who has appropriated bits of the past for present purposes. Vitez' interest had shifted in 1986 from the gap between past and present to the active processes of remembering the past and reconstituting it in the imagination.

The major currents of European theatre in the second half of the twentieth century are all present in Vitez' work: political theatre, ritual theatre, psychoanalysis, post-modernism. The post-modern 1986 *Electra* can either be welcomed for its sophistication, or discarded as a neoconservative form, lacking ideals, and accommodating itself to institutional structures which it feels powerless to

change. The strength of the Sophoclean text is its ability to adapt to currents that will continue to shift.

TRANSLATION

What is translation?

Traduttore traditore – the Italian catch-phrase 'translator traitor' sums up a common feeling that translation is a form of betrayal. Greekless readers of Greek plays, the majority of those who will read this book, are likely to feel a sense of inadequacy because they only know Sophocles in translation. Yet it is debatable how far readers of Greek have privileged access to the 'real' Sophocles. The 1927 *Prometheus* was performed in modern Greek translation partly to make contact with the most important audience, the local villagers, and partly to avoid a political dilemma: to perform ancient Greek in the standard academic style fixed by Erasmus would have enraged the Greeks, and to perform the ancient text using the pronunciation of modern Greek would have enraged the foreign visitors.[31] Though modern Greek has a rather restricted range of vowel sounds, Vitez found that ancient Greek pronounced as modern was released from 'its funeral shroud', and he could sense the relationship to a living language.[32] The fact is that people who read ancient Greek still do not know how the play sounded when it was performed.

The Greekless reader may draw considerable comfort from the remarks of a French translator of Shakespeare. Jean-Michel Déprats cites Peter Brook's view that Shakespeare is more accessible performed in French than in English because so much of the English text is only comprehensible to scholars, and he continues: 'From this perspective, the translation of a foreign text into another language is far from being a last resort. It is not the necessary evil claimed by those who stress the inevitability of loss. Translation is an opportunity, the chance to establish live contact with a work that has become unapproachable in its original tongue.'[33] Translation can be seen positively as part of a continuing process of renewal. In a famous essay on translation written in 1923, Walter Benjamin claimed that translation is 'charged with the special mission of watching over the maturing process of the original language and the birth pangs of its own'.[34] The language of yesterday becomes hackneyed, and translation forces the language of today to test out new possibilities.

Let us consider what the translator does. Tom Stoppard puts it this way: 'When you write a play, the cocktail comes out of the same bottle: vocabulary, idiom, meaning, sub-text, speech rhythm, they all arrive together, or not. But when the material itself is, by definition, an approximation of an original work, aiming for equivalence, everything in the cocktail presents itself for separate consideration.'[35] The translator may therefore elect to concentrate on individual words, the style, ideas behind the words, or rhythm and sound. Given these options, the idea that a translation can ever be 'faithful' is wishful thinking. To render one aspect of the cocktail is always to lose another. Benjamin offers a different metaphor, the broken vase. Each word is like a fragment that has to be glued together to make the complete shape. If you translate one fragment directly into another, the new pieces will never fit together to form a new vase.[36] Vitez claims to have learned the art of translation as a jobbing actor hired to dub films. He realized that if the actor doing the voice-over captures the movement of the sentence, and the behaviour that lies behind that movement, then the viewer will never notice the mismatch of the lips. The Greek text for Vitez comprises the 'traces' of lost behaviour, and the translation provides the actor with different 'traces' of the same behaviour.[37]

The nature of translation has been much debated. Timberlake Wertenbaker makes a distinction between 'adaptation', when you fit the play to an audience, and 'translation', when you 'transport an audience into the play'.[38] For Déprats, this notion of 'transportation' is a mistake. He supports the aim of Vitez, which was rather to 'show the fracturing of time', to make something new out of the pieces. Though the translator may choose to privilege the time of the writer or the time of the audience, the translator's job should not be to 'transport' the one to the other but to set up a relationship of difference. Déprats praises the 1986 *Electra* for the way it represented simultaneously a classical Greece and the contemporary Greece of Ritsos.

Ezra Pound

Vitez in 1986 counterpointed what he called his 'kitchen sink' setting against a text that displayed its historical remoteness – though his translation by now seemed to him too lyrical, made in accordance with the taste of the sixties.[39] The translation itself had a single

texture. Ezra Pound, probably the most influential translator of poetry in the twentieth century, translated Greek tragedy with a view to fusing historical and contemporary languages within the text itself, so that the past could always be *heard* alongside the present. In 1949, locked up as a lunatic so as not to stand trial for treason, he secretly undertook Sophocles' *Electra*, projecting on to the situation of the play feelings about his incarceration and about the evil usurpers who had thrown out fascism in Italy. The mixture of American street slang, extracts of Greek and passages of biblical simplicity create an implicit dialogue between Pound's present situation and the classical past. Translations are normally considered unperformable in the professional theatre after some ten years because of the speed at which language changes, but Pound's text retains its energy fifty years later. A few lines are enough to illustrate the three main registers:

ELEKTRA: housed neath my father's bed
kenneled and fed on trash
in a shapeless sack.
CHORUS: THARESI MOI etc. ... ANASSOON.[40]

Pound set out five principles that underpinned his version:

1. There must be real person speaking possible speech NOT goddam book-talk. 2. Must be the stage SEEN, the position of the person speaking and their movements. 3. Modification of speech MINIMUM or NONE for the sung parts. They shd/ be as straight as Drink to me only with thine eyes. BUT cantabile. 4. When danced, the foot-beat must be indicated BY the words, from them to the tune. 5. For the sung part the translation need NOT adhere to literal sense (intellectual) of the original but must be singable IN THE EMOTION of the original.[41]

With rare exceptions (such as Steven Berkoff), twentieth-century dramatists have not succeeded in using verse. Most modern translators, rejecting the triviality or naturalism of prose, and failing to find any viable form of verse-drama in the contemporary theatre, have felt obliged to fall back on the verse idiom of an earlier generation, commonly the Shakespearean iambic pentameter: in short, 'goddam book-talk' and not 'possible speech'. Pound's method was to visualize the speaker on stage, but since his taste was for Japanese Noh plays rather than twentieth-century drama, he was not constrained by a vision of realist proscenium theatre. The sung parts, Pound main-

tains, should not allow any obscurity, but have music in the words. By 'modification of speech' he means that translators should not force English to adopt the complicated grammatical forms of an inflected language, but keep to a natural syntax.[42] The rhythm of the dancer should be embedded in the words, and not left as something for a musician or choreographer to superimpose. With the complex choral odes, Pound's objective is to create sharply different moods so that each seems unique.

Back in 1840 it was possible for a translator of Aristophanes, rejecting both literalism and modernization, to claim: 'The language of translation ought, we think, as far as possible to be a pure, impalpable and invisible element, the medium of thought and feeling.'[43] The idea that words can be invisible, and separate from the thought hidden behind them, made sense at a time when there was, among the elite, consensus about the nature of ancient Greece, good theatre and the English language. Now that consensus has gone, choices have to be made. Pound's bold solution remains on the margins of modern practice, for most classicists feel there needs to be more respect for the formality and detail of the Greek text, while most theatre directors prefer to demonstrate how their own creativity works upon the Greeks, without calling attention to the intermediate creativity of a modern writer.

Modern translations currently on the market derive from three basic sources: poets whose first commitment is to a vital language; theatre people committed to a performance that works for a specific audience; and classicists whose first commitment is to the Greek original. Successful theatre poets of the present generation include Tony Harrison, Robert Fagles, Tom Paulin and contributors to the American Oxford University Press series in single volumes edited by William Arrowsmith. Theatre people include Timberlake Wertenbaker, Ranjit Bolt and contributors to the Methuen series edited by J. Michael Walton. Academic translations include the Chicago University Press tragedies edited by Richmond Lattimore and David Grene, and the emerging Oxford World's Classics series. Penguin offer a mixed bag. The categories overlap, and almost all translations nowadays – apart from those in parallel text editions – claim to be performable. When reading a Greek tragedy in translation, you have to be acutely vigilant as to the origins of your text. The recurrent and difficult question is this: does an academic translation transport

the reader towards the Greek original, or does it obscure the purpose of the original, which was to present an alert and responsive crowd with something new and unexpected?

Two versions of The Agamemnon

Through comparing the way two different translators render a passage from Aeschylus' *Agamemnon*, we can see some of the choices that a translator has to make. I shall begin with the 'Browning version' of 1877, best known today from the title of Terence Rattigan's comedy.[44] In the finale of *The Browning Version*, a boy gives Robert Browning's translation to his pedantic schoolmaster, who like Agamemnon is a victim of adultery. The speaker in the following extract is Cassandra, a Trojan priestess who knows that Clytaemnestra is about to kill her.

> Papai: what fire this! And it comes upon me!
> Ototoi, Lukeion Apollon, ah me – me!
> She, the two-footed lioness that sleeps with
> The wolf, in absence of the generous lion,
> Kills me the unhappy one: and as a poison
> Brewing, to put my price too in the anger,
> She vows, against her mate this weapon whetting
> To pay him back the bringing me, with slaughter.[45]

In Rattigan's play, the Browning version symbolizes a failure of communication: the boy is unable to respond to the verse because it is meaningless to one who lacks a classical education. Browning attempted to follow the Greek phrase by phrase, keeping as far as possible the sentence structure, alliteration and some sense of the rhythm, but in trying to push the English language to its limits, Browning created a text that was unperformable. No Victorian actor could have rendered the emotions of the beginning, or clarified the thought in the conclusion. Nevertheless Terence Gray in his formal, masked production of 1926, unbothered by obscurity, used a text that was distinctly Browningesque.[46]

The translation published in 1991 by Frederic Raphael and Kenneth McLeish is rather different. McLeish was a professional translator for the theatre, who undertook plays in many European languages; Raphael is a professional writer, whose work includes screenplays and fiction. This stage version is based on a 1979 translation for television:

Ah-o-oh! Ah-o-oh!
The flames possess me.
A two-legged lioness couches with a wolf,
Beds with a wolf. While the true lion hunts,
She plots his death. And my death too:
I came with him, I die with him.
The knife is sharp.[47]

The dominant theatrical idiom of the 1980s and early 1990s was minimalist, in the wake of writers like Beckett, Pinter and Mamet, and of course television. Accordingly, much here has been stripped away. The ritual cries of grief – *papai, ototoi* – have been suppressed as archaic or exotic, replaced by a simple groan: 'ah-o-oh!'. Two other semi-formal expressions of pain – 'ah me!' and 'unhappy one' – have also vanished because modern English has no set vocabulary for venting grief in public. We have seen how difficult Fiona Shaw found the task of playing deritualized grief in McLeish's *Electra*. Apollo has vanished from the translation as a piece of cultural baggage that the modern audience cannot easily relate to, and so has the allusion to witchcraft. The metaphor of the wolf is doubled, because the modern listener is not good at picking up poetic images. The focus of the ending is no longer the prophecy of Agamemnon's death, but the human predicament of Cassandra, and the strange prophetess now has a human face. The result of this rigorous pruning is a text that certainly has 'modification of speech MINIMUM' and 'NOT goddam book-talk' as Pound put it. The rhythm is strong, varied and performable. Many classicists would claim that Raphael and McLeish have skilfully adapted the text to the audience, but have failed to transport the audience to the play. Whatever the rights and wrongs of that debate, it is entirely clear that Raphael and Mcleish have sought to avoid any sense of Vitez' 'fracturing of time'.

Aristophanes and the joke

Aristophanes raises slightly different issues because his plays were not set in historic or mythic time but in the world of his audience. I begin with a *Lysistrata* published in 1996 by Jeffrey Henderson, an American academic who edited the Greek text for Oxford University Press. Henderson claims to have opted for 'straightforward, idiomatic prose' in 'the interests of clarity and accuracy',[48] but I shall set

out a sample passage as verse to reflect the line structure of the original Greek, and also the rhythms of blank verse which Henderson has introduced partly to parody tragic language, but partly, I suspect, unconsciously.

> LYSISTRATA: Oh what a low and horny race are we!
> No wonder men write tragedies about us:
> we're nothing but Poseidon and a bucket.
> Dear Spartan, if you alone would
> side with me, we might still salvage the plan;
> give me your vote!
> LAMPITO: By Twain Gods, is difficult
> for females to sleep alone without the hard-on.
> But anyway, I assent; is need for peace.[49]

As far as he can, within the constraints of writing a close translation, Henderson is keen to efface the gap between the modern American reader and the Greek spectator. He maintains elsewhere that women were present in the Greek audience, and offers Aristophanes' focus on gender conflict as an argument to support this view. He claims that Aristophanes wrote for the reader as much as the spectator, so as a translator he is not troubled by competing objectives. And he has a goal to aim for: 'Ideally we should write what Aristophanes might have written had he and his audience been speakers of American English but otherwise people of their own time and place.'[50] It is a fundamental proposition of modern linguistics that the language people use determines the way they think, so I find it hard to accept Henderson's conception that one can in theory separate the 'people' of a particular culture from the way they talk.

An obvious issue for the translator is obscenity, and Henderson prides himself on avoiding the coyness of earlier versions. In Laurence Housman's version written for the suffrage movement, Lampito spoke of being debarred from 'her lover's lips'.[51] In a translation used at the Royal Court in 1957 for a production starring Joan Littlewood, the American Dudley Fitts tried 'a great big bed with nobody there but herself'.[52] Alan Sommerstein in the Penguin edition of 1973 advanced to a 'prick'.[53] Whether Henderson has actually achieved the goal of authenticity with his 'hard-on' is debatable, since the Greek actually refers to a 'drawn-back' (foreskin). In his determination not to be coy, Henderson offers 'hard-on' as the laugh-word at the end of the sentence, whilst Aristophanes

places the obscenity as a throw-away, and the Greek word which prompts the laugh is 'alone' (which refers ambiguously to just one 'drawn-back' as well as just one woman). The term which Henderson translates 'low and horny' refers specifically in the Greek to anal penetration. This only makes sense in terms of the Greek sexual code, whereby the junior male partner disgraced himself if he offered his body to a man with any enthusiasm. The difficulty of translating the practices of one culture into another causes Henderson to substitute a passive image of sexuality with an active, safely heterosexual image.

Henderson deals with the incomprehensible joke about Poseidon by writing a long note, explaining that the allusion must be to a lost play by Sophocles in which a young woman is seduced by the sea-god and disposes of her newborn twins by setting them adrift in a dug-out. The word *bucket* is obviously used here because it sounds vaguely funny. Since the tragedy in question is now lost, even the reader of the note cannot fully grasp the comic implications of the dug-out, and the spectator is obviously in a hopeless position. Most translators for the stage opt for an explanatory paraphrase – like Fitts' 'All we want's a quick tumble!' McLeish, knowing that the rhythm of the scene requires a laugh-line at this point to counterbalance the wheedling plea to Lampito, invents his own joke.

> *Frailty, thy name is woman.* As someone said
> We just won't kick against the pricks.[54]

The oath sworn by the 'Twain Gods' raises more problems. The reference is to Demeter and her daughter Persephone, and the oath is characteristically feminine in order to offset the coarseness which follows. The translator must choose whether to keep the cultural otherness of a reference to Greek gods, or keep the mood of an everyday exclamation – like Fitts' phrase written for a southern drawl: 'Ah sweah.' There is also the question of translating for rhythm, since the oath sworn by the *twain* in the Greek falls at the end of the line to balance *alone* at the end of the next. Lampito's oath sworn by the Twain Gods is directly echoed by Lysistrata six lines later, when another woman wheedles her precisely as she has wheedled Lampito. Making Aristophanes funny in the theatre is fundamentally a matter of rhythm, and the problem with translations made for the reader is that they translate jokes for their thought content, not their timing.

Perhaps the most difficult issue is Lampito's southern accent, clearly marked in the Greek text. Here the quest for what an English-speaking Aristophanes might ideally have said reveals its absurdity, for any choice makes a political statement about the present. Fitts' southern drawl is a Broadway convention, but the American civil war lurks in the background. Sommerstein opts for Scots, assuming the reader to be English. Henderson records that the Russian accent which he hinted at in an earlier 1987 translation already seemed passé in 1991 with the end of the Cold War.[55] His text in 1996 evokes someone who is perhaps Hispanic, someone whose English is faulty and not simply different. McLeish avoids a collision between Greek and modern realities by erasing dialect completely.

There are rich possibilities if one does decide that the new text should contrast ancient and modern situations. Tony Harrison collaborated with an Irish poet in 1964 to create a version for students in northern Nigeria, evoking tribal tensions that were soon to erupt in the Biafran war.

– Oh women! Women! The weak, weak sex.
We're only good for bed and humping babies
On our backs ... *We* can still pull this thing off.
Please back me up. Please, Iyabo, say yes.

– True to God, we know say 'e hard make woman no meeting lova, but if
    we want make dis war stop, na de only ting we fit go do be dat.[56]

Standard pronunciation is used to suggest the politically dominant northerners, and pidgin for southern Yoruba, the actors themselves being southerners. The gains from this cultural transposition were great. The political situation in Athens had a direct bearing on the world of the audience, and the performance had a purpose. The two European poets found a language that freed them from the constraints of BBC English, and 'goddam book-talk'. Yoruba traditions of masquerade and Travelling Theatre made it possible to develop a performance style that seemed closer than any available European style to the masked, ritualistic, satirical and populist theatre of Aristophanes. However, the logic of transposition, starting with small details like carrying babies on the back, rapidly meant that the invisible line between translation and adaptation was crossed. Where this line actually runs is an open question.

The chorus in Aristophanes

In many ways it is hard to improve on the choruses translated by the deaf Victorian barrister Benjamin Bickley Rogers. In this extract, Lysistrata and her colleagues have barricaded themselves inside the skênê, which represents the Propylaea, the gatehouse of the Acropolis. After two lines in marching rhythm which allow the chorus of men to bring on logs and a brazier, the first dance begins (256ff):

> O dear, how many things in life bely one's expectations!
> Since who'd have thought, my Strymodore, that these abominations,
> Who would have thought that sluts like these,
> Our household pests, would have waxed so bold,
> As the Holy Image by **fraud** to **seize**,
> As the City Castle by **force** to **hold**,
> With block and bolt and barrier vast,
> Making the **Propylaea fast**.

At this point the marching rhythm resumes and it appears that the men pick up the props which they deposited for the dance. Rogers continues:

> Press on, Philurgus, towards the heights; we'll pile a great amazing
> Array of logs around the walls, and set them all a-blazing...[57]

Rogers follows the original closely, and translates on a line by line basis. The decision to generate rhymes, not a feature of the Greek, results in several surplus words, some misogynistic – 'abominations','sluts', 'waxed so bold' – some to sound impressive – 'barrier vast', 'great amazing', 'blazing'. Rogers attempts to replicate the metre of the original, and I have printed a few syllables in bold to clarify the underlying rhythm of the Greek. In the march Rogers injects a certain jollity by using a rising rhythm where the Greek has a mainly falling rhythm to catch the weary determination of the old men. One of the problems of turning Greek metre into English verse based on stress is that English cannot produce any direct equivalent to the seven short syllables which lie behind 'As the Holy Image by', quickly spoken words which imply rapid footwork on the part of the dancers. Dudley Fitts demonstrates the best that can be done in English with a run of unstressed syllables to suggest speed (my italics):

> Women that used to board with us, bed with us –
> Now, by the gods, *they've got ahead of us* ...

Rogers' verse bounces along, ignoring an element of syncopation in the Greek which suggests that the old men become out of breath and cannot quite keep up with themselves. Rhyme was not a feature of ancient Greek songs because so much was expressed through rhythm, but for modern European song-writers rhyme is a basic resource, and rhyme is not directly linked to dance steps. The translator is in a quandary. Today most opt for rhyme in Aristophanes because of the comic potential, and avoid rhyme in tragedy.

If we compare Rogers to a reputable academic translation published 120 years later, the modern text seems a little leaner. This is Stephen Halliwell in the 1998 Oxford World's Classics edition:

OLD MEN.   *Strophe*
   Long life brings many surprises, shiver me timbers!
   Who would have thought, my friend, we'd ever hear
      That *women*, whom we reared
      As blatant mischiefs in our homes,
      Should seize Athena's statue,
      And occupy our sacred hill,
      And fasten up these massive gates
      With bolts and bars?
LEADER.
   Come on, my ancient comrade, let's push on up to the summit.
   We've got to pile these logs around the site that's occupied . . .[58]

The most useful feature of Halliwell's text is that, unlike those of most twentieth-century translators it clarifies the structure of the original, recognizing that the form of a play is part of its meaning. It is clear to the eye, if not to the ear, which passages are strophic dances, which are monodies, which are in marching rhythm and which spoken. More hesitantly than Rogers, Halliwell gives an impression of the metrical form of the Greek. The lack of rhyme helps him avoid the spirit of Gilbert and Sullivan, which bedevils the Penguin series of translations. The problem with the Halliwell text is that, by comparison with Rogers, it is not much fun to perform. The key to performability lies in the way words organize time. Let us take line one: the thought order in the Greek is that there are many surprises in a long life, and the Greek line ends with an exclamation '*pheu*', which Halliwell translates as 'shiver me timbers' to fill out the line length. The rhythm of the Greek appears to miss a short beat before the *pheu*, as also before 'long life', to create an impression that age has difficulty in dancing, and a contrast with the speed that

follows when the men's fury takes them over. Dudley Fitts, having absorbed the rhythms of the American musical, demonstrates the kind of momentum that is possible in an English translation:

> Forward, forward, comrades! Whew!
> The things that old age does to you!

The thought here builds up to the key notion of old age, and the rhymes allow for an exhausted exhalation of breath. The 'sense of performance' is not something we should consider a mystery: what Fitts displays is technique.

Other points of detail seem less important. Halliwell decides without any particular evidence that the marching section should be delivered by the coryphaeus alone. And he eliminates the proper names Strymodoros and Philourgos, which are actually rather remarkable evidence of the degree to which individual chorus-men were characterized in Aristophanic comedy. Fitts saw the comic potential here, creating a sense of intimate nattering within the group. Halliwell avoids the terms Acropolis and Propylaea to minimize the sense of cultural otherness, but he loses also the force of the Greek word order: 'Acropolis-mine-take!' The Greek communicates mounting outrage and an absurd claim that the Acropolis is a male preserve. Aristophanes ends the dance with the line '*ta Propylaia paktoun*' ('the Propylaea to seal up'). Halliwell preserves the alliterative thump, but unlike Rogers loses the final thought, that the women have closed the place that is signified by doors visible to the audience. The choreographer looking for a final tableau is forced to look for irrelevant gestures that relate to bolts and bars. Though Fitts' last line is self-indulgence, he knew that the final verbal–visual image of the dance routine needs to sum up the whole:

> And barred the doors,
> The aggravating whores.

I have perhaps painted a rather bleak picture for the Greekless reader, in showing just how far you have to take account of the translator when reading a play that purports to be by Aristophanes. I have three crumbs of comfort. First, the 'authentic' Aristophanes is an infinitely receding illusion. Meaning does not lie out there on the page of Greek text, but can only be constructed in the mind of the reader or spectator. Second, the Greek words are, to quote Vitez, mere 'traces' of lost behaviour; all that can be done is create

something new by following the traces. To put it another way, any surviving text is a fragment, just the notation of what was said, and meaningless if you have no sense of the space, the costumes, the audience, and the whole cultural context; many of these other fragments of the broken vase can be inspected by the Greekless reader. Thirdly, no amount of dictionaries or grammar books will teach you how plays communicate in the theatre. There are other skills besides language relevant to understanding Greek drama.

Chronology

590 BC	pre-democratic reforms of Solon
530s	competition in tragedy at the Dionysia
530s approx.	competition in performing Homer at the Panathenaia
507	Athenian constitution democratized by Cleisthenes
494	Persians destroy Miletus
492	Phrynichus fined for tragedy about Miletus
490	Aeschylus fights in Battle of Marathon
486 approx.	competition in comedy at the Dionysia
480/79	Persians defeated at Salamis, but burn Athens
472	Salamis described in Aeschylus' *Persians*
468	Sophocles defeats Aeschylus at the Dionysia
462	power removed from the Council of the Areopagus
460–429	dominance of Pericles
458	Aeschylus' *Oresteia* dramatizes Areopagus
456	death of Aeschylus in Sicily
449	competition for best tragic actor at the Dionysia
447–432	building of the Parthenon; also the Odeon
441	Euripides' first victory
441 approx.	contest of comic poets and actors at the Lenaia
431	Peloponnesian war begins
430	plague in Athens
426	Aristophanes wins his first victory at the Dionysia
	Cleon takes legal action in response to Aristophanes
416/5	genocide in Melos
413	Athenians defeated in Sicily
411	democracy temporarily overthrown
406	death of Euripides in Macedonia
	death of Sophocles in Athens
405	*The Frogs* performed twice
404	Athens defeated by Sparta

	dictatorship of the 'thirty'
388	Aristophanes' *Wealth* – his last extant play
386	'old' tragedies performed at the Dionysia
330s	Lycurgus registers official version of Greek play-texts
	Lycurgus rebuilds theatre in stone
335–323	Aristotle in Athens: *Poetics* written
315 approx.	Menander's first victory at the Dionysia
195–180	Aristophanes of Byzantium edits Greek plays

Notes

I MYTH

1 'A short organum for the theatre', in *Brecht on Theatre*, ed. J. Willett (London: Methuen, 1964), 183.
2 The account by Plutarch can be found in his *Moralia*, 998e. The lost Euripidean play is the *Kresophontes*.
3 The Performance Group, *Dionysus in 69*, ed. R. Schechner (New York: Farrar, Strauss & Giroux, 1970).
4 *Eumenides*, 46ff
5 Rudkin's essay 'Aspects of *Hippolytus*' distributed at the performance: The Other Place, Stratford-upon-Avon.
6 *Phaedra*, after Seneca and Euripides, performed by the National Theatre of Craiova, and presented at the Riverside Studios, London, 21–4 June 1995.
7 Herodotus, vi.21. Translation from Herodotus, *The Histories*, tr. A. de Sélincourt (Harmondsworth: Penguin, 1954), 366.
8 *Rhesus*, attributed to Euripides, may be by a later author. Euripides' *Andromache* was written for another city, according to one later authority. Euripides' *Bacchae* may, like his lost *Archelaus*, have been written for the king of Macedon. Two comedies of Aristophanes were written in the next century.
9 *Republic*, 377e – translation adapted from Plato, *The Republic*, tr. D. Lee (Harmondsworth: Penguin, 1974), 131.
10 Homer, *Hymn to Apollo*, 146ff.
11 Plutarch, *Life of Nikias*, 10.
12 *Odyssey*, viii.
13 The text of Plato, *Ion* is in *ALC*, 39–50.
14 The classic statement is in Aristotle, *Poetics*, xxiv, 1459b – *ALC* 126.
15 John Herington, *Poetry into Drama* (University of California Press, 1985), chapter 3. The phrase is adapted from Baudelaire.
16 *Mythologies*, tr. A. Lavers (St Albans: Paladin, 1973).
17 *Laws*, 888c – translation adapted from the Penguin edition, tr. T. J. Saunders (Harmondsworth, 1970), p. 415.
18 *Laws*, 948c.

19 *Republic*, 383b – Penguin ed., p. 139. The original play is lost.
20 See George Steiner, *Antigones* (Oxford University Press, 1984), 11; Plato, *Laws*, 909.
21 See W. B. Tyrrell and F. S. Brown, *Athenian Myths and Institutions* (Oxford University Press, 1991), Chapter 7.
22 Isocrates, *Panathenaia*, 118.
23 The versions are compared in Plutarch, *Life of Theseus*, 29.
24 For a survey of different versions see Lowell Edmunds, *Oedipus: the ancient legend and its later analogues* (Johns Hopkins University Press, 1985).
25 See B. M. W. Knox, *Oedipus at Thebes* (Yale University Press, 1957), 63.
26 Antiphanes, fr. 191 (Kock) – translated by Peter Burian in *CCGT*, 183.
27 See, for example, Christopher Norris, *Deconstruction: theory and practice* (London: Methuen, 1986), 32.
28 Freud made his major statements in *The Interpretation of Dreams* in 1900 and in his *Introductory Lectures on Psycho-analysis* of 1915–17.
29 See Fiona Macintosh in *CCGT*, 289.
30 'Psychopathic characters on the stage' in *Complete Works, vol.* VII (London: Hogarth Press, 1953), 305ff.
31 'The structural study of myth' in *The Structuralists from Marx to Lévi-Strauss*, ed. R. and F. De George (New York: Anchor Books, 1972), 168–94.
32 See Nicole Loraux, 'Kreousa the autochthon: a study of Euripides' *Ion*', *NTDWD*, 168–206; J. M. Hall, *Ethnic Identity in Greek Antiquity* (Cambridge University Press, 1997), 51–6.
33 For a critique of this approach, see Brian Vickers, *Towards Greek Tragedy* (London: Longman, 1973), 526ff.
34 Antiphanes, fr. 191 – my translation.

2 RITUAL

1 Peter Brook, *The Empty Space* (London: MacGibbon & Kee, 1968), 45–6.
2 Antonin Artaud, *The Theatre and its Double*, tr. V. Corti (London: Calder & Boyars, 1970), 40–3.
3 Demosthenes, *Against Meidias*, 52, extracted in *COAD*, 112.
4 Emile Durkheim, *The Elementary Forms of Religious Life*, tr. K. E. Fields (New York: Free Press, 1995), 419, 421.
5 Clifford Geertz, 'Deep play: notes on the Balinese cockfight' in *Rethinking Popular Culture*, ed. C. Mukerji and M. Schudson (University of California Press, 1991), 239–77, p. 269. Originally published in 1972.
6 *Politics*, 1341b – tr. T. A. Sinclair (Harmondsworth: Penguin, 1962), 314.
7 *Poetics*, iv.1449a – *ALC*, 95. For the antiritualist view, see G. Else, *The Origin and Early Form of Tragedy* (Harvard University Press, 1965).
8 For arguments about the programme, see *COAD*, 107.
9 *COAD*, 110–11.
10 E. E. Rice, *The Grand Procession of Ptolemy Philadelphus* (Oxford University Press, 1983).

11 *COAD*, 125–6.
12 Philochoros cited in *COAD*, 301 – my translation.
13 *Poetics*, iii.1448a – *ALC*, 92 – my translation.
14 These are inferences from the organization of the dithyramb: see *COAD*, 149–50.
15 Tony Harrison, *Trackers of Oxyrhynchus* (London: Faber, 1991); performed at Delphi and at the Olivier Theatre, London.
16 Richard Schechner, *Performance Theory* (New York and London: Routledge, 1988), 120.
17 The account is in Xenophon, *Hellenica*, ii.3.
18 Book 11.
19 Cited in Athenaeus, 675a – discussed in Richard Seaford, *Reciprocity and Ritual* (Oxford University Press, 1994), 86.
20 Herodotus, v.67 – discussed in Seaford, *Reciprocity and Ritual*, 112–13, 325–6.
21 See B. M. W. Knox, 'The date of the *Oedipus Tyrannus* of Sophocles' in *Word and Action* (Johns Hopkins University Press, 1979), 119–24.
22 Cited from an interview in *Hot Tickets*, 6 September 1996. See Richard Hornby's account of the production in the *Hudson Review* 49 (1997), 645–51. The productions were performed at the Olivier Theatre, London, and Epidaurus.
23 *Making an Exhibition of Myself* (London: Sinclair-Stevenson, 1993), 313.

3 POLITICS

1 Pseudo-Xenophon (the 'Old Oligarch'), *Constitution of the Athenians*, i.13.
2 Lysias, xxi. Extract in *COAD*, 146–7.
3 *Acharnians*, 505–6.
4 The evidence for the review belongs to the next century, but I assume the tradition was older: A. Pickard-Cambridge, *Dramatic Festivals of Athens*, revised by J. Gould and D. Lewis (Oxford University Press, 1968), 68–70.
5 *Laws*, 701 – my translation.
6 Pericles' funeral speech in Thucydides, *History of the Peloponnesian War*, ii.40.
7 Cleon's speech in the debate about Mytilene: Thucydides, iii.38.
8 *Gorgias*, 502.
9 *Menexenus*, 235.
10 Diodoros, xii.53.
11 *Republic*, 492.
12 *Daily Telegraph*, 31 August 1996. Hall writes apropos his production of *Lysistrata*.
13 *Rhetoric*, i.1.
14 Sophocles, *Antigone*, 724–5.

15 B. Brecht, *The Messingkauf Dialogues*, tr. J. Willett (London: Methuen, 1965), 82.

16 Following K. J. Dover in *Aristophanes: Clouds* (Oxford University Press, 1968), lvi.

17 J.-P. Sartre, *Three Plays* (Harmondsworth: Penguin, 1969), 288.

18 Directed by Holek Freitag for Habimah, Tel Aviv, 1983. See Shimon Levy and Nurit Yaari, 'Theatrical responses to political events: the Trojan War on the Israeli stage during the Lebanon War, 1982–1984', *Journal of Theatre and Drama* 3 (1999), 1–15.

19 Cited in Peter Reynolds, *Unmasking Oedipus* (London: Royal National Theatre Publications, 1996), 13.

20 *Brecht on Theatre*, tr. J. Willett (London: Methuen, 1978), 87.

21 See *Hegel on Tragedy* ed A. and H. Paolucci (New York: Harper & Row, 1975), 178, 325; Fiona Macintosh in *CCGT,* 286–8.

22 See J. Anouilh, *Antigone*, tr. L. Galantière (London: Methuen, 1951 – text of the 1949 production directed by Laurence Olivier). On the New York text, see Ian Reid, 'Hazards of adaptation: Anouilh's *Antigone* in English' in *The Languages of Theatre: problems in the translation and transposition of Drama*, ed. O. Zuber (Oxford: Pergamon, 1980), 82–91.

23 B. Brecht, *Antigonemodell 1948* (Berlin: 1949), 34 – my translation. This volume contains a comprehensive photographic record of the original production in Switzerland. The preface is translated in *Brecht on Theatre*, tr. Willett, 209–15.

24 The production is documented in *Les Voies de la création théâtrale*, vol. 1 (Paris: CNRS, 1985), 217–43.

4 GENDER

1 Sappho, fragment 114.

2 Sappho, fragment 140a. The texts are analyzed by Richard Seaford in *Reciprocity and Ritual* (Oxford University Press, 1994), 278–80; see also Denys Page, *Sappho and Alcaeus* (Oxford University Press, 1955), 122, 127.

3 Thucydides, *History of the Peloponnesian War*, ii.45.

4 Simon Goldhill's arguments seem to me compelling in 'Representing democracy: women at the Great Dionysia' in *Ritual, Finance, Politics*, ed. R. Osborne and S. Hornblower (Oxford University Press, 1994), 347–69. For the alternative view, see *COAD*, 286–7.

5 Jean Genet, *The Blacks*, tr. B. Frechtman (London: Faber, 1960). I owe this point to an unpublished paper by Nurit Yaari: 'Women as spectators in classical Athens'.

6 See Nicole Loraux, *The Children of Athena*, tr. C. Levine (Princeton University Press, 1993), 179–81.

7 Plutarch, *Life of Solon*, 20–1, 12; Seaford, *Reciprocity and Ritual*, 78–86.

8 See Plutarch, *Life of Lycurgus*, 14.

9 *Eumenides*, 658–61.

10 First performed in the Berlin Schaubühne in 1980 and revived with a Russian cast in 1994.
11 First performed in Limoges in 1996, and revived by the National Theatre of Craiova in 1998.
12 *Histories*, ii.35, 48.
13 *Eumenides*, 685–9.
14 Euripides, *The Captive Melanippe*. The surviving fragments can be read, in a translation by M. J. Cropp, in Euripides, *Selected Fragmentary Plays*, vol. 1, ed. C. Collard *et al.* (Warminster: Aris & Phillips, 1995), 249–65.
15 Aristophanes, *Women at the Thesmophoria* (translated in the Penguin edition as *The Poet and the Women*; in the Methuen edition as *Festival Time*); on the festival, see A. M. Bowie, *Aristophanes: myth, ritual, society* (Cambridge University Press, 1993), 205–12.
16 *The Frogs*, 405–16.
17 See Kevin Clinton, *Myth and Cult: the iconography of the Eleusinian Mysteries* (Stockholm: Svenska Institutet i Athen, 1992), 87–9.
18 C. G. Jung, *Freud and Psychoanalysis* (London: Routledge & Kegan Paul, 1961), 152–5.
19 The fragments of *Myrmidons* can be read in vol. 11 of the Loeb edition of *Aeschylus*, tr. H. W. Smyth (London: Heinemann, 1967), 422–6.
20 *On the Generation of Animals*, 1.20.
21 Judith Butler, *Gender Trouble: feminism and the subversion of identity* (London: Routledge, 1990), 137.
22 Sarah Pomeroy, *Goddesses, Whores, Wives and Slaves: women in classical antiquity* (New York: Schocken, 1975), 107–8.
23 *Ibid.*, 112.
24 See Daniel Ogden, *Greek Bastardy in the Classical and Hellenistic Worlds* (Oxford University Press, 1996), 63, 194–6.
25 See Edith Hall, 'Medea and British legislation before the First World War', *Greece and Rome* 46 (1999), 42–77; Duncan Wilson, *Gilbert Murray OM* (Oxford University Press, 1987), 181.
26 Sue-Ellen Case, 'Classic drag: the Greek creation of female parts' *Theatre Journal* 37 (1985), 317–27; reprinted in substance in *Feminism and Theatre* (London: Macmillan, 1988).
27 Tony Harrison, interview in Marianne McDonald, *Ancient Sun, Modern Light: Greek drama on the modern stage* (Columbia University Press, 1992), 143.
28 Sue-Ellen Case, in *Feminism and Theatre* 11.
29 Case, in *Feminism and Theatre* 7.
30 Case, in *Feminism and Theatre* 17, citing *Poetics*, xv.1454a – *ALC*, 110.
31 Froma Zeitlin, 'Playing the other: theater, theatricality and the feminine in Greek drama' in *NTDWD*, 68; originally published in *Representations* 11 (1985), 63–94.
32 Lauren K. Taafe, *Aristophanes and Women* (New York and London: Routledge, 1993), 144–6.
33 Luce Irigaray, 'The bodily encounter with the mother' (1981) in *The*

Irigaray Reader, ed. M. Whitford (Oxford: Blackwell, 1991), 34–46, pp. 36–7.
34 Hélène Cixous, 'The laugh of the Medusa' in *New French Feminisms*, ed. E. Marks and I. de Courtivron (Brighton: Harvester, 1980), 245–64, p. 256.
35 Hélène Cixous, 'Aller à la mer' in *Modern Drama* 27 (1984), 546–8.
36 *The Hélène Cixous Reader*, ed. S. Sellers (London: Routledge, 1994), 'Preface', xix.
37 *Ibid.*, xviii.

5. SPACE

1 See A. W. Dilke, *Greek and Roman Maps* (London: Thames & Hudson, 1985), 23–4, 56–9.
2 Aristides, *Panathenaic Oration*, 11–19.
3 *Symposium*, 175e – *COAD*, 135.
4 See Barry Strauss, *Athens After the Peloponnesian War* (London: Croom Helm, 1987), 70–86; also David Stockton, *The Classical Athenian Democracy* (Oxford University Press, 1990), 15–18. The estimated numbers refer to residents of Attica, and exclude many of Athenian citizen status who had set up colonies elsewhere in the Mediterranean world.
5 Isocrates, *Panathenaic Oration*, 121–2, 168
6 Froma Zeitlin in *Nothing to do with Dionysos?*, ed. J. J. Winkler and F. Zeitlin (Princeton University Press, 1992), 144.
7 *Bacchae* was first performed in Tokyo in 1977; *Clytaemnestra* in the Toga theatre, 1983. The latter is translated in *The Way of Acting: the theatre writings of Suzuki Tadashi*, tr. J. T. Rimer (New York: Theatre Communications Group, 1986).
8 W. Dörpfeld and E. Reisch, *Das griechische Theater* (Athens, 1896).
9 Isadora Duncan, *My Life* (New York: Boni & Liveright, 1927), 128–30.
10 William Dinsmoor, 'The Athenian theater of the fifth century' in *Studies Presented to David Moore Robinson*, ed. G. E. Mylonas (Washington University Press, 1951), 309–30.
11 S. G. Miller 'Ikria and orchestra – in which agora?' in *Sources for the Ancient Greek City-State*, ed. M. H. Hansen (Copenhagen: Royal Danish Academy of Sciences and Letters, 1995), 218–19.
12 See Margarete Bieber, *History of the Greek and Roman Theater* (Princeton University Press, 1961), 74–5.
13 For the opposite view to the one argued here, and at length in David Wiles, *Tragedy in Athens* (Cambridge University Press, 1997), 63–7, see for example Stephen Scully, 'Orchestra and stage in Euripides, *Suppliant Women' Arion* 4 (1996), 61–84.
14 *Poetics*, iv.1449a – *ALC*, 95.
15 See R. S. Shankland, 'Acoustics of Greek theatres', *Physics Today* (October 1973), 30–5.

16 Performed at the Olivier Theatre in 1987. First performed in Tokyo in 1978, and still running in 1998.

17 See Richard Beacham's analysis of the production in *Living Greek Theatre*, ed. J. Michael Walton (Westport: Greenwood Press, 1987), 302–12.

18 Silvia Purcarete, interview with Georges Banu printed in the programme to the *Oresteia* (Barbican Theatre, London, 1998).

19 Jacques Lecoq, *Le Corps poétique*, Actes Sud – Papiers 10 (Arles: Anrat, 1997), 137, 139.

20 See Wiles, *Tragedy in Athens*, 51.

21 Patsy Rodenburg, *The Actor Speaks: voice and the performer* (London: Methuen, 1997), 313.

22 Roland Barthes, *The Responsibility of Forms* (Oxford: Blackwell, 1986), 79.

23 Anne Anthony in *Eva Palmer-Sikelianou* (Athens: Papadema, 1998), 193 – originally published as *Eos* 9–10 (1966–7).

24 Jerzy Grotowski, *Towards a Poor Theatre* (London: Methuen, 1969), is the classic treatment.

25 *Iphigeneia at Aulis, Agamemnon* and Sophocles, *Electra* directed by Garland Wright at the Guthrie Theater: see the review by R. Sonkowsky in *Arion* 4 (1996), 152–4, 225–33, p. 232.

26 *COAD*, 117, 161.

27 Oliver Taplin, *The Stagecraft of Aeschylus: the dramatic use of exits and entrances in Greek tragedy* (Oxford University Press, 1977).

28 *Ibid.*, 438–40.

29 Aeschylus' *Eumenides* and Sophocles' *Ajax*. For a detailed analysis of the issues, see Scott Scullion, *Three Studies in Athenian Dramaturgy* (Stuttgart and Leipzig: Teubner, 1994).

30 M. M. Bakhtin, 'Forms of time and the chronotope in the novel' in *The Dialogic Imagination*, tr. C. Emerson and M. Holquist (University of Texas Press, 1981), 85–258.

31 *Poetics*, v.1449b – *ALC*, 96.

32 See M. M. Bakhtin, *Rabelais and His World*, tr. H. Iswolsky (Indiana University Press, 1984).

33 See Richard Beacham's account in *Living Greek Theatre*, ed. J. Michael Walton (New York: Greenwood Press, 1987), 305–13.

34 A. Baksky in *Max Reinhardt – His Theatre*, ed. O. M. Sayler (New York: Brentano, 1924), 338.

35 Richard Schechner, *Environmental Theatre* (New York: Applause, 1994), 2–6, 40–5.

36 See Marvin Carlson, 'Accueil on the road: Mnouchkine's *Les Atrides* in context', *Assaph C* 8 (1992), 153–60.

37 Marcel Freydefont, 'Tout ne tient pas forcément ensemble: essai sur la relation entre architecture et dramaturgie au XXème siècle', *Etudes Théâtrales* 11–12 (1997), 13–45, pp. 38–9.

38 My remarks draw in part upon an unpublished conference paper by Katerina Arvaniti.

6. THE PERFORMER

1 Herodotus, v.67. See Richard Seaford, *Reciprocity and Ritual* (Oxford University Press, 1994) 112.
2 *Laws*, 654.
3 See Claude Calame, *Choruses of Young Women in Ancient Greece*, tr. D. Collins and J. Orion (Lanham: Rowman & Littlefield, 1997), 210–14 (on Sappho), 34–40 (on the circle).
4 Or eleven months, according to an unreliable source: *COAD*, 143–4.
5 See John Gould, 'Tragedy and collective experience' in *Tragedy and the Tragic*, ed. M. S. Silk (Oxford University Press, 1996), 217–43, pp. 222–4.
6 Plutarch, *Life of Nikias*, 29.
7 *The Gospel at Colonus* (New York: Theatre Communications Group, 1989) – first performed 1983.
8 David Wiles, *Tragedy in Athens* (Cambridge University Press, 1997), 95.
9 Jacques Lecoq, *Le Corps poétique*, Actes Sud – Papiers 10 (Arles: Anrat, 1997), 139–40.
10 The militarist view of the tragic chorus is supported by Jack Winkler in 'The ephebes' song: *tragōidia* and *polis*', *NTDWD*, 20–62. Post-classical texts relating to choreography are gathered in *COAD*, 361–4.
11 Text in *COAD*, 360–1.
12 Texts in *COAD*, 13, 154–5.
13 Aristotle, *Poetics*, v.1449b – *ALC*, 96; *Constitution of Athens*, 56.3.
14 *Laws*, 816–17.
15 A vase in Heidelberg is often alleged to show a figure from comedy, but resembles more closely a maenad from a satyr play. See Margarete Bieber, *The History of the Greek and Roman Theater* (Princeton University Press, 1961), fig. 208.
16 Demosthenes, *On the False Embassy*, 287.
17 *Laws*, 668.
18 *COAD*, 365–6.
19 As in the vase reproduced in Stephen Lonsdale, *Ritual Play in Greek Religion* (Johns Hopkins University Press, 1993), fig. 20, p.146.
20 *Laws*, 797–800.
21 Ibid., 795–6.
22 Adolf Wilbrant, cited by W. Schadewaldt in 'Ancient tragedy on the modern stage' in *Sophocles: the classical heritage*, ed. R. D. Dawe (New York: Garland, 1996), 283–308, p. 292.
23 Friedrich Schlegel, cited in Marvin Carlson, *Theories of the Theatre* (Cornell University Press, 1984), 179.

24 *Poetics*, xviii.1456a – *ALC*, 116.
25 See for example Albert Henrichs, 'Why should I dance?', *Arion* 3 (1995), 56–111.
26 *Poetics*, xxvi.1461b – *ALC*, 131.
27 *Politics*, viii.6–7 – 1340b–2b.
28 L. Tieck, cited by Schadewaldt in 'Ancient tragedy', 289 n.16. The performance in Potsdam in 1841 is documented in Hellmut Flashar, *Inszenierung der Antike* (Munich: C. H. Beck, 1991), 66–76.
29 Nirupama Natyanandan in an interview with Denis Salter: 'Théâtre du Soleil: *Les Atrides*', *Theater* 24 (1993), 66–74, p. 69.
30 Pratinas, cited in Athenaeus, 617: – *COAD*, 338–9.
31 Pherecrates – *COAD*, 336–8.
32 *The Frogs*, 1314.
33 From *Orestes* – *COAD* 341–2, with the music on plate 21A.
34 [Aristotle] *Problems*, 918 – *COAD*, 348.
35 J. R. Green, 'Dedications of masks', *Revue archéologique* (1982), 237–48.
36 See also A. Pickard-Cambridge, *Dramatic Festivals of Athens*, revised by J. Gould and D. Lewis (Oxford University Press, 1968), figs. 17–24.
37 Walter F. Otto, *Dionysus: myth and cult*, tr. R. B. Palmer (Indiana University Press, 1965), 91.
38 Robertson Davies *et al.* (eds.) *Thrice the Brinded Cat Hath Mew'd* (Toronto: Clarke, Irwin & Co., 1955), 123–8.
39 J.-L. Barrault, *The Theatre of Jean-Louis Barrault*, tr. J. Chiari (London: Barrie & Rockliff, 1961), 76.
40 Michel Saint-Denis, *Theatre: the rediscovery of style* (London: Heinemann, 1960), 104.
41 Jacques Lecoq, *Le Corps poétique*, Actes Sud – Papiers 10 (Arles: Anrat, 1997), 48–9, 63–6.
42 Richard Hornby, 'Historic theatres', *Hudson Review* 49 (1997), 645–51, p. 646.
43 Tony Harrison, letter of 20 September 1981 to Peter Hall, printed in *Omnibus* 4 (1983); cf. programme note to *The Oresteia* (National Theatre, 1981).
44 Peter Hall, 'The mask of truth': lecture cited in Stephen Fay, *Power Play* (London: Hodder & Stoughton, 1995), 285.
45 K. Koun, *Kanoume theatro gia tin psyche mas* (Athens: Kastaniotes, 1987), 164–5. I am grateful to Yana Zarifi for help with the translation, and to K. Arvaniti for providing me with a copy of 'The representation of women in contemporary productions of Greek tragedies based on the myth of Orestes, with special reference to the theme of matricide' (Ph.D. thesis, University of Kent, 1996).
46 Plutarch, *Life of Demosthenes*, 7, 11.
47 G. Bassus, cited in Aulus Gellius, *Attic Nights*, 5.7.
48 Thanos Vovolis, 'Form and function of the tragic mask', unpublished lecture, London, April 1966.

49 Patsy Rodenburg, *The Actor Speaks: voice and the performer* (London: Methuen, 1997), 95.
50 *Ion*, 535 – *ALC*, 44.
51 See Philip Zarrilli, 'What does it mean to "become the character": power, presence and transcendence in Asian in-body disciplines of practice', *By Means of Performance*, ed. R. Schechner and W. Appel (Cambridge University Press, 1990), 131–48.
52 My analysis draws in particular on William G. Thalmann, 'Aeschylus' physiology of the emotions', *American Journal of Philology* 107 (1986), 489–511.
53 *The Acharnians*, 395–400.
54 Euripides, *Medea*, 1019–80. The word *thumos* has proved notoriously hard to translate.
55 The production visited the Olivier Theatre, London in 1987, and was still running in Tokyo in 1998.
56 The inelegant pose of the king, his weight balanced on one leg, and the presence of a concubine on the right of the image, show that this vase in Syracuse represents a more frivolous subject than the messenger scene from *Oedipus the King*.
57 *The Frogs*, 1061–3; also Athenaeus, 21.
58 *COAD*, 222–3.
59 *Moralia*, 816 and *Lysander*, 23 – *COAD*, 230.
60 *On the False Embassy*, 247 – *COAD*, 230.
61 Sophocles, *Plays: Two*, ed. J. Michael Walton (London: Methuen, 1990).
62 Fiona Shaw, 'Electra speechless' in *Sophocles' 'Electra' in Performance* (*Drama* vol. IV), ed. F. M. Dunn (Stuttgart: Metzerlschen & Poeschel, 1996), 131–8, pp.134, 131.
63 Timberlake Wertenbaker, *The Thebans* (London: Faber, 1992).

7. THE WRITER

1 *Laws*, 817d.
2 Plutarch, *Lives of Ten Orators – Lycurgus*, 841F.
3 I follow amongst others P. Ghiron-Bistagne, *Recherches sur les acteurs dans la Grèce antique* (Paris: Belles Lettres, 1976), 127–34, and Thomas K. Hubbard, *The Mask of Comedy: Aristophanes and the textual parabasis* (Cornell University Press, 1991), 227–30.
4 The ancient biographer and commentator on *Clouds*, 527 both infer that Kallistratos was an actor. A man called Kallistratos produced tragedies at the Lenaian festival: *COAD*, 136.
5 Scholiasts on *Clouds*, 554, *Knights*, 531.
6 Text from the translation of lines 1069–74 by Robert Fagles in *The Three Theban Plays* (Harmondsworth: Penguin, 1984). It is possible but not probable that Sophocles introduced a marker to indicate changes of speaker.

7 Alcidamas, *On Those Who Write Speeches*, translated in *Early Greek Political Thought from Homer to the Sophists*, ed. M. Gagarin and P. Woodruff (Cambridge University Press, 1995), 276–83.

8 *Rhetoric*, iii.2.2–5.1404b – *ALC*, 137.

9 *Phaedrus*, 271–9.

10 *Republic*, 393 – *ALC*, 61. The reference to movement is silently omitted by the Penguin translator.

11 Jeffrey Halcher, *The Art and Craft of Playwriting* (Cincinatti: Story Press, 1996), 21.

12 See Augusto Boal, 'Aristotle's coercive system of tragedy' in *Theater of the Oppressed*, tr. C .A. and M.-O. Leal McBride (London: Pluto, 1979), 1–50. Brecht's own critique is rather of 'aristotelian drama' than of Aristotle's text.

13 Timberlake Wertenbaker, speech at the University of Birmingham, April 1997; printed in *Studies in Theatre Production* 15 (1997), 88–92.

14 *Poetics*, vi.1450b; xiv.1453b; xxvi.1462a – cf. *ALC*, 100, 108, 132.

15 *Rhetoric*, iii.1.1403b–1404a – cf. *ALC*, 135–6.

16 *Poetics*, vi.1450b; *Politics* viii.7.1341b – *ALC*, 99, 133–4.

17 The biographies are translated in Mary R. Lefkowitz, *The Lives of the Greek Poets* (London: Duckworth, 1981), and most relevant biographical data is collected in her chapters.

18 For possible exceptions see p. 211 above, note 8.

19 Athenaeus, i.20.

20 Theophrastus, cited in Athenaeus, x.424e refers to the wine-pouring.

21 Cratinus, cited in Athenaeus, xiv.638d.

22 Lefkowitz, *Lives of the Greek Poets*, 102, 166 n.7.

23 Plutarch, *Life of Kimon*, 8; discussed in William Calder III, 'Sophocles, Oinomaos and the west pediment at Olympia', *Philologus* 118 (1974), 203–14.

24 *Rhetoric*, iii.18.6 – 1419a. For the context see M. H. Jameson, 'Sophocles and the four hundred', *Historia* 20 (1971), 541–68.

25 See Robert Parker, *Athenian Religion: a history* (Oxford University Press, 1996), 184–5.

26 Seamus Heaney, *The Cure at Troy* (London: Faber; Derry: Field Day Theatre Co., 1990). First performed in Derry in 1990.

27 W. M. Calder III, 'Sophoclean Apologia: *Philoctetes*', *Greek, Roman and Byzantine Studies* 12 (1971), 153–74.

28 The ancient biography tells how the Spartan general had a vision of Dionysos and permitted burial to take place: Lefkowitz, *Lives of the Greek Poets*, 162.

29 My interpretation follows Lowell Edmunds, *Theatrical Space and Historical Place in Sophocles'* 'Oedipus at Colonus' (Lanham: Rowman & Littlefield, 1996), 91–5.

30 *Women at the Thesmophoria*, 52–7.

31 *The Frogs*, 52–3.

32 *Poetics*, ix.9.1451b, xvii.1.1455a; *Rhetoric*, ii.81386a – *ALC*, 103, 113.
33 David Wiles, *The Masks of Menander* (Cambridge University Press, 1991), 26–7.
34 *Ion*, 533–5 – *ALC*, 42–4.
35 *Poetics*, xvii.2.1455a – *ALC*, 113 with note 5.
36 *Poetics*, xxv.6.1460b – *ALC*, 128.

8. RECEPTION

1 Primary sources are gathered in Leo Schrade, *La Représentation d'Edipo Tiranno au Teatro Olimpico* (Paris: CNRS, 1960), and Alberto Gallo, *La prima rappresentazione al Teatro Olimpico* (Milan: Polifilo, 1973). Pigafetta's adulatory account of the performance is translated in *A Sourcebook of Theatrical History*, ed. A. M. Nagler (New York: Dover, 1959), 81–6; Riccoboni's poisonous account is translated in *Sophocles: the classical heritage*, ed. R. D. Dawe (New York: Garland, 1996) 1–12.
2 Schrade, *Representation*, 53.
3 Riccoboni's criticism is echoed in the gossip picked up by Pinelli: Gallo, *Prima rappresentazione*, 59.
4 Ibid., 11; cf. 18, 6.
5 I have consulted a forthcoming study of Vitruvian theatres by Karina Mitens.
6 Attributed to Anghelos Sikelianos in Eva Palmer-Sikelianos, *Upward Panic*, ed. J. Anton (Chur, Switzerland: Harwood Academic Publishers, 1993), 65.
7 *E archaia ellenika tragodia melete V. Kanellou* (Athens: Ethnikon typografpheion, 1964). Basic documentation of the festival is in *Eva Palmer-Sikelianou* (Athens: Papadema, 1998) – reprint of *Delphikes eortes* from *Eos* 98–108 (1966/7). Secondary material in R. Jaquin, *L'Esprit de Delphes* (Université de Provence, 1988).
8 Hellmut Flashar, *Inszenierung der Antike: das griechische Drama auf der Bühne der Neuzeit, 1585–1990* (Munich: C. H. Beck, 1991), 142.
9 See Oliver Taplin, *The Stagecraft of Aeschylus* (Oxford University Press, 1977), 460–9.
10 Philip Sherrard, 'Anghelos Sikelianos and his vision of Greece' in *The Wound of Greece* (London: Rex Collings, 1978), 72–93, p. 90.
11 Gabriel Boissy in *Eva Palmer-Sikelianou*, 231–2.
12 See Richard Beacham's account in *Living Greek Theatre*, ed. J. M. Walton (New York: Greenwood Press, 1987), 315–16; Flashar, *Inszenierung der Antike*, 130, 159.
13 Nietzsche, *The Birth of Tragedy*, tr. S. Whiteside (Harmondsworth: Penguin, 1993), 49–50.
14 Palmer-Sikelianos, *Upward Panic*, 156 n. 4.
15 Richard Cave, *Terence Gray and the Cambridge Festival Theatre* (Cambridge: Chadwyck-Healey, 1980), 38.

16 Nietzsche, *Birth of Tragedy*, 44–6.
17 Palmer-Sikelianos, *Upward Panic*, 224–5.
18 *Eva Palmer-Sikelianou*, 301.
19 Palmer-Sikelianos, *Upward Panic*, 130, 182, 222–4.
20 The most influential study was Maurice Emmanuel, *La Danse grecque antique d'après les monuments figurés* (1896, reissued Paris and Geneva: Slatkine, 1987).
21 Palmer-Sikelianos, *Upward Panic*, 150.
22 *Eva Palmer-Sikelianou*, 134.
23 Palmer-Sikelianos, *Upward Panic*, 113.
24 Cited by Georges Banu in ' "Aujourd'hui je traduis du grec" ' in *Antoine Vitez: le devoir de traduire*, ed. J.-M. Déprats (Paris: Maison Antoine Vitez, 1996), 11–19, p. 12. Basic documentation is in A.Vitez, *Ecrits sur le théâtre*, vol. II, *La scène 1954–1975*, and *Ecrits sur le théâtre*, vol. IV, *La scène 1983–1990* (Paris: POL, 1995, 1997); Anne Ubersfeld, *Antoine Vitez: metteur en scène et poète* (Paris: Quatre-Vents, 1994).
25 Vitez, *Ecrits*, II.137–8.
26 *CCGT*, 302–4; on Murray generally, see P. E. Easterling, 'Gilbert Murray's reading of Euripides', *Colby Quarterly* 33 (1997), 113–27.
27 Palmer-Sikelianos, *Upward Panic*, 130.
28 A.Vitez, *Le Théâtre des idées* (Paris: Gallimard, 1991), 14.
29 Ibid., 323; cf. Ubersfeld, *Antoine Vitez, 138*.
30 Vitez, *Théâtre des idées*, 15–16.
31 Palmer-Sikelianos, *Upward Panic*, 108.
32 Vitez, *Ecrits*, IV.159–160.
33 J.-M. Déprats, 'Le temps de l'oeuvre et le bel aujourd'hui' in *Translation: here and there, now and then*, ed. J. Taylor, E. McMorran and G. Leclercq (Exeter: Elm Bank, 1996), 103–21, p. 112.
34 Walter Benjamin, 'The task of the translator' in *Illuminations*, ed. H. Arendt (London: Cape, 1970), 73.
35 Tom Stoppard, programme note to *The Seagull*, tr. Stoppard.
36 Benjamin, *Illuminations*, 78.
37 A.Vitez and E. Copfermann, *De Chaillot à Chaillot* (Paris: Hachette, 1981), 51.
38 Timberlake Wertenbaker, *Platform Papers 1: Translation* (London: Royal National Theatre, 1972): panel on 20 October 1989.
39 Vitez, *Ecrits* IV.161.
40 Sophocles, *Elektra*, a version by Ezra Pound and Rudd Fleming (London: Faber, 1990), 14.
41 Ibid., 103.
42 Ezra Pound, *Making it New* (London: Faber, 1934), 148.
43 John Hookham Frere in *Translation/History/Culture: a sourcebook*, ed. A. Lefevere (London: Routledge, 1992), 41.
44 *The Browning Version* in *Playbill* (London: Hamish Hamilton, 1949), 36.

45 *The Agamemnon of Aeschylus*, transcribed by Robert Browning (London: Smith, Elder & Co., 1877), 107 – *Agamemnon*, 1256–63.

46 R. C. Trevelyan, *The Oresteia of Aeschylus* (Cambridge: Bowes & Bowes, 1920).

47 Aeschylus, *Plays: two* (London: Methuen, 1991), 39; based on *The Serpent Son* (Cambridge University Press, 1979).

48 Jeffrey Henderson, *Three Plays by Aristophanes: staging women* (New York: Routledge, 1996), 30.

49 *Lysistrata*, 137–44; Henderson, *Three Plays*, 48.

50 Henderson, *Three Plays*, 17; J. Henderson, 'Translating Aristophanes for performance' in *Intertextualität in der griechisch-römischen Komödie* (*Drama*, vol. II), ed. N. W. Slater and B. Zimmermann (Stuttgart: Metzlersche & Poeschel, 1993), 81–91, pp. 81, 84. The second proposition is derived from A. H. Sommerstein, 'On translating Aristophanes: ends and means', *Greece and Rome* 20 (1973), 140–54, p. 152.

51 *Lysistrata* (London: Women's Press, 1911), 15.

52 *Lysistrata* (London: Faber, 1955), 13.

53 *Lysistrata/The Acharnians/Clouds* (Harmondsworth: Penguin, 1973), 185.

54 Aristophanes, *Plays: one* (London: Methuen, 1993), 202.

55 Henderson, 'Translating Aristophanes', 86.

56 *Aikin Mata*, translated and adapted by T. W. Harrison and James Simmons (Ibadan: Oxford University Press, 1966), 21. Stage directions omitted. Performed in Zaria in 1964.

57 B. B. Rogers, *The revolt of the Women: a free translation of the Lysistrata of Aristophanes* (London: George Bell, 1878), 9. Bold print added.

58 Stephen Halliwell, *Birds and Other Plays* (Oxford University Press, 1998), 104.

Further reading

I MYTH

The gods and Greek religion

Bremmer, Jan N. *Greek Religion*, New Surveys in the Classics 24 (Oxford University Press, 1994)
Bruit Zaidmann, Louise and Pauline Schmitt Pantel. *Religion in the Ancient Greek City*, tr. P. Cartledge (Cambridge University Press, 1992)
Burkert, Walter. *Greek Religion*, tr. J. Raffan (Oxford: Blackwell, 1985)

Introductions to the study of myth

Buxton, Richard. *Imaginary Greece: the contexts of mythology* (Cambridge University Press, 1994)
Detienne, Marcel. 'Rethinking mythology' in *Between Belief and Transgression: structuralist essays in religion, history and myth*, ed. M. Izard and P. Smith (University of Chicago Press, 1982), 43–52
Graf, Fritz. *Greek Mythology: an introduction*, tr. T. Merier (Johns Hopkins University Press, 1993)

Tragedy and choral performance

Herington, John. *Poetry into Drama* (University of California Press, 1985)

The performance of Homer

Nagy, Gregory. *Poetry as Performance: Homer and beyond* (Cambridge University Press, 1996), chapter 3
Segal, Charles. 'Bard and audience in Homer' in *Homer's Ancient Readers*, ed. R. Lamberton (Princeton University Press, 1992), 3–29

225

The storylines of tragedy

Burian, Peter. 'Myth into *mythos*: the shaping of tragic plots', *CCGT*, chapter 8

Tragic myth and the historical past

Easterling, P. E. 'Constructing the heroic' in *Greek Tragedy and the Historian*, ed. C. Pelling (Oxford University Press, 1997), 21–37

Knox, B. M. W. 'Myth and Attic tragedy' in *Word and Action* (Johns Hopkins University Press, 1979), 3–24

Vernant, J.-P. 'The historical moment of tragedy in Greece: some of the social and psychological conditions', *MTAG*, 23–8

Freud

Bremmer, Jan. 'Oedipus and the Greek Oedipus complex' in *Interpretations of Greek Mythology*, ed. J. Bremmer (London: Croom Helm, 1987), 41–59

Vernant, J.-P. 'Oedipus without the complex', *MTAG*, 85–111

An analysis of tragedy inspired by Lévi-Strauss

Segal, Charles. *Tragedy and Civilization: an interpretation of Sophocles* (Harvard University Press, 1981)

2 RITUAL

General

Gould, John. 'On making sense of Greek religion' in P. E. Easterling and J. V. Muir (ed.), *Greek Religion and Society* (Cambridge University Press, 1985), 1–33

On the ritual origins of drama

Adrados, Francisco. *Festival, Comedy and Tragedy: the Greek origins of theatre* (Leiden: Brill, 1975)

On the roots of Athenian tragedy in ritual

Seaford, Richard. *Reciprocity and Ritual: Homer and tragedy in the developing city-state* (Oxford University Press, 1994)

The festival of Dionysos – primary sources

COAD, 103–85

On drama and Dionysos

Easterling, P. E. 'A show for Dionysus', *CCGT*, chapter 2
Friedrich, Rainer. 'Everything to do with Dionysos? Ritualism, the Dionysiac and the tragic', with a response by Richard Seaford, in M. S. Silk (ed.), *Tragedy and the Tragic* (Oxford University Press, 1996), 257–94
Henrichs, Albert. '"He has a god in him": human and divine in the modern perception of Dionysus' in *Masks of Dionysus*, ed. T. H. Carpenter and C. Faraone (Cornell University Press, 1993), 13–43

On ritual elements within plays

Bowie, A. M. *Aristophanes: myth, ritual and comedy* (Cambridge University Press, 1993)
Easterling, P. E. 'Tragedy and ritual' in R. Scodel (ed.), *Theater and Society in the Classical World* (University of Michigan Press), 7–23
Foley, Helene. *Ritual Irony: poetry and sacrifice in Euripides* (Cornell University Press, 1985)
Yaari, Nurit. '"What am I to say while I pour these funeral offerings": stage image, word and action in Aeschylus' libation scenes', *Journal of Dramatic Theory and Criticism* 14 (1999), 49–64

On specific rituals

Burkert, Walter. 'Greek tragedy and sacrificial ritual', *Greek, Roman and Byzantine Studies* 7 (1966), 87–121
Horst-Warhaft, Gail. *Dangerous Voices: women's laments and Greek literature* (London: Routledge, 1992)
Parker, Robert. *Miasma: pollution and purification in early Greek religion* (Oxford University Press, 1983)
Sinn, Ulrich. 'Greek sanctuaries as places of refuge' in N. Marinatos and R. Hägg (ed.), *Greek Sanctuaries: new approaches* (London: Routledge, 1993), 88–109

3 POLITICS

Primary sources

'The Old Oligarch', *Early Greek Political Thought from Homer to the Sophists*, ed. M. Gagarin and P. Woodruff (Cambridge University Press, 1995), 133–44
Plutarch. *The Rise and Fall of Athens*, tr. I. Scott-Kilvert (Harmondsworth: Penguin, 1960)
Thucydides. *The Peloponnesian War*, tr. R. Warner (Harmondsworth: Penguin, 1954)

The democratic system

Ober, Josiah. *Mass and Elite in Democratic Athens: rhetoric, ideology and the power of the people* (Princeton University Press, 1989)
Stockton, David. *The Classical Athenian Democracy* (Oxford University Press, 1990)

Politics and the festival of Dionysos

Cartledge, Paul. 'Deep plays: tragedy as process in Greek civic life' *CCGT*, chapter 1
Seaford, Richard. *Reciprocity and Ritual: Homer and tragedy in the developing city-state* (Oxford University Press, 1994)
Wilson, Peter. 'Leading the tragic *khoros*: tragic prestige in the democratic city' in *Greek Tragedy and the Historian*, ed. C. Pelling (Oxford University Press, 1997), 81–108
Winkler, John J. and Froma I. Zeitlin (ed.). *Nothing To Do With Dionysos? Athenian drama in its social context* (Princeton University Press, 1990) – especially the essays by Goldhill, Strauss and Ober, and Henderson

Tragedy and rhetoric

Bers, Victor. 'Tragedy and rhetoric' in *Persuasion*, ed. I. Worthington (London: Routledge, 1994), 176–95
Hall, Edith. 'Law court dramas: the power of performance in Greek forensic oratory', *Bulletin of the Institute of Classical Studies* 40 (1995), 39–58

Politics and plays

Carey, Christopher. 'Comic ridicule and democracy' in *Ritual, Finance, Politics*, ed. R. Osborne and S. Hornblower (Oxford University Press, 1994), 69–83
Cartledge, Paul. *Aristophanes and his Theatre of the Absurd* (Bristol: Bristol Classical Press, 1990)
Croally, N. T. *Euripidean Polemic: The Trojan Women and the function of tragedy* (Cambridge University Press, 1994)
Foley, Helene. 'Tragedy and democratic ideology: the case of Sophocles' *Antigone*' in *History, Tragedy, Theory*, ed. B. Goff (University of Texas Press, 1995), 131–50
Griffith, Mark. 'Brilliant dynasts: power and politics in the *Oresteia*', *Classical Antiquity* 14 (1995), 62–129
Knox, B. M. W. *Oedipus at Thebes* (Yale University Press, 1957) – chapter 2: Athens
Meier, Christian. *The Political Art of Greek Tragedy*, tr. A. Webber (Cambridge, Mass.: Polity Press, 1993)

4 GENDER

Women in Greece

Fantham, Elaine and H. P. Foley, N. B. Kampen, S. B. Pomeroy, and H. A. Shapiro. *Women in the Classical World* (Oxford University Press, 1994)
Gould, John. 'Law, custom and myth: aspects of the social position of women in classical Athens', *Journal of Hellenic Studies* 100 (1980), 38–59
Pomeroy, Sarah B. *Families in Classical and Hellenistic Greece: representations and realities* (Oxford University Press, 1997)

Women in tragedy

Foley, Helene P. 'The conception of women in Athenian drama' in *Reflections of Women in Antiquity*, ed. H. P. Foley (New York: Gordon & Breach, 1981), 127–67
Hall, Edith. 'The sociology of Greek tragedy' in *CCGT*, chapter 5
Loraux, Nicole. *Tragic Ways of Killing a Woman*, tr. A. Forster (Harvard University Press, 1987)
Zeitlin, Froma. 'Playing the Other: theater, theatricality and the feminine in Greek drama' in *NTDWD*, 63–96; reprinted in F. Zeitlin, *Playing the Other* (University of Chicago Press, 1996), 341–74

Women in comedy

Loraux, Nicole. 'The comic Acropolis: Aristophanes, *Lysistrata*' in *The Children of Athena*, tr. C. Levine (Princeton University Press, 1993), 147–83
Taafe, Lauren K. *Aristophanes and Women* (New York and London: Routledge, 1993)
Zeitlin, Froma. 'Travesties of gender and genre in Aristophanes' *Thesmophoriazousae*' in *Reflections of Women in Antiquity*, ed. H. P. Foley (New York: Gordon & Breach, 1981); reprinted in F. Zeitlin, *Playing the Other* (University of Chicago Press, 1986), 375–416

Women in ritual performance

Bruit Zaidman, L. 'Pandora's daughters and rituals in Grecian cities' in *A History of Women in the West*, vol. 1, ed. Pauline Schmitt Pantel (Harvard University Press, 1992), 338–76
Calame, Claude. *Choruses of Young Women in Ancient Greece*, tr. D. Collins and J. Orion (Lanham: Rowman & Littlefield, 1997)
Foley, Helene P. 'The politics of tragic lamentation' in *Tragedy, Comedy and the Polis*, ed. A. H. Sommerstein *et al.* (Bari: Levante, 1993), 101–43

Lonsdale, Stephen. 'Rehearsals for womanhood: dance and play in female transition rites' in *Dance and Ritual Play in Greek Religion* (Johns Hopkins University Press, 1993), 169–205

Women in art

Blundell, S. 'Marriage and the maiden: narratives on the Parthenon' in *The Sacred and the Feminine in Ancient Greece*, ed. S. Blundell and M. Williamson (London: Routledge, 1998), 47–70

Women as spectators at the Dionysia

Goldhill, Simon. 'Representing democracy: women at the Great Dionysia' in *Ritual, Finance, Politics*, ed. R. Osborne and S. Hornblower (Oxford University Press, 1994), 347–69

Dionysos and sexuality

Jameson, M. 'The asexuality of Dionysos' in *Masks of Dionysos*, ed. T. Carpenter and C. Faraone (Cornell University Press, 1993), 44–64
Segal, C. P. *Dionysiac Poetics and Euripides Bacchae* (Princeton University Press, 1982), chapter 6
Winkler, John J. 'Phallos Politikos: representing the body politic in Athens' *Differences: a journal of feminist cultural studies* 2.1 (1990), 29–45

Homosexuality and gender

Halperin, David M. *One Hundred Years of Homosexuality* (New York: Routledge, 1990)

Gender issues in twentieth-century performance

Bryant-Bertail, Sarah. 'Gender, empire and body politic as *mise en scène*: Mnouchkine's *Les Atrides*', *Theatre Journal* 46 (1994), 1–30
Laks, B. C. *Electra: a gender sensitive study of the plays* (Jefferson, North Carolina: McFarland, 1995)

5 SPACE

Most aspects of performance space

Wiles, David. *Tragedy in Athens: performance space and theatrical meaning* (Cambridge University Press, 1997)

Classical concepts of space

Vernant, Jean-Pierre. *Myth and Thought Among the Greeks* (London: Routledge & Kegan Paul, 1983) – part 3: 'The organization of space'

The representation of place in Greek drama

Crane, Gregory. 'Oikos and agora: mapping the polis in Aristophanes' *Wasps*' in *The City as Comedy: society and representation in Athenian drama*, ed. G. W. Dobrov (University of North Carolina Press, 1997), 198–229

Edmunds, Lowell. *Theatrical Space and Historical Place in Sophocles' Oedipus at Colonus* (Lanham: Rowman & Littlefield, 1996)

Loraux, Nicole. 'The comic Acropolis: Aristophanes, *Lysistrata*' and 'Autochthonous Kreousa: Euripides, *Ion*' in *The Children of Athena: Athenian ideas about citizenship and the division between the sexes*, tr. C. Levine (Princeton University Press, 1993), 147–236; the second essay also in *NTDWD*, 168–206

Saïd, Suzanne. 'Tragic Argos' in *Tragedy, Comedy and the Polis*, ed. A. H. Sommerstein *et al.* (Bari: Levante, 1993), 167–89

Zeitlin, Froma. 'Thebes: theater of self and society in Athenian drama' in *NTDWD*, 130–67; reprinted in F. Zeitlin, *Playing the Other* (University of Chicago Press, 1996)

Archaeology

Dinsmoor, William. 'The Athenian theater of the fifth century' in *Studies Presented to David Moore Robinson*, ed. G. E. Mylonas (University of Washington Press, 1951), 309–30

Leacroft, Richard and Helen Leacroft. *Theatre and Playhouse: an illustrated survey of theatre building from Ancient Greece to the present day* (London: Methuen, 1984), chapters 1–3

Wycherley, R. E. *The Stones of Athens* (Princeton University Press, 1978)

Resources of the theatre

Gould, John. 'Tragedy in performance' in *The Cambridge History of Classical Literature, vol. 1, Greek Literature*, ed. P. E. Easterling and B. M. W. Knox (Cambridge University Press, 1985), 263–81

Rehm, Rush. *Greek Tragic Theatre* (London: Routledge, 1992), chapter 4: 'The theatre of Dionysus'

Taplin, Oliver. *The Stagecraft of Aeschylus: the dramatic use of exits and entrances in Greek tragedy* (Oxford University Press, 1977) – appendix B, pp. 434–51: 'The stage resources of the fifth-century theatre'

Space in performance

Croally, N. T. *Euripidean Polemic: The Trojan Women and the function of tragedy* (Cambridge University Press, 1994)

Hourmouziades, N. C. *Production and Imagination in Euripides: form and function of the scenic space* (Athens University Press, 1965)

Lowe, N. J. 'Greek stagecraft and Aristophanes' in *Farce: themes in drama*, vol. x, ed. J. Redmond (Cambridge University Press, 1988), 33–52

Padel, Ruth. 'Making space speak' in *NTDWD*, 336–65

Taplin, Oliver. 'Sophocles in his theatre' in *Sophocle*, ed. J. de Romilly (Geneva: Entretiens Hardt vol. xxix, 1983), 155–83

6 THE PERFORMER

The chorus

Aylen, Leo. *The Greek Theater* (Associated University Press, 1985), chapter 5: 'Dance drama'

Bacon, Helen H. 'The chorus in Greek life and drama', *Arion* 3 (1995), 6–24

Gould, John. 'Tragedy and collective experience', with a response by Simon Goldhill, in *Tragedy and the Tragic*, ed. M. S. Silk (Oxford University Press, 1996), 217–56

Lawler, Lilian. *The Dance in Ancient Greece* (London: A. & C. Black, 1964)

Lecoq, Jacques. *The Poetic Body*, tr. David Bradby (London: Methuen, forthcoming)

Lonsdale, Steven H. *Dance and Ritual Play in Greek Religion* (Johns Hopkins University Press, 1993)

Naerebout, F. G. *Attractive Performances. Ancient Greek dance: three preliminary studies* (Amsterdam: Gieben, 1997)

Wiles, David. *Tragedy in Athens: performance space and theatrical meaning* (Cambridge University Press, 1997), chapters 4 and 5

Music

Anderson, W. *Music and Musicians in Ancient Greece* (Cornell University Press, 1994), chapter 5: 'Fifth-century music'

Wilson, Peter. 'The *aulos* in Athens' in *Performance Culture and Athenian Democracy*, ed. Simon Goldhill and Robin Osborne (Cambridge University Press, 1999), chapter 3

Zimmermann, Bernhard. 'Comedy's criticism of music' in *Intertextualität in der griechisch-römischen Komödie* (*Drama*, vol. ii), ed. N. W. Slater and B. Zimmermann (Stuttgart: Metzlersche & Poeschel, 1993), 39–50

Acting: general

Arnott, Peter D. *Public and Performance in the Greek Theatre* (London: Routledge, 1989)
Walcot, Peter. *Greek Drama in its Theatrical and Social Context* (University of Wales Press, 1976)
Walton, J. Michael. *The Greek Sense of Theatre* (London, Methuen, 1984), chapter 4: 'The performers'

Acting: aspects

Hall, Edith. 'Actor's song in tragedy' in *Performance Culture and Athenian Democracy*, ed. Simon Goldhill and Robin Osborne (Cambridge University Press, 1999), chapter 4
Halliwell, Stephen. 'The function and aesthetics of the Greek tragic mask' in *Intertextualität in der griechisch-römischen Komödie* (*Drama*, vol. II), ed. N. W. Slater & B. Zimmermann (Stuttgart: Metzlersche & Poeschel, 1993), 195–210
Sifakis, G. M. 'The one-actor rule in Greek tragedy' in *Stage Directions – essays in ancient drama in honour of E. W. Handley*, ed. A. Griffiths (London: Institute of Classical Studies, 1995), 13–24
Stanford, W. B. *Greek Tragedy and the Emotions* (London: Routledge & Kegan Paul, 1983)
Webster, T. B. L. 'Some psychological terms in Greek tragedy', *Journal of Hellenic Studies* 77 (1957), 149–54

Visual sources

Bieber, Margarete. *The History of the Greek and Roman Theater* (Princeton University Press, 1961)
Brooke, Iris. *Costume in Greek Classical Drama* (London: Methuen, 1962)
Green, J. R. *Theatre in Ancient Greek Society* (London: Routledge, 1994)
Prag, A. J. N. W. *The Oresteia: iconographic and narrative tradition* (Warminster: Aris & Phillips, 1985)
Taplin, Oliver. *Comic Angels: and other approaches to Greek drama through vase-paintings* (Oxford University Press, 1993)
'The pictorial record', *CCGT*, chapter 4
Trendall, A. D. and T. B. L. Webster. *Illustrations of Greek Drama* (London: Phaidon, 1970)

7 THE WRITER

The emergence of the writer

Havelock, Eric A. 'The oral composition of Greek drama' in *The Literate Revolution and its Consequences* (Princeton University Press, 1982), 261–313

Wise, Jennifer. *Dionysus Writes: the invention of theatre in ancient Greece* (Cornell University Press, 1998)

The biographies of playwrights

Lefkowitz, Mary R. *The Lives of the Greek Poets* (London: Duckworth, 1981)

Comedy and politics

Cartledge, Paul. *Aristophanes and his Theatre of the Absurd* (Bristol: Bristol Classical Press, 1990)

De Ste Croix, G. E. M. 'The political outlook of Aristophanes' in *Oxford Readings in Artistophanes*, ed. E. Segal (Oxford University Press, 1996), 182–93 – originally published in 1972

The writer and production

Rehm, Rush. *Greek Tragic Theatre* (London: Routledge, 1992), chapter 3: 'Production as participation'

Dramatic form

Easterling, P. E. 'Form and performance', *CCGT*, chapter 7

Halliwell, Stephen. 'Formality and performance' in Aristophanes, *Birds and other plays* (Oxford University Press, 1998), xxx–xxxix

The language of tragedy

Goldhill, Simon. 'The language of tragedy: rhetoric and communication', *CCGT*, chapter 6

Oral tradition

Thomas, Rosalind. *Literacy and Orality in Ancient Greece* (Cambridge University Press, 1992)

Plato and Aristotle

Halliwell, Stephen. *Aristotle's Poetics* (London: Duckworth, 1986)
Havelock, Eric A. *Preface to Plato* (Oxford: Blackwell, 1963)
Jones, John. *On Aristotle and Greek Tragedy* (London: Chatto & Windus, 1962)

8 RECEPTION

Modern performances of Greek drama

Barthes, Roland. 'Putting on the Greeks' in *Critical Essays*, tr. R. Howard (Northwestern University Press, 1972), 59–66
Burian, Peter. 'Tragedy adapted for stage and screens: the Renaissance to the present', *CCGT*, chapter 10
Chioles, John. 'The *Oresteia* and the avant-garde: three decades of discourse', *Performing Arts Journal* 45 (1993), 1–28
Hall, Edith and Fiona Macintosh. *Hellas Rehearsed: Greek tragedy on the British stage, 1660–1914* (Oxford University Press, forthcoming)
Macintosh, Fiona. *Oedipus Rex: a production history* (Cambridge University Press, forthcoming)
   'Tragedy in performance: nineteenth- and twentieth-century productions', *CCGT*, chapter 11
McDonald, Marianne. *Ancient Sun, Modern Light: Greek drama on the modern stage* (Columbia University Press, 1992)
Steiner, George. *Antigones: the Antigone myth in western literature, art and thought* (Oxford University Press, 1984), chapter 2
Walton, J. Michael (ed.). *Living Greek Theatre: a handbook of classical performance and modern production* (New York: Greenwood Press, 1987)

The most comprehensive survey is only available in German:
Flashar, Hellmut. *Inszenierung der Antike: das griechische Drama auf der Bühne der Neuzeit, 1585–1990* (Munich: C. H. Beck, 1991)

Productions discussed in this chapter

Neuschäfer, Anne. 'Antoine Vitez: the script and the spoken word – intercultural dialogue in the theatre' in *The Intercultural Performance Reader*, ed. P. Pavis (London: Routledge, 1996), 131–9
Palmer-Sikelianos, Eva. *Upward Panic*, ed. J. Anton (Chur &c: Harwood Academic Publishers, 1993)
Vidal-Naquet, Pierre. 'Oedipus in Vicenza and in Paris: two turning points in the history of Oedipus' in *MTAG*, 361–80; reprinted in *Sophocles: the classical heritage*, ed. R. D. Dawe (New York: Garland, 1996), 13–31

Translating for the theatre – general

Johnston, David (ed.). *Stages of Translation* (Bath: Absolute Classics, 1996)
Platform Papers I: translation (London: Royal National Theatre, 1992)

Manifestoes by (or about) translators of Greek plays

Arrowsmith, William. 'The lively conventions of translation' in *The Craft and Context of Translation*, ed. W. Arrowsmith and R. Shattuck (University of Texas Press, 1961), 122–40

Carne-Ross, D. S. 'Aeschylus in translation', *Arion* 5 (1966), 73–88

Carson, Anne. 'Screaming in translation: the Elektra of Sophocles' in *Sophocles 'Electra' in Performance* (*Drama*, vol. IV), ed. F. M. Dunn (Stuttgart: Metzlerschen & Poeschel, 1996), 5–11

Eliot, T. S. 'Euripides and Professor Murray' in *Selected Essays* (London: Faber, 1951), 59–64

Ewans, Michael. 'Aischylos: for actors in the round' in *The Art of Translation: voices from the field*, ed. R. Warren (Northwestern University Press, 1989), 120–39

Harrison, Tony. '*The Oresteia* in the making', *Omnibus* 4 (1982), 16–19

Pound, Ezra. 'Translation of Aeschylus' in *Making it New* (London: Faber, 1934), 146–56

Sommerstein, A. H. 'On translating Aristophanes: ends and means', *Greece and Rome* 20 (1973), 140–54

Vitez, Antoine. 'The duty to translate' in *The Intercultural Performance Reader*, ed. P. Pavis (London: Routledge, 1996), 121–30

Wilamowitz-Moellendorff, U. von. 'What is translation?' in *Translation/History/Culture: a sourcebook*, ed. A. Lefevere (London: Routledge, 1992), 166–71 – published in German in 1925

Index

237